BISON
BOOKS

P9-AOI-054

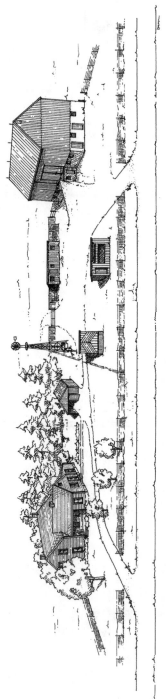

The Farmstead

Illustration by Scott Duenow

The Farm on the North Talbot Road

Allan G. Bogue

University of Nebraska Press
Lincoln and London

© 2001 by the University of Nebraska Press
All rights reserved
Manufactured in the United States of America

Library of Congress Cataloging-in-Publication Data
Bogue, Allan G.
The farm on the North Talbot Road / Allan G. Bogue.
p. cm. Includes bibliographical references (p.) and index.
ISBN 0-8032-6189-6 (pbk. : alk. paper)
1. Dairy farming–Ontario. 2. Dairy farms–Ontario.
3. Farm life–Ontario. 4. Bogue, Allan G.   I. Title
SF227.C2 B64 2001
636.2'142'0971325–dc21
2001017488

Illustrations are courtesy of the author unless otherwise credited.

*Dedicated to my family and to all the others who helped
give special meaning in my mind to the North Talbot Road*

Contents

Illustrations

Maps

Tables

Preface

In this book I have tried to describe how we did things on an Ontario farm during the 1930s. I have not tried to write an autobiography or detail the growing pains that I experienced while I moved through my early and middle teens. Nor did I wish to write a family history. When completed, my account contained elements of all of these things. But livestock husbandry and market gardening and the impact of the depression of the 1930s upon our farm life provide the book's central focus. Some readers may wish to know our family and our neighbors somewhat better than the first two chapters allow by reading chapter 9, "Neighborhood and Family," before meeting the Holsteins, experiencing the joys of picking tomatoes, and rattling off to market as described in chapters 3–8. Others may be more interested in the story line than in the specifics of herd management and agricultural prices detailed in the two appendixes.

But why devote a book to so ordinary a thing as a family farm? As a history teacher at the University of Iowa and the University of Wisconsin, Madison, I was lucky enough to become acquainted with a number of the young economic historians who were creating a "new economic history" between the mid-1950s and the late 1970s. During those years I attended symposia and professional meeting panels in which these scholars discussed their work and responded to the questions and criticisms of members of the audience. They were particularly intrigued by the institution of slavery in the American South, and argument often centered upon the details of daily agricultural practice as well as upon the broader issues of profit and loss, regionalism, and mortality. These researchers and their critics discovered a surprisingly broad array of source materials that yielded information about the peculiar institution. Some also found that firsthand contemporary experiences and observations were an invaluable part of the whole if we were to fully understand the problems and challenges that the southern cultivator faced. I realized at the time that I might be able to draw upon my own experiences as a farm boy in a very different time and kind of agricultural region to prepare such a document describing the farm operation of which I was a part for almost twenty years.

During my years as a doctoral candidate and the first fifteen years of my life as a college history teacher, I spent much of my time trying to understand the agricultural history of the midwestern prairie states and the grasslands immediately beyond. At an early point in these years I read *Sod and Stubble* by John Ise, a story of family and homesteading in west-central Kansas, and when I put it down I was convinced that I had learned more from this book about settler life and the pioneer era of the mid-American grasslands than from any other historical source. I returned to this little book time and again thereafter and often assigned it as a text in my course on the history of the American West. My experience with *Sod and Stubble* reinforced my belief that accounts of individual families and their farms in other times and places could have broader meaning and usefulness. In the following pages I have tried to provide such a study.

I hope also that I have been able to convey some of the complexity of farm life, its ups and downs, its moments of triumph or laughter, and its times of despair. The history of the farm on the North Talbot Road was not a chronicle of a dominant father or mother or of conflict between them; it was a family story in which children played significant roles in shaping outcomes, and influences other than rational economic decision making helped to explain the conclusion. I suspect that this could be said of most of the farm histories in our neighborhood and the larger community of which our stretch of the North Talbot Road was part. But each farm experience was unique also, and Veeman, Madolyn, and Ethel and their companions of the milk row—as well as endless baskets of tomatoes—helped to give a special character to our farm experience.

All the incidents I describe in this account took place on our farm and I have been as accurate in describing them as memory allowed. In so far as possible I have verified my work from other historical sources. The people who appear in the story were or are all real people. I have withheld or changed a few names in order to avoid any possible embarrassment on the part of descendants.

Onno Brouwer and his staff at the Cartographic Laboratory of the University of Wisconsin prepared the neighborhood, farm, and soil maps and amply sustained the high reputation of their work. A generation ago, a purchaser of the farm razed the farmstead and I had no photographs that showed it as it had been in our family's years on the farm. Working from my crude sketches and a number of slides showing some aspects of the house and farm yards, Scott Duenow of Architecture Network, Inc. prepared a sketch for me. A believer in good fences, Scott somewhat underestimated the amount of sag in those at the road front of our farmstead, and his medium does not reveal the degree to which our house needed paint, but he recreated the buildings and general layout of the farmstead in fine fashion and I am most grateful for his kindness in accepting an assignment that I am sure was much less interesting than his usual work.

Few authors can claim total credit for producing a manuscript, although we must always shoulder the blame for defects. This book is a family story in part and I have received much assistance from my Canadian relatives. I have drawn repeatedly upon the knowledge and memories of my sister-in-law Irene Barney Bogue, my nephew Arthur Bogue, and my niece Margaret Aziz. Over the years Irene and Margaret also kept an eye out for local history publications and newspaper stories and sent me those in which they knew that I would be interested. Irene made or preserved most of the family pictures used to illustrate this volume. On trips to Canada and with Arthur at the wheel, I periodically revisited the Lambeth-Byron neighborhood, and refreshed my memory of the agricultural geography of the 1930s—not without some friendly argument with Arthur. In this same respect I must mention my first cousin, Gordon Bogue, who talked to me on various occasions about the history of our part of the North Talbot Road. Gordon was the last of the Bogues to live on the road between Lambeth and Byron.

Years ago, Raymond K. Crinklaw, farmer, scholar, and Westminster Township and Middlesex County officer, developed plans to use local newspapers as a source for compiling data of historical interest relating to Westminster Township. I found the volumes of such material prepared under his supervision highly useful in helping me to understand the historical background of my family, although unfortunately, from my standpoint, Crinklaw ended his coverage of Westminster Township in the mid-1920s. I am indebted to him as well for a pleasant morning of conversation about local history.

As in many years past, I have been heavily in debt in my research to the librarians of the State Historical Society of Wisconsin and the various branches of the University Library System at the University of Wisconsin. The society's magnificent collection of Canadian government documents and Canadiana is matched in few other American libraries. Society Interlibrary Loan librarian Ellen Burke was ever helpful, particularly when she valiantly extracted two dozen volumes of the *Holstein-Friesian Herd Book* from a disinterested neighboring university after we learned that Wisconsin's dairy scientists had decided that their run of the yearbook was of little use and returned it to Canada. In the State Archives Reading Room operated by the society, Harry Miller and his colleagues often assisted me. At the University of Western Ontario, John H. Lutman and Theresa Regnier in the J. J. Talman Regional Collection of the D. B. Weldon Library kindly helped me on several occasions. I was fortunate in making contact with Michael Dove, then a doctoral candidate in the History Department at the University of Western Ontario. After my initial reconnaissance in the Abstract Books of Westminster Township in the office of the Middlesex County Land Registry Office, in London, Ontario, Michael agreed to dig out the references to our family's land transactions during my father's farming career and to supervise duplication of those in which I was interested. I appreciate the care and promptness with which he carried out these tasks and also his enthusiastic interest in the project.

For some fifty years I have happily shared family, home, and profession with Margaret Beattie Bogue, and as always, during the preparation of this book, I have been sustained by both her affection and her knowledge and skills as historian.

The Farm on the North Talbot Road

ONE

Of Time and Place and People

During the 1920s and 1930s the stretch of the North Talbot Road that linked the villages of Lambeth and Byron was an "improved" gravel road between the junction of Provincial Highways 2 and 4 in Lambeth and the Springbank Drive, cutting the latter slightly to the east of Byron. Place yourself in time on a September afternoon in 1935 in Lambeth at the two-story red-brick continuation school located a couple hundred yards south of the highway junction. Now follow me as I mount a rattly blue bicycle, leave the school grounds, and point my machine north along the uneven cement sidewalk. Soon I am at the crossroads, just past the white clapboard Masonic Hall. A branch of the Royal Bank of Canada is on my right, and across Highway 4 is the one-story Anglican Chapel beside its graveyard.

I cross Highway 2 to take the village sidewalk on the west side of the North Talbot Road, passing beside a one-story gray-brick establishment owned by the local Farmer's Cooperative Society. Stepping beneath its front portico and inside, customers can find candy, groceries, or dry goods. At a side entrance is coal oil in a horizontal drum. Big bags of livestock feed are inside at the rear side door, which faces on the North Talbot Road, and locals fill their need for yellow wooden fence posts and rolls of fence wire from the piles in a yard at the back of the store. Across the street on the other corner is a small gray-brick hotel, the Longwoods Inn, and a little farther along, the edifice of the United Church of Canada, also of gray brick.

If you look to the left as we cross the highway to the Farmer's Co-op, you see the gasoline pumps and show window of the Ford Agency, and beyond that, the open door and faded board front of the blacksmith shop. A glance in the other direction, up Highway 2 in the direction of London, reveals a couple of gasoline stations, a drug store, and the recreation hall, ice cream bar, and bus stop called The Bluebird.

Leaving Lambeth's major intersection behind, I cycle through three short blocks of residences, some of substantial size, built mostly of gray brick. One serves as residence and office for our family doctor. The sidewalk ends at a sign that proclaims on its northern face: "Live in Lovely Lambeth," a motto often altered by paint-wielding pranksters to read "Love in Lively Lambeth."

Now I take to the gravel road, which at this time of year is a hard-packed washboard, bordered by a treacherous fringe of loose gravel that can throw a careless rider into a wrenching skid and abrasive fall. I shall follow the road for a mile and a quarter until I reach Dale's Side Road. This stretch is one of gentle undulation, dipping to cross a small bridge and a number of culverts and rising in between these points, sometimes sufficiently to make me shift from the bike seat into stand-up pumping. To the immediate left, as I leave the "Lovely Lambeth" sign, is a small field of asparagus planted in a sunken area that was once part of a gravel pit. This is owned by my father's cousin Bill, and beyond stretch his two greenhouses. His modest white frame house is set close to the road, and to the north another small field drops down to a creek that passes under the road below a diminutive cement bridge, scarcely more than a glorified culvert. Bill's Jersey cow grazes beside the little waterway.

Farther along the road are several small one-story residences. One is occupied by a mysterious retired pianist; another, so it is said, by an aged relative of Sandy Somerville, the London hero who won the United States Amateur Golf Championship a few years earlier. Across the road to my right, farmsteads have sprung up. As soon as I have crossed the little bridge I begin to work against a gentle slope that continues until I have pedaled half a mile from the four corners at Lambeth and reached the line fence of the third farm on my right. Here the Third Concession-line Road of Westminster Township intersects the North Talbot Road from the left and apparently proceeds no further.

At this point I have reached the boundary of my family's immediate neighborhood. In the fat V formed by the Third Concession Road and the North Talbot Road is the schoolyard and gray-brick school of School Section (ss) 17. Its two substantial rooms join at right angles, a stubby bell tower sitting at the junction. Behind the school a white board fence divides the grounds and separates the two-holer outhouses into domain of boy and girl—females to the north, males to the south. My brother, my two sisters, and I all received our public schooling at ss 17. Across from ss 17 is the farm of Cousin Norman, known to the family as Tink because of his love of tinkering with machinery. Next, to the north, is the holding of my grandfather, David. He and Tink's father, John Jr., spent much of their lives in expanding the original clearings on these farms after John Sr. acquired the title in the early 1850s.

Just past the school, the road begins to slope gently toward the north and continues to do so until past the David Bogue farm. Thus far it has angled to the west of north, but now at the north line fence of my grandfather's old place, a quarter mile past the Third Concession Road, it bends to head more directly to the north. The change in direction seems to increase the velocity of the head winds that cyclists face. West of the road the frontage of the Sadler family's dairy farm and well-tended orchard has stretched from the school to the bend. Next is the farm to which my father, George Bogue, took Eleta Britton, my mother, on their marriage in 1904; it is now owned by Sam Kilbourne, who is employed in London but works at odd times as a plasterer and farms with the aid of a grown son. An ugly two-story brick house that my father built dominates this farmstead.

Most of the farms between Lambeth and Byron are fifty or one hundred acres in size, but immediately to the north of the Bogue homesteads on the east side is a two-hundred-acre holding, its frontage stretching for a quarter of a mile. George usually refers to it as the Burley Burch farm since it was first owned and long occupied by the Burch family, who obtained it from the Crown as a United Empire Loyalist entitlement. In my earliest memories it was the Pringle farm, owned by a London businessman believed to be rich, and stocked with purebred Jersey cattle, some of them wearing the chain and small padlock around the horns that denoted origin in the Jersey Islands, or so we believed. Across the road and next to the Kilbourne place is the Bilyea farm. In the corner made by their line fence and the road fence is a small cemetery plot with an impressive monument marking the resting place of a family patriarch.

Beyond the north line fence of the Bilyea farm the road dips gently for some fifty yards and then levels to run to its junction with Dale's Side Road a quarter of a mile ahead. To the left the Vanstone farm stretches for the whole distance, first an open field, then an orchard and a weathered two-story frame house shrouded by large pines, with maple trees along the road fence, and then again an open field. To my right is the fifty-acre farm of Fred Merriam, a younger farmer who recently bought the place after the deaths of Mrs. Vanstone's aged parents. Next I reach the land that George Bogue farmed during the teens and most of the 1920s. Its farmstead sits at the corner of the North Talbot Road and the side road. Here, quite close to the North Talbot Road, George built another two-story brick house. But I pass by this residence because the family now lives in the farmstead on the northeast corner of the road junction.

On the right-hand corner of the road junction two mail boxes are mounted on posts, and I open the one closest to the corner. Back on the cycle, I pedal along the side road for some fifty yards before turning left into the driveway of our farm. Had I continued past our farm to the north toward Byron, I would have found the cycling more challenging, for after a slight dip in front of our house to a small bridge spanning a little stream that emerges from our night pasture, the road crosses hillier terrain. Beyond our line fence on the left side of the road is an old frame house usually occupied by renters, and across our line fence is a one-story dwelling, little better than a shack, built by a bachelor who recently inherited the twenty-five acres on which it sits. Now the road dips again before surmounting a hill steep enough to make some cyclists dismount and push their wheels up past the mailboxes of the McLaughlins' place on the right and that of the Griffiths to the left. From here there are no more farm residences to the east of the road until it reaches the Second Concession-line Road, three quarters of a mile from our side road. To the west of the road however, Ed Brown's farm lies adjacent to that of his sister Mrs. Griffith, and Basil Cornell has a small acreage in fruit beyond him. The Second Concession Road rises rather sharply as it runs west from its junction with the North Talbot Road, and on the crest of the hill Stan Cornell manages a prosperous small fruit operation. His gray stucco house commands a magnificent view of the countryside to the south, and he has named his home the Valley View Fruit Farm.

Beyond the second concession the road continues to loop upward. The first farmstead on the left is unoccupied, owned by a widow, Mrs. McGregor, the land rented during the mid-1930s by Tink Bogue. Opposite that farmstead is a smallholding occupied by nonfarming retirees. Beyond the McGregor place on the west side of the road to the north is the small farm occupied by the Duncans, father and son. Just beyond their farmstead the road crests, and here there is a large gravel pit. Now the rider has reached the summit of the Thames River bluffs. From here the road descends steeply through wooded banks in a series of tight curves. To the school cyclist, this is the "Big Hill." Sometimes my brother Len amuses himself and his passengers when returning from Byron by pushing the accelerator of our Model A. Ford to the floor as the car labors out of the last upward curve of this big hill, gains all the speed possible over the short stretch of level road ahead, and bursts over the hill crest behind Duncan's barn with a stomach-twisting wrench. Then he turns off the ignition to see whether the car will coast all the way home.

For the cyclist returning home on his one-speed bike, the Big Hill is too much; he is soon afoot, pushing his machine up the winding inclines. But going north, as I did on school mornings during my last two years of high school at London Central Collegiate Institute, the Big Hill was pure exhilaration. Coasting downward, the bike accelerates swiftly. Soon the wind whistles in the ears, eyes tear, and the intoxication of speed takes full command. In the late spring of 1938 that intoxication was almost to end in serious injury. Sweeping out of the last curve, I tried to avoid a rut and my handlebars broke apart. In the clanging, scraping, dust-raising crash that followed, pure luck placed me on top of the rear wheel as the machine slid along the road.

My companion, Ron C., helped me search for broken bones. There were none, but there was a six-inch rent in the seat of my trousers. We borrowed needle and thread from Jeanie L., at whose place we left our bikes during the day, and Ron did his best to stitch up the problem. But my probing hand detected flesh as we walked from our London bus stop to the school, and I blessed the dimness of London Central's corridors when I moved from class to class. As I emerged into the light of a classroom, I darted quickly to a seat, holding my notebook well to the rear.

The two miles of road stretching from Cousin Tink's southern line fence to the Duncan property gave lengthwise dimension to our neighborhood. Dale's Side Road, on which our driveways opened, provided latitude. If we followed that little road west from its junction with the North Talbot Road, the Vanstone farm ran along on our left, and on our right lay the fields of Fora Cornell, who occupied the holding on the northwest corner at our crossroad. Beyond its junction with the North Talbot Road the side road inclined downward for some 150 yards to a small bridge above the same stream that exited from our night pasture. On a rise some fifty yards past the bridge sat Fora's two-story brick residence.

Now the road ditches became increasingly sandy and we came to a smallholding where young Harvey Kilbourne lived in a one-story dwelling for some years during the 1930s, supporting himself by market gardening and by work as a plasterer. Once past his sandy field, we came to the woods that bordered the east bank of Dingman's Creek and a final mild downward dip of the road took us to a small iron bridge across the "crik." Here a path through the trees along the stream led to a neighborhood swimming hole. Beyond the bridge on both right and left were the farms of the Pack brothers, although in these years, Bill, living south of the side road, spent much of his time trucking livestock, particularly animals being shipped to the Toronto stockyards.

If, on the other hand, we turned east from our gateway on the side road, we traveled between George's former and current farms for half a mile and thence another half mile between the Dale and the old Topping place. This distance brought us to the T junction where the side road met the Bostwick Road, named for the early nineteenth-century surveyor who had surveyed it during the 1820s. By turning to the right and traveling along "the Bostwick" for half a mile, we reached, on the right, the edge of the back fifty of the David Bogue farm, a tract that George had inherited. The family of George's younger brother Chester held the matching fifty, fronting on the North Talbot Road, Chester having been killed in the woods by a falling tree in 1911.

The presence of Bogues on the North Talbot Road during the 1930s traced back to the decision of a lowland Scot, John Bogue Sr., to emigrate to Upper Canada when he was already in early middle age. Born in 1800 in Lanarkshire, Scotland, he arrived in London, Ontario, with his wife and four young children in 1837, the year of the Upper Canada Rebellion, and they settled on lot 33 in the First Concession of Westminster Township. Unfortunately any records and correspondence belonging to Bogues of the first and second generations disappeared with their passing. John's biographical sketch in the *History of the County of Middlesex* of 1889 explains that he migrated as a young man to Widby in northern England, where he worked as a gardener for some twenty years, married Elizabeth Parrott, and fathered the children that they brought with them to Upper Canada.

In the new land John was a farmer and brick maker, benefiting from the excellent brick clay that underlay some of the holdings in the First Concession of lots in Westminster Township. This activity of John and some of his neighbors gave the road its early name, Brick Street. The census taker of 1852 recorded a household that included John, Elizabeth, and their children, Allan, Emma, James, David, and Richard, ranging in age from twenty to seven years of age. Of the younger Bogues, Allan and Emma were born in England, while the place of birth of the remaining three was listed as Upper Canada. The household also included a laborer, James Smart, identified as a Scot and eventually the husband of Ann Bogue, a daughter who was not present when the enumerator called in 1851. The census reveals a thriving agricultural operation producing a wide range of crops, livestock, and dairy products.

By this time, the Bogue family on Brick Street was already subdividing. The census taker also reported that twenty-four-year-old John, English born, and eleven-year-old Thomas Bogue, Canadian by birth, were living on a farm in the Second Concession of Westminister, where they tended sixty-nine acres in crops in 1851. But this John's later history, along with that of his younger brother David, was played out on the North Talbot Road between Lambeth and Byron.

North of Lambeth on both the east and west sides of the North Talbot Road, the government surveyor marked off two-hundred-acre lots, beginning with number 71. These continued the sequence of lot numbers running from south to north along the road from Talbotville, south of Lambeth. On the north side of lot 75, the surveyor left space for the crossroad that we called Dale's Side Road, and beyond this street lot 76 fronted on the North Talbot road. Since the lot lines along the North Talbot road did not run in parallel with the concession-line roads of the township as a whole, lot 78 (east), lying immediately south of the Second Concession-line road, was triangular in shape. Reflecting the fact that the land surveys in Westminster Township incorporated at least two organizational principles, the lots to the north of the Second Concession Road fronted on that road rather than on the North Talbot Road (see map 1).

In 1835 the Crown vested the title to the 202 acres of lot 73 (east) in Abram Sloot, and by 1853 David M. Rymals and his wife owned this property. In that year this couple deeded it to John Bogue Sr., accepting from him a note and mortgage in the amount of one thousand dollars. Ten years later the Rymals released the mortgage, John Bogue's obligation to satisfy the note or bond having been satisfactorily discharged. John Bogue Jr. and his younger brother, David, developed farms and raised families on the southern and northern halves of this property. The patriarch on Brick Street did not rush to place ownership of these lands in his sons' hands, deeding them to John Jr. and David, my grandfather, in 1886. By that time John Jr. was fifty-eight and David was forty-three years of age. John and David Bogue lived out their lives on the North Talbot Road. John passed on his property to his son Norman, and David divided his half of lot 73 between his son George and the family of his deceased son Chester.

Elsewhere, three other sons of John Bogue Sr. also became land-owning farmers, presumably with the assistance of their father. Thomas and James settled in Adelaide Township, close to the town of Strathroy. Allan, the second son, inherited the Brick Street property when his father died at the age of ninety-one in 1891. Of the six sons of John Bogue Sr., therefore, five

North Talbot Road neighborhood lot and property lines, 1878

succeeded in acquiring farms in Middlesex County. Only Richard left the county, emigrating to the prairies of the Canadian West and becoming a storekeeper in Moose Jaw, Saskatchewan.

Obviously the combined occupations of farmer and brick maker allowed John Bogue Sr. to do well by his family. He reported to the census taker of 1871 that he had produced 250,000 bricks in that year to the value of some twelve hundred dollars, using a labor force of six workers during five months of operation—somewhat lower figures than those reported by the proprietors of seven adjacent brickyards.

David Bogue celebrated the birth of his eldest son, George Allan, in 1879. The youngster attended public school and then saved the money that allowed him to attend the Business College directed in London by James Westervelt. Here he learned basic accounting procedures, mental arithmetic, and other skills appropriate to bookkeepers and clerks. Late in his life he could still demonstrate the rigor of this training by reciting multiplication tables up to fourteen times fourteen and saying the alphabet backwards. His business skills gave his later life a different quality than that of the usual farm boy. One of his best decisions, however, led him to court and in 1904 to marry Eleta Britton, one of the three daughters of Ellen Brannagan Britton, who lived on the Third Concession Road between the school grounds of ss 17 and Dingman's Creek. When he started farming, George's possessions consisted of two horses and probably a buggy or wagon. But Eleta had inherited five hundred dollars from the estate of her father, and George used it as down payment on a farm in lot 74 (west) on the North Talbot Road. It was apparently a sensible decision, but Eleta later believed that the importance of her stake in the union was not always acknowledged.

Solidly built and a scant five feet, nine inches in height, George had hazel eyes, a small wave in his black hair, and a ginger mustache. He was articulate, although no orator. Nor was he a wit or a great raconteur, although not without some sense of humor. In later years I recall him repeating with great relish the story about Mitchell F. Hepburn, the provincial Liberal Party leader, who mounted the box of a manure spreader at a barnyard political rally and announced that for once he had the opportunity to stand upon the party platform of his opponents. A female relative in George and Eleta's generation told me that as a young man, George had been thought to be a great catch by the young women of the neighborhood.

Eleta Britton, eldest of Ellen Britton's three daughters, was a slim girl almost as tall as George, with brown hair, gray eyes, and regular features. Her stepfather called her a tomboy, and one of her shins was deeply pitted where a doctor had chiseled out an infection that had developed in a bruise suffered in a fall from a horse. She did not smile for photographers because her teeth were unevenly placed. In the years that I knew her she was a serious and prim woman. "That wasn't very nice," she remarked to me as the audience laughed during a grandstand performance at London Fair when a clown lost his outer trousers to reveal red flannel long johns. She did enjoy the occasional joke and drew upon a fund of proverbs. "If wishes were horses, all beggars would ride," she told me when I learned that I was expected to walk to a young people's function in Lambeth, adding "Shank's mare for you."

We know little about George and Eleta's first farm operation. Their first daughter, Myrtle, arrived in 1905 and three years later came a son, Leonard Wilfred. The household at this time was Grit—that is, Liberal— in sentiment and my brother's hated middle name attested to George's admiration for the great party leader Wilfred Laurier. Eleta and George apparently prospered in other respects as well, if the substantial brick house that they built on this holding is any indication. During George's early years in agriculture, the farmers of the Lambeth area became converts to the gospel of cooperation, he among them. In later years Eleta told of early cooperative activity when the local society ordered railroad carloads of fertilizer and other farm supplies for distribution to members. George kept the books for such enterprise. Later the society maintained two general stores and a cheese factory. Hired employees managed the stores and a cheese maker contracted with the society to run the dairy enterprise. Throughout my memory of the co-op activity, George was the secretary, holding the seal of the society, preparing and sending out the annual reports, and going to the store in Lambeth on Saturday nights to write checks for the manager.

In the days of its greatest popularity, the cooperative combined a dinner and entertainment with its annual meeting. When I was four or five I first encountered the oyster at one such gathering, an oyster supper. I filed reservations about oyster stew and rebelled utterly at oysters on the shell. Members of the board of directors of the organization sometimes held evening meetings at our house, and some of them were dedicated smokers. Eleta hated the smoke, ashes, and residual stink, but when the smokers apologized, or asked permission to smoke, she was always gracious, affirming that her houseplants found the smoke to be a beneficial fumigant. The discussions I heard as I waited for sleep meant little to me, but I remember George's repeated ploy in trying to move meetings forward— "Now boys, what have we decided about this?"—as well as general expressions of concern from members of the group about the tendency of co-op rank and file to buy their groceries at the big stores in London. In truth, the secretary's family was not free from this sin, nor, I suspect, were the families of other directors. The cooperative stores gave credit, and periodically George and other officers spent a day in calling upon customers whose bills had accumulated unduly, sometimes protecting the association by arranging a chattel mortgage on some of the delinquent's livestock.

George sold the farm on lot 74 (west) in 1909, and moved to the fifty-acre holding in lot 75 (east) on the southeast corner at the junction of the North Talbot Road and Dale's Side Road. The family was living on the southeast corner farm when Eleanor, my sister and senior by eight years, was born. That was still the family location when I arrived at London's Victoria Hospital in 1921, where I am sure the reception committee was somewhat different than that which met Myrtle and Leonard, my elder sister and brother, who were born at home.

George once told me that he had "made money" during the years of World War I because of the high prices for which wheat and other grains sold at that time. He considered himself to be a progressive farmer, and during the wartime era he began to convert his milking herd to purebred Holstein-Friesians. This impulse toward stock improvement was in line with family background. In early October 1851, John Bogue Sr. exhibited the best two-year-old filly at the agricultural fair held at the London fair grounds. Several of his sons, including my grandfather David, became enthusiastic poultry fanciers, showing their birds at fairs in the region. My great-uncle Allan pursued this interest so actively that he served on the board of directors of the Western Exhibition in London and became, so family members told me, the first Canadian to be named president of the North American Poultrymens' Association as well as serving as a judge at many fairs or exhibitions. Among articles left to George and Eleta by my grandfather and grandmother Bogue was a stand of bedroom drawers in which several compartments were stuffed with red, blue, yellow, and white prize ribbons awarded to my grandfather's fowl at local or regional fairs. I thought them pretty when first I saw them; later I myself succumbed to the mystique of the livestock show.

Given our family background, George's decision to develop a herd of registered Holsteins was not so much innovation as another expression of the family interest in improved livestock. The animals in his initial milking herd were unpedigreed or "grade" animals. The first step in the transition to purebred stock was his decision to buy a registered heifer for Len to enter in calf club competition.

My memory of the farmstead on the southeast corner is well fixed in mind because I knew it under owners who succeeded George and Eleta as well as during our family's tenure there. As farmsteads go, it was quite well developed. The brick house stood at the road corner, a short driveway to the south leading to a metal windmill, beyond which were clustered a garage building, the barn with attached machine shed and granary wing, a henhouse, and a hog pen.

The garage housed a stationary gasoline engine that could be belted to the windmill pump. Beneath the floor of the engine room was a cement cistern or water tank that projected beyond the building on the north. A stretch of this had a wooden cover that the men lifted to allow animals to drink directly from it. Behind the engine compartment was a small milk house, entered from the other side of the garage building. Inside this small room was another opening into the water tank, so that cans of milk could be lowered into it for cooling. Some thirty feet beyond and somewhat to the north of the garage, the barn paralleled the side road, about thirty feet within the property line. At the west end of the barn a one-story wooden structure ran out from its south side to provide an implement shed and granary, their front in parallel with the back of the garage and milk house.

When coming from the house we usually entered the barn by passing through the wide door of the implement shed and then opening a door set in the south wall of the barn. This took us into the first of three major ground-level areas within the barn, where we saw before us a box stall and a raised square cistern, its well containing water piped underground from the garage tank. Beyond a cleanup alley was a row of horse stalls, hinged-board flaps making the mangers accessible from the adjacent barn drive floor that formed the second major ground-level area of the barn. A door at the south end of the row of horse stalls led onto this drive floor, which had big access doors both on the side facing the road and into the yard behind the barn. As in the rest of the barn, the floor here was made of concrete. Beyond the drive floor was the cow stable, containing three rows of wooden stanchions, one fronting toward the barn floor and two running at right angles to the east end of the barn. The cows or younger animals confined in these stanchions stood on platforms raised a few inches above the floor level and terminating in gutters at the rear. A feeding alley ran between the east-west rows of stanchioned cattle, leading to a door in the middle of the east wall of the stable. This gave access to the silage chute of a wooden-stave silo. A small bay at the southeast corner of the stable provided additional floor space for a calf pen and tethered calves.

Above both the horse and cow stables, the squared-timber framework of the barn enclosed large mows. Suspended close below the peak of the roof, a wooden track ran from one end of the barn to the other; mounted on this was a hay car. We used this with a system of ropes and a harpoon fork to unload wagon loads of hay and with sling ropes to transfer loads of grain sheaves into the mows, preparatory to threshing. At threshing time, the separator man of the threshing crew typically positioned the machine's blower to shoot straw into a partially filled hay mow or into the mow from which the grain bundles had been taken. Roughly in the center of the ceiling in the cow stable, a chute provided the route by which hay or straw could be pitched down into the stable. Given its major internal divisions and the barn-floor access to mangers, the barn was a great place for games of hide-and-seek.

This barn had numerous access doors: the great drive-floor doors on either side; the door into the implement shed from the horse stable; single-width access doors at either end of the alley behind the horse stalls; similar doors opening both toward the road and on the barnyard side behind the row of cows facing the barn floor; the silage door in the east end of the barn; and another one opening into the alley behind the north row of east-west stanchions. Situated across the barnyard and beyond the end of the granary, a henhouse and a small hog house completed the barnyard layout.

We entered the house from the barnyard through a woodshed that was enclosed within the foundation and framing of the house. Here we could descend steps into the cellars or climb a short flight of stairs to enter a large kitchen. Beyond lay the dining room and parlor, with a downstairs bedroom in the northwest corner of the first floor. Stairways from the dining room took one down to the cellar or up to the second floor, where there were several more bedrooms.

Attached to the interior wall of the kitchen was a brown wooden telephone box with a black mouthpiece projecting from the front below silvery twin bells. On the right side of the box the earpiece rested in a forked metal holder, and below it was a small crank. Users stood while operating this device that linked the farm to the wider world. A big black cooking range stood opposite the exterior kitchen door. It had a square oven door and a water cistern at the right-hand end, supplying hot water in addition to that provided by the tea kettle or surface pans. A kitchen table stood by a southern window. I remember flames dancing within the glass chimney of a coal-oil lamp set upon that table at night and my brother sitting there with his crystal set, wearing headphones, and announcing that he was bringing in station KDKA in Pittsburgh.

At another time, I watched a sandy-haired man clamp a squat goosenecked device to the outer edge of the table, a drive crank projecting from it into the room. He set four small long-necked bottles of milk into copper cups suspended around a central connector positioned at the top of the machine and above the table. Then with a turn of the crank, he set the four samples of milk to spinning around the pivot, centrifugal force causing the copper cups to flip up at right angles to their original position and to lose their separate identities within a blurry copper-colored circle. He was forcing the butter fat to separate and move into the thin necks of the test bottles, explained Eleta, where he could measured it to determine the butter fat content in the milk of the cows that were "on test." This machine operator was an employee of the Record of Performance program of the Canadian Department of Agriculture. We knew such men as "ROP testers." Both Eleta and I would have been amazed to learn that years later I would be employed by the same university that employed the inventor of the Babcock Test and would even examine the rude prototype of the ROP tester's centrifuge, displayed in the lobby of Babcock Hall at the University of Wisconsin, Madison.

Our connection to ROP, I remember, led to my first civics lesson. As I approached school age, my siblings introduced me to the alphabet, and one evening as George sat at the kitchen table preparing his monthly report on the daily production of the various cows on test, I noticed that the big white preaddressed envelopes provided by the Record of Performance Program had the four capital letters of the government frank, OHMS, stamped in the upper right-hand corner.

"What does this mean?" I asked.

"Those capital letters stand for On His Majesty's Service," said George.

"Well who is His Majesty?"

"George the Fifth. He is our King."

"Do we have to do what he says?" I asked.

"Things don't quite work that way," George replied. "George V approves the laws our parliament makes and Canada is part of the British Empire [actually Commonwealth by this time], but we run our own show. A great English poet named Kipling wrote a poem called 'Our Lady of the Snows' about this."

Then George recited with great feeling:

"Daughter am I in my mother's house,
But mistress in my own,
And I abide by my Mother's House,"
Said our Lady of the Snows.

George was not a great reader and I never knew the source of this surprising show of erudition, but he mingled with politicians, and it was the Canadian government's decision to pass a preferential tariff that inspired Kipling to write his poem. This exchange at the kitchen table was my introduction to the political world of which we on the North Talbot Road were a part.

My household memories of the southeast corner farm also go back to the last days of Henry's appearance at the table. For a number of years during the 1920s and perhaps earlier as well, George hired Henry to spend a week or so doing our fall plowing. Due to a deformed back, the top of Henry's head was some four feet, six inches above and somewhat to the left of the soles of his shoes; he was, in the words of that day, a hunchback. He may also in George's vocabulary have been somewhat "slow." But he spoke little, which in George's view of hired men was much in his favor. He was also a good horseman and an excellent plowman. The meticulous straightness of his furrows left no opening for derisive comments from passersby. Henry's arrival always signaled a change in table settings. From the back of the kitchen cupboard, Eleta retrieved a set of butter dishes and each of us had our separate allocation of butter at the table for the duration of Henry's stay. This change in table etiquette was, I believe, linked to the havoc that Henry could produce in a communal butter dish with his gravy-laden knife rather than arising from a desire to stint his use of butter. Overindulgence in the more costly foods by hired help occasionally revealed a vein of Scots frugality or meanness in George, but this was not present in my mother.

I remember following Eleta down the interior cellar steps of the house to supervise her while she checked the temperature of an incubator set up beside the hot-air furnace and turned the chicken eggs within it and, at a later time, removed little chicks from a litter of egg shell and placed them in a cardboard box. But I can also remember seeing mother hens proudly leading little convoys of chicks here and there in the barnyard during those years.

On the southeast corner farm in spring, a pond usually collected in the middle of the field that lay immediately adjacent to the farmstead. Standing at the woodshed door, I once saw motor cars park on the side road and a well-dressed man with close-cropped gray mustache cross the yard to ask permission to enter the field behind our barn. He and his friends wanted to bring their binoculars to bear upon the wading birds that used the pond as a way station on their route north. This was Dr. Saunders, a pleasant man whose fame as an ornithologist had even reached our farm. My parents gladly gave permission, pleased that our farm was uniquely recognized by feathered navigators.

Although boisterous when my confidence was up, I was a rather timid child with little of the derring-do that marked my brother Leonard's childhood career around the farmstead. I was never attracted by the skeletal ladder attached to one side of the triangular steel-framed windmill standing some seventy feet from the back door of the house. But when Len was hardly big enough to walk a straight line, Eleta ended a search for him by spotting him some thirty feet above the yard and climbing resolutely upward. Never one to wring her hands in the face of challenge, she scaled the ladder and shielded him with her body as he climbed down. On another occasion George found him in a horse stall trying to pick stones from the hoof of its occupant with a large nail, imitating the Lambeth blacksmith at work. Luckily Len had chosen one of the more placid horses on which to begin his career as farrier.

Although I lacked my brother's venturesome spirit, I still found the barn to be an exciting and attractive place. There were colts and calves there and tempting piles of hay on the central barn floor. Eleta, George, and Len cautioned me to take care around the animals, and experience reinforced their advice. During the late teens and early twenties, George had the best cattle dog he had ever owned, a brown-and-tan farm collie. At a word from George at the stable door, Bob would dash out into the adjacent pasture, gather the milking herd into a compact platoon, and bring them at a gentle pace to the stable. But as I reached the active age of four or five, Bob was aging and becoming increasingly grouchy. A member of the family fed him after milking was finished in the alley below the hay chute, and at this point on a winter day I ventured within a foot or so of his feed dish. Bob bit me on the leg. It was one in a series of incidents in which he had been overly protective of the farm or of his own space. For a long time no one told me of the outcome of this encounter, but it was the last of such occasions. George had a neighbor shoot poor Bob.

I can remember standing in the stable alley behind the east-west row of milk cows, watching and listening to brother Len recite from *The Lays of Ancient Rome,* declaiming the deeds of Horatius, Sextus, and the twin Tarquins as he hunched on a small box, his head tucked into a black and white flank, milk spurting alternately in rhythmic streams below his clenching hands. Under his supervision in those years, I walked across the manure gutter into the space between two stanchioned cows, gingerly grasped a bovine teat, and tried myself to make the milk come. The initial experiment was a failure. For the time being I could only admire my brother's dexterity in producing pails of milk topped with an inch or so of white foam and occasionally, with an air of utter innocence, whipping a white stream across the bare legs of a passing sister.

At this time George was producing milk for sale in the city, and I joined an expedition to bring home an additional milk cow he had purchased on Brick Street, several miles away. Our Chevrolet touring car of those years inched along the rural roads as the cow walked somewhat indignantly in the shallow road ditch in front of my brother and sister, snatching mouthfuls of timothy grass as she was driven farther and farther from her home pastures.

Producers of milk for our dairy outlet, Silverwood's Dairy, were required to follow hygienic rules. Milk must be strained and cooled immediately after being taken from the cow, stables were to be whitewashed, and they must be cleaned daily. Hogs were not to be kept in quarters within or closely adjacent to the cow stable. Sanitary inspectors checked the premises without prior warning for compliance on such matters. Father of a family of six boys and one daughter and a great talker, Bill Topping owned the hundred-acre farm beyond ours on the side road. He produced milk for the same dairy and believed that the sanitary regulations were overly strict. George liked to tell of the day Bill was at our place and an inspector arrived in our barnyard. Going immediately to our house, Bill asked permission to use the phone and was soon telling one of his boys to take precautions. By the time the inspector had completed his visit at our barn and driven on along the side road to Bill's farm, the barn there contained not a pig, although a vacant pen showed suspicious traces of hog droppings.

The southeast corner farm had a simple field layout. An orchard and night pasture lay directly to the south of the farmstead. We had expeditions in early summer to the Yellow Transparent and Red Astrakhan trees bearing the fruit that was first to ripen in the orchard. The four other fields all ran from the side road fence to the south line fence. The first of these was usually in pasture, although George cropped it in some years. About two thirds of the way across this field from the road, a pond collected in the late fall and remained into the spring; a tile run limited its dimensions and drained away most of the water during the latter season. In winter the pond provided good skating. As I was being readied for bed in my first few years, I could sometimes hear the swish and scrape of skates and the shouts of my older siblings and neighborhood youngsters as they skated or played shinny with a puck or tin can on winter nights. Each would try to control the puck for as long as possible. It was a great triumph when at four or five I was allowed one evening to try out a pair of hand-me-down skates on the pond. I remember the pond as backdrop also on a spring day when I watched George and a stocky white-mustached man, "the vet," come from the field after inspecting the colt of Mae, one of our gray Percheron mares. Joint ill was the diagnosis, but young Major survived.

Beyond the first field lay one that was in cultivation or in hay each year. It had a gentle upward slope, cresting about halfway back on the farm. Here I had my first experience, at age six or seven, in driving the team on the hay wagon as the horses straddled the windrow of cured hay. I remember the groan of the wagon as I turned too sharply at the end of the windrow and the front wheels grated against the wooden underframing of the hay rack. In the third field the ground dropped down from the road to a smaller pond surrounded by a fringe of sumac and scrub timber. This also we pastured and sometimes used as a night pasture.

Beyond this enclosure, and stretching to the east line fence, was a large and relatively level field, consistently kept under grain or forage crops. At one time some of the frontage of this field had apparently been hedged with thorn. By the time I knew it, the thorn plants had become scraggly trees almost covered with vines of bittersweet. One day when George was cultivating corn in that field, a sister escorted me to the field at noon so that I could ride the cultivator horse up the road to the barn. Still in memory I feel the hot, still pool of air that I rode through on the sunny side of the barrier of vines, my hands grasping the brass knobs at the top of the harness hames, and the horse's flanks sweaty against the inside of my bare knees. George walked behind with the reins (lines, we usually said) still knotted behind his back. In the fall the bittersweet berries turned this barrier into an orange wall some fifteen feet high, a sight Eleta said was well worth the walk back on the side road.

By the time my memory began to store images of farm life along the North Talbot Road, George had incorporated the back half of his father's farm into his own farming operation. At the time of transfer, this included some twenty acres of prime maple sugar bush immediately behind the front fifty on the North Talbot Road, where Chester's widow, Aunt Leila, and her sons lived. David had made a considerable quantity of syrup in this bush. George continued the practice on a lesser scale while we were on the southeast corner farm. In perhaps the last year before George cut the big timber on the Bostwick fifty, I accompanied Eleta and one of my sisters on a buggy trip to the sugar shanty in order to bring out several milk cans of concentrated maple sap that was to be given a final boiling down and straining at home.

I found it a tiresome journey, to and fro over Dale's Side Road and the Bostwick Road—then in a condition of spring breakup—and an even more problematic passage up the lane and into the bush on the back fifty. As horsewoman Eleta was competent and fearless, and she took us safely to the shanty where George was supervising a big evaporator pan in which sap was boiling and steaming furiously.

The twenty-five acres of the back fifty that stretched from the Bostwick Road to the bush was improved land, used for forage or grain crops. To the south of our fifty acres lay the back end of Tink's farm, much of it still wooded. Unlike George, Tink was an only child and had no brother with whom patrimony must be shared. The gateway into our Bostwick fifty was set on the south side of the property, adjacent to the line fence separating Tink's farm and our land, and it opened into a fenced holding of perhaps an acre, the lane beyond it running along Tink's fence line all the way back to the woods. Close by the road, George had built a thirty-foot steel windmill and watering trough, picking the site for its well by using a dowsing wand. Len joked that a well dug at any point on this part of the back fifty would have struck water at about the same depth, but in such decisions George tried to have as much working for him as possible. Although the back fifty increased the size of our farm unit to about 150 acres, the distance between the front and back tracts meant that the men wasted a good deal of time in traveling back and forth.

Historians often write of neighborhoods and communities without attempting to define their terms. Our neighborhood of the 1920s and 1930s was a stretch of open country bisected by the North Talbot Road and quartered by our side road. The names on the mailboxes were mainly of English and Scottish derivation, but among them were one Welsh and one Pennsylvania Dutch name. Quite a number of the heads of households were the sons of men and women who had improved the raw farms emerging from the woods along the North Talbot Road during the last two thirds of the nineteenth century. But a glance at the *Historical Atlas of Middlesex County, Ontario*, published in 1878, shows that the names of at least ten of the landholders of that date in our neighborhood had vanished from the ownership plat of the area by my time, their property now occupied by incomers or by the sons and daughters of other members of the local settler generation.

George used to say to family members or acquaintances who wished to buy a new farm that it was important to investigate the neighbors as well as the farm in question. Bad ones, he said, could make life intolerable. My recollections of the people who lived in the stretch of open country I have described are of individuals who were approachable and friendly but not excessively forthcoming. The farmers traded work at threshing and silo-filling time, each farmer estimating a fair exchange in terms of workers or team and wagon when he contacted his neighbors. I never heard complaint about anyone asking for too much or giving too little. Erection of a new farm building might be marked by an invitation to neighbors to help in raising the frame, and such occasions were well attended. A reasonable request to borrow a tool or other scarce article inspired a willing response, although we expected that such demands would not be made too often and that items would be returned with reasonable promptness.

There was social mingling within the neighborhood. Perhaps half of the families along our stretch of the North Talbot Road were members of the Lambeth congregation of the United Church of Canada. They saw one another at Sunday services and Sunday school and in good weather exchanged greetings and pleasantries for a few minutes on the church lawn after the weekly service. The activities of the church auxiliaries and the weeknight prayer meeting drew individuals to the church as well. Several families along the road were Anglican, however, and attended services in that church's beautiful little one-story chapel at the main corner in Lambeth. In the late 1920s one family joined the congregation of a charismatic Baptist preacher in London, committing themselves to his ministry on a short-run basis, given that he was preaching that the world would end in 1929. Faithfulness to church going varied, however, both within and among families. George sometimes chose to do chores on Sunday morning rather than attend service with Eleta and younger members of the family. Other farmer heads of households behaved similarly. Len never went to church on Sunday morning in the years of my recollection, but he sometimes attended the evening service with male or female friends. Family attendance at the ss 17 Public School and Lambeth Continuation School also gave the neighborhood families common interests. Death in a household prompted neighbors to leave prepared foods quietly in the grieving family's kitchen and to drop by for a few minutes of commiseration as well as to attend the funeral.

We should not overemphasize the restrictions that local geography placed upon the residents of this or any other Ontario rural neighborhood of the time. Only one family on our stretch of the North Talbot Road lacked an automobile during my years of recollection. There was local bus service between Lambeth and London and also between Byron and London over the Springbank Drive. And each family's neighborhood differed from that of adjacent families. I doubt that the members of any individual farmer's threshing ring in the open country between Lambeth and Byron were identical with those of another. When Len went threshing on a farm at the northern limit of our exchange group, he mingled with sheaf pitchers or teamsters from farms on the Second Concession Road or adjacent side roads with whom we did not exchange work. Although our southeast corner farm shared a line fence with Bill Topping's farm at the eastern end of Dale's Side Road, and we passed by his farmstead frequently in the course of going to or coming from the back fifty, and George and Bill were on good terms, the two farms did not exchange work. At that time Bill maintained neighborly relations with farmers on the Second Concession Road and Brick Street.

Kin relationships for most of the families along our stretch of the North Talbot Road extended beyond our neighborhood. The farm occupied by my grandmother, Ellen Britton, and her second husband and their son faced on Highway 2, just to the east of Lambeth. Daughter Eleta and other members of our family often visited there. There was the occasional exchange of farming machinery between the two farms as well. Eleta's younger sister and her husband farmed on the Gore Road, adjacent to Delaware Township, and we visited them and rotated joint celebrations at Christmas in family gatherings that the grandparents also attended. We did not exchange labor or agricultural implements with that family, however.

Lines of business interaction radiated out from George's farm, especially to Lambeth, where as we have seen he was involved in the administration of the Farmer's Co-op store where the family purchased many supplies. There was a social dimension involved in the co-op relationship as well. George and Eleta became good friends of some of the directors and their wives, and there was a certain amount of family visiting back and forth. The coming of the auto age facilitated such socializing, since most of the directors lived in the wider Lambeth service area. George and some of these men would also be active in the political movement known as the United Farmers of Ontario and its successor, the Progressive Party. The activity earned George stints as a returning officer in two provincial elections.

In recent years scholars have written much about a sense of place. That such a thing exists none can argue. Driving down the North Talbot Road between Lambeth and Byron today evokes a flood of memories and emotions in me. I am sure that other surviving children of the 1930s who trudged or rode their bikes along the Byron extension of the North Talbot Road during the 1930s have similar reactions when they ride along it today. But I also know that their sense of living in that place and time is not the same as mine. In viewing its surface detail, they share with me some sense of place, but for each of us the inward personal meaning is unique. The individual comes to understand—as I did not when I rode the old bicycle along the road—that layer after layer of information exists, each, as we acquire it, deepening our understanding of place.

I had no inkling as I biked along the North Talbot Road that the landscape owed its basic contours to the Wisconsin Glacier, the last of the series of great ice sheets that covered the area thousands of years ago. I knew that the farm lands to the west of the road tended to be sandier or more gravelly than were ours and that the soil on the east side was darker brown in color and softer to the touch when rolled between finger and thumb. George told me that the soil on our farm was a clay loam—he pronounced the word "loom." In this he differed from the judgment of later soil scientists, who decided that most of our land was surfaced with sandy silt loam, although there was some clay soil at the east end. Neither George nor I understood that our stretch of the North Talbot Road roughly paralleled the northeastern edge of a glacial spillway; that insignificant little Dingman's Creek, half a mile to the west, rested in the bed of what had been a great flow of glacial icemelt; or that the intervening sands and gravels had been deposits in the bed or along the shore of that great stream. To the east of the road in our vicinity, however, such deposits were less prevalent in the rolling glacial till plain left there by the retreating glacier. George's progression northward from farm to farm along the North Talbot Road and inheritance of the back fifty of his father's farm had been fortunate insofar as his farming operations were concerned, because the spillway sands and gravels crossed the road into the front fields of the ancestral front fifty, and his first farm unit in the next lot to the north had been west of the road. The soils of our farms at the crossroads were more drought resistant and generally more productive than the sandier soils to the south and west.

Unknowing, I contested the area's glacial legacy on most school mornings during my last two years of high school when I toiled my bicycle north along the North Talbot Road to catch a bus on Springbank Drive. Laboring up the series of slopes and hills that began a few hundred yards past our northern line fence, I was mounting the southern side of the Ingersoll Moraine, shaped by glacial activity along the side of the Wisconsin Glacier lobe that had on its southern side the spillway feebly marked today by Dingman's Creek. The glacial waterway on the northern side of the lobe was much larger than its southern counterpart, and in its deepest part the Thames River now flows. Of all this I was completely ignorant, as apparently were my teachers in public and high school. A life-long fan of the mystery story, I might have approached my choice of career quite differently had I known how fascinating a detective story the glacial physiography of southern Ontario provided.

Nor did I know that climatologists would later place our neighborhood in a climatic subregion that they named the "South Slopes," an area of southward-inclining topography upslope of the lakeshore counties along Lakes Erie and Ontario. Our neighborhood was at its coldest in January, when the mean daily temperature there is some 23 degrees Fahrenheit, and at its warmest in July, when that measure is about 69 degrees. Between spring and fall the farmers in this region could expect a frost-free period of between 140 and 150 days on average and a growing season that began about mid-April and ended in early November, including something more than 200 days. They would usually see their fields moistened each year by some thirty-seven inches of precipitation in the form of rainfall or snow, distributed fairly evenly through the year. At the time I might have challenged this last fact, impressed as I was by the apparent tendency of the weatherman to dump endless buckets of rain upon us in the week of the great Western Fair or exhibition in London.

George could not have quoted accurately the climatic limits within which he farmed, but he understood from years of observation and practice when it was safe to plant particular crops and the times at which they must be harvested if a good yield was to be expected. He never, for example, made the mistake of planting winter wheat in mid-August, thus making it vulnerable to the Hessian fly, as did a young farmer on the Second Concession-line Road whose fields we sometimes passed on our way into London. Neither George nor any member of the family had heard of corn heat units, which, when calculated on the basis of the daily differences between minimum and maximum temperatures summed, gave totals that predicted the success to be expected in growing corn for different purposes. Such knowledge was one of the advances in agricultural science and hybridization that took place in Ontario during the 1950s and 1960s.

On the farms at the crossroads my siblings and I knew nothing of the lives of the Native Americans who had ranged the area before the arrival of Europeans, although Len and his friend from across the side road, Andy M., dug up a bag full of crude pottery shards from the edge of our woods on the northeast corner farm. We were also largely ignorant of the earlier story of the settler neighborhood of the mid- and late nineteenth century. George and Eleta were born and raised no more than a mile away, but they seldom talked about their younger days. I was in university before I learned that the North Talbot Road bore the name of a crusty old soldier who had supervised the transfer of the land title from the Crown to private citizens in some thirty southwestern Ontario townships including our Westminster. The prefix *North* distinguished our Talbot Road from other roads along which Colonel Thomas Talbot had placed settlers. Initially running from the St. Thomas area to Lambeth, the North Talbot Road was extended to Byron on the Thames River. One of the early settlers in the Lambeth-Byron area claimed that he had hacked out the original trace between the emerging villages about 1810. Although I knew our land was divided from that of our neighbors by line fences, I had no idea of the pattern of rectangles and corrective gore roads and triangles that government surveyors like Mahlon Burwell and John Bostwick had traced upon the land in Westminster Township during the first decades of the nineteenth century, following survey procedures more flexible but also more confusing than those on the public lands in the United States. The knowledge that shapes an individual's sense of place may be either deep or shallow; the sense of place is a very personal thing.

TWO

We Move to the Northeast Corner

Two long rings followed by a short one on our party-line telephone, I soon learned, could signal good or interesting things to come—news that my oldest sister would be home for the weekend, that the family Christmas celebration would be held at my grandmother's house, or that a milk tester was expected to arrive at the farm within a few days. Other calls caused Eleta's voice to drop to a low, sober tone and at some point in the conversation she would ask, "When is the funeral?" More frightening were the times when the phone rang for a minute or so continuously, then stopped briefly and began to peal again. This signaled an emergency and most frequently meant that there was a fire at one of the homes on the line. Someone at every house picked up the receiver for such calls and then hastily hung up upon learning the nature and location of the emergency, so as not to interfere with calls for assistance.

In midafternoon on a perfect day in midsummer, 1927, our phone began to peal. Eleta soon shouted to Len in the barnyard that the Toppings' barn was on fire. A gentle rise in elevation several hundred yards beyond our buildings prevented us from seeing the buildings in their farmstead. But Len climbed partway up our windmill and reported that a big column of smoke was rising to the east. Soon it could be seen from the ground as well. The pumper truck of the Lambeth Fire Department came down the North Talbot Road and lumbered along the side road. George, returning from London in late afternoon, reported that the barn was completely in flames and that family members and the assembled onlookers were carrying furniture from the house in case it too should catch fire. Later that evening we learned that Bill Topping had lost all of his buildings, his well having failed to supply enough water to keep the house sufficiently wet to resist the burning brands flying from the barn.

In these years the *London Advertiser,* the Grit newspaper to which we

subscribed, and its Tory rival, the *London Free Press,* periodically carried accounts of such fires, which were usually attributed to spontaneous
combustion in mows of inadequately cured hay. Bill Topping was also a
smoker and the father of five sons, one or two of whom might have been
experimenting with the combustion of tobacco that afternoon. The exact
cause of the disastrous fire at the Topping place was never identified. But
it had far-reaching effects upon George Bogue and his family.

On September 20, 1902, George had purchased his first farm, a fifty-
nine-acre parcel in lot 74, west of the North Talbot Road. For this tract
he paid $3,300 to a widow, Mary Mathers, who accepted a down payment
of $500 and a note and mortgage for the remaining $2,800 of the sale
price. After their marriage in 1904, George and Eleta remained on this
farm for six years and contributed a substantial two-story brick house to
its improvements. In 1910 George and Eleta sold the property in lot 74 for
$5,450, having purchased fifty acres in lot 75E in 1909 and a like acreage
in lot 76E in 1910, paying $4,000 and $3,500 for the two parcels. They
made up the difference between the sale price of the farm in lot 74 and the
total of the two acquisitions by mortgaging the lot 75 property for $2,000.
The prosperity that Ontario farmers enjoyed as a result of the demand for
agricultural products during World War I allowed George and Eleta to pay
off this mortgage in the fall of 1918.

In addition to looking forward to obtaining title to the north half of
John Bogue Sr.'s 1853 purchase of 202 acres on the North Talbot Road,
my grandfather David had in 1879 obtained a tract across the road in lot
73W. He sold this in two parcels, the last transferred to another owner in
1915, and then he moved to a six-acre holding in lot 76E. Here he and my
grandmother occupied a set of farm buildings located across Dale's Side
Road from the farmstead in lot 75E where George and Eleta lived.

Meanwhile George's younger brother, Chester, had lived on the front
fifty of David Bogue's original location in lot 73E with his family until his
death in 1911. My Aunt Leila continued to reside there with her two sons, her
second husband, and a third son. David died in 1923, and my grandmother
Sarah followed two years later. Now George's title was confirmed to the
back fifty of lot 73E with its sugar bush, and he also acquired David's small
holding in 76E. At about this time he added to his acreage in that lot by
purchasing a twenty-acre tract that brought this unit up to seventy-five
acres. This was the situation when Bill Topping's buildings went up in
smoke and flames in the summer of 1927.

Within a few weeks of this catastrophe, Bill decided that he could best
mend his fortunes by purchasing our farm on the southeast corner. It was

a reasonable decision. Although the barn on our southeast corner farm was somewhat smaller than the one he had lost, it was adequate, and the other buildings on the farmstead were superior in some respects to those that had burned. Bill would now have a farm unit of 150 contiguous acres, and his six sons seemed to guarantee the labor force needed to operate it. He agreed to pay the Bogues $6,500 for the fifty acres and improvements in lot 75E. His payment included a note and mortgage for $2,500 as part of the transaction. This George promptly sold to a third party. We would continue in possession on the southeast corner farm until the late spring of 1928.

Now George and Eleta owned seventy-five acres with old and somewhat dilapidated buildings in lot 76E and the back fifty of what had been David's hundred acres in lot 73E. After selling the southeast corner farm, George logged off the bush on the back fifty, selling some of the logs to his first cousins, James and Edgar, who operated a sawmill and lumber yard in Strathroy. Others he used as massive floor joists above the stables in reconstructing the barn on the northeast corner farm. In the fall of 1928 he sold the back fifty subject to completion of the logging operation. He then bought another farm on the Fifth Concession-line Road but disposed of it on unfavorable terms after harvesting one year of crops from it.

For one or two years thereafter he rented the Dale farm, located directly behind our farm on the side road. In 1932 he took back the Bostwick Road fifty when the buyer was unable to meet the terms of purchase. He resold this tract at the end of the 1930s in order to obtain funds with which to purchase a house in London, which members of the family first occupied in the spring of 1939. Perhaps George believed that Bill Topping's offer of $6,500 in 1927 was too good to turn down. Whatever George's motives, the sale of the southeast corner farm was part of a series of transactions that probably left the value of his assets in 1939 at a figure well below that of 1927. But said Eleta later, "George could not bear to have money in his pocket; spend it he must." These transactions, as we shall see, very much reflected the different visions of the future held by George, Eleta, my brother Len, and my sister Myrtle. They helped to shape my future as well.

In 1927, George, I believe, miscalculated the costs of bringing the seventy-five acres on the northeast corner into profitable production. In general the fencing was old and in need of repair. The barn had a dirt floor and a ground-level foundation, the weathered board siding was shrunken, cracked, and in some places rotten or missing. The wind had blown off some of the old wooden roofing shingles. As it stood, the barn was unsuited for a dairy operation that met the standards of the day. The massive hand-hewn oak timbers of the structure's frame, however, were sound. George planned to raise this skeleton to sit on concrete walls, enclosing a cement-floored lower story divided into a cow stable, a horse stable, and a section of box stalls. There was to be fresh board siding as required for the barn's upper story, he told us, and a corrugated galvanized metal roof. Lengthwise the barn would run from north to south, and on the west side would be an elevated approach or bridge giving access to two great doors in the second story wall opening onto the drive floor. He planned a double or two-bay mow in the north end of the barn and a granary and single mow at the other side of the drive floor.

I cannot remember many of the details of our move across the road to the northeast corner house and farm during the late spring and summer of 1928. Work on rebuilding the barn began in the spring and was completed during the summer. The Topping boys brought loads of newly cured hay up the side road to store in the empty mows of the barn on the southeast fifty, and I can remember hearing my brother or sister shouting, "Here come the Toppings," and straining to hear the rumbling sound of loaded horse-drawn wagons coming down the gravel side road from the east. We continued to milk our cows in the stable on the southeast corner farm until the new barn was completed.

We transferred our household furniture and kitchenware to the house on the northeast corner place at the end of June. This faded white clapboard dwelling consisted of a two-story section that ran north and south with a one-story wing projecting toward the barnyard. The wing had a woodshed attached on the north side, its walls faced with metal shingling, its roof made of corrugated iron. George employed carpenters to modernize the house somewhat prior to our occupancy, but it lacked the furnace and central heating of the house on the southeast corner farm. Instead of the outdoor toilet to which we were accustomed, however, we could now use a privy in the corner of the woodshed. The wooden receptacle of this one was set in a dry well and could be removed and hauled away for disposal of its contents. Our move across the road occurred at the same time as the Ontario Hydro Electric Power Commission began to provide electrical service on this section of the North Talbot Road. By the time we occupied it, George had had the old house wired for electricity. This house had a porch built into the south side of the single-story wing facing the driveway, and the electrician placed the electricity meter and a control box containing several fuses over the door leading from the west end of the porch into the living room. We learned how to replace the fuses temporarily with copper pennies when we did not have new ones on hand.

George warned me to stay out of the construction area in which the new barn was taking shape, and my memory of the details of how the work progressed is incomplete. I was present when he hitched a team of horses to a two-handled earth scoop and proceeded to level the ground before the cement crew poured the concrete floor of the barn's lower level. The day when trucks equipped with revolving mixers brought freshly mixed concrete to construction sites had not yet arrived on our section of the North Talbot Road. The cement contractor brought in a portable mixer. In the concrete floor of the lower level of the barn, the carpentry crew set a line of substantial wooden posts running down the center of the barn and providing interior support for the upper story. On the cap beam linking these posts, the carpenters set the interior ends of the joists on which the flooring of the barn's second story was to rest, the outer ends resting on planks that topped the exterior walls. These joists were straight logs some fifteen to eighteen inches in diameter, leveled top and bottom with a carpenter's broad axe; the bark remained on the sides.

The carpenters then supervised the erection above the joists of the massive square beams that had framed the old barn, their sides still showing the marks of the broad axes used in making them. Somehow I missed the interesting process by which these great beams were disassembled and then once more joined together on top of the lower story of the barn. Vaguely I remember an afternoon when some of the neighbors came in to help the carpenters with the erection of the barn frame, using a block and tackle arrangement. The carpenters joined the great beams to each other by pounding wooden pegs into end holes bored with an auger. The occasion was not the great neighborhood gathering that some social historians describe, although I believe sandwiches, cake, and lemonade were served.

Later the building crew laid siding from the old barn over the new rafters to provide backing for a shiny layer of corrugated metal roofing. Truckers had brought loads of new boards from the Strathroy lumber yard to be used as siding for the upper barn walls and massive planks to serve as flooring for the drive floor. When completed, this was to be accessed through large double doors opening to the raised earthen approach or bridge that crossed over the top of the cement-walled and -roofed milk house. Siding from the old barn provided flooring for the hay mows and walls for the granary set in the southeast corner of the upper barn level. I remember the staccato hammering of the gang of three or four carpenters as they put the boards of the sheeting layer in place on the barn rafters and nailed new boards in place to fashion the side walls of the upper story. Despite long experience, the carpenters did not always hit the nail on the head; two came to the house for iodine and bandages after hammering their thumbs. Eleta made thumb stalls with tails that fastened around the wrist to hold the bandages in place.

The stable layout of the reconstructed barn was simple. A line of concrete mangers ran the length of the barn, with a feed alleyway running in front of the mangers. The only break was a passageway crossing from the milk house door between stabled cows and then through the horse stable to end at a door leading to the manure pile at the back of the barn. The line of center posts supporting the floor joists of the second story stood in the molded cement of the outer manger wall. George had found the sunken gutters of the barn on the southeast fifty hard to clean, and in the new barn the floor dropped down at the rear of the cow row for some six or eight inches and then rose with gentle pitch to the exterior stable wall. A row of new green metal stanchions was set into the low back side of the mangers, and round tubular steel dividers separated the cows in the stanchion line into pairs, although there were a couple of single-animal stalls and a stretch in which three animals stood together without an intervening divider. At the rear of the cows' platform, the cement men had scored several parallel grooves in the concrete to provide better footing for the animals.

The central alley of the stable floor ran the length of the barn, the cattle mangers on one side and the horse stable and two large box stalls on the other. As we entered the stable level of the barn from the exterior door at the south end of this central alley, we had the cow mangers on our left. On the immediate right, a narrow alley ran in front of the first set of horse stalls. At its interior end a grain chute ran down from the granary above. This allowed us to bag grain just a few feet away from the door at which it was loaded for its trip to the grist mill at Lambeth. Next one walked beside a pair of generous horse stalls, sided with planks and also floored with wood of the same dimension, elevating the horses by a couple of inches above the stable's concrete floor. Behind this set of horse stalls ran the cross passage from the milk house to the manure pile. With an upward glance just before reaching this point, we saw the square opening of a hay chute through which we pitched down hay and straw for the animals from the mows in the upper story of the barn. To the right and on the far side of this cross passage were two more horse stalls, and then another cross alley, which contained a ladder to the upper floor. Beyond were two large box

stalls, their walls constructed of round iron tubing. At the north end of
the central alley stood a hand pump that brought up water from a large
concrete cistern sunk in the ground outside at the north end of the barn.

The stable level of the reconstructed barn had a generous allotment of
doors and windows. There were two doors in the south end, one leading
into the alley behind the stanchioned cattle and one into the central alley.
If George's plans for developing the farm had matured, a silo would have
stood adjacent to the second door, but this he was never able to build. At
the north end of the barn, a single door allowed entrance at the end of the
cow stable alley. Doors on the east side of the barn led into the horse stable
alley and into the corner box stall or bull pen. The first of these was a Dutch
door, the top half usually left open in summer for ventilation. On this side
of the building also, two wide doors were set in the upper barn wall, some
four feet above the surface of the drive floor and directly opposite the big
doors that opened on the approach. These doors on the east side of the
barn provided ventilation on hot summer days when we were filling the
mows but were also useful at threshing time, when the blower pipe of a
grain separator could be extended through them to blow threshed straw to
a stack being built outside the barn.

Somewhat more than a third of the way along the west wall of the barn,
a small one-story concrete structure protruded from the ground-floor wall.
Within this concrete box, a divider separated a milk house from a ground-
level cistern. As noted, the approach to the large doors opening into the
upper barn level of mows and granary passed directly across the roof of this
combined milk house and cistern. At the lower level, the outside door to
the milk house was the only one in the west side of the barn.

The pitch of the shiny barn roof was rather steep and uninterrupted
by hips or gambrels. Four lightning rods stood at equal distance along the
length of its peak, each wearing a white glass ball near its spearlike top. A
few years later I lived in terror of George's uncertain temper for a day or so
after a stone from my slingshot punctured the ball on the south end rod.
When I confessed my sin and terror to Len, he laughed and said, "Don't
worry, with Dad's eyesight, he will never see it." And so it proved. Rain
drained from the great shiny expanse of roof via eave troughs and piping
to the cisterns at the north end of the barn and adjacent to the milk house.
Suspended in the interior peak of the barn was a track for the hay car.
With its big harpoon fork and sling rope hook, this device eased the task
of unloading wagons of hay or sheaves of grain.

Although the layout of the new barn allowed greater efficiency in
handling the milking operation and in choring generally, the barnyard

on the northeast corner farm was never as well developed as was that on the southeast fifty. I am sure that George expected to be able to install a track and litter carrier in the stables in due course, to erect a silo at the south end of the barn, and to build an implement shed for machinery that either stood outside or was housed in winter on the barn floor or in an old barn in the lower pasture.

There were still unused boards and scantlings on hand from the old barn when the workers had completed its renovation. George used these to construct a chicken house at the north side of the barnyard, consisting of two pens and a compartment that sometimes housed chickens but was more usually occupied by pigs or overflow calves. He and Len used small-mesh wire to build exterior pens at each end of the chicken house.

The side entrance to the house faced the side road gate, and from this access to the property a gravel driveway curved into the house yard between a Northern Spy apple tree on the right and a walnut tree on the left, passing beyond the house to a two-stall drive shed—now converted to a garage for our car—and beyond that to a gate set in the fence dividing the house yard from the barnyard. Also on the right-hand side of the house yard were two more Northern Spy apple trees, and in the lawn adjacent to the side entrance of the house stood a large basswood tree. At the house corners facing the barnyard were a peach tree on the driveway side and a plum tree at the back of the woodshed. A Snow apple tree and a King apple tree grew between house and drive shed. Still farther back was a windbreak line of tall and ragged Norway spruce trees, the source of moaning sound when north or northwest winds blew against the farmstead. Just beyond these trees stood the mesh wire fence marking the south boundary of the night pasture, an enclosure that wrapped around the house yard and extended south to the side road and west to the North Talbot Road. Here, for convenience, we often kept the horses and milking cows during the night hours.

Leaving the house to go to the new barn, we followed a gravel path past the garage, opened a wide swing gate into the barnyard, and continued past a tall pole that supported a yard light and the power line extending from the kitchen end of the house to the barn. Initially a couple of chicken brooder houses were stationed to the right, and there was often a woodpile there. After several years Len converted the oldest of the brooder houses into the entrance shed of a small greenhouse, standing just inside the barnyard gate. Another fifty yards took us to the cow stable door at the southwest corner of the barn. If we walked behind the cows to the far end of the barn and passed through the door there, a gate to the right gave access to the first of the fields east of the barn. A turn to the left carried us past the chicken house to the northwest corner of the barnyard, where a gate led into the lane to the lower pasture and another accessed the night pasture. Between this gate and the barnyard gate into the house yard stood the windmill, still in working condition, although the wind wheel lacked a couple of its sheet-metal blades and the narrow angle-steel frame and stringers of the four-sided tower were somewhat rustier than those on the southeast corner farm. At the side closest to the night pasture gap was an octagonal concrete water trough.

The field layout of the northeast corner farm was more complex than that of the farm across the side road (see map 2). A lane ran north from the barnyard, passing between the night pasture on the left and the kitchen garden on the right, situated behind the henhouse. This lane opened into the lower pasture, a field that carried to the north line fence of the farm. At the end of the short lane was a small tilled field on the right, around which the lower pasture hooked, so that both the pasture and the field ran east to a fence marking the western end of an old orchard. On the other side of the orchard a small field separated it from a woodlot of six or seven acres that reached to the farm's eastern line fence. This stretch of pasture and tillage, orchard, and woodland made up the north side of the farm, and between it and the side road were three large cultivated fields, divided by fencerows and stretching from the barnyard to the east end of the farm.

In terms of soil fertility there was not much difference between the farm that George had sold and that to which the family moved in the late 1920s. The predominant soil was an easily worked sandy silt loam, although the soil of the old orchard and the little field beyond it was somewhat sandier than the rest. The terrain, however, imposed some restrictions on cultivation. Its rolling surface was not sufficiently hilly to bar cultivation, but there were drainage problems. A pond stood at the north side of the middle field adjacent to the orchard fence. Two smaller marshy ponds lay at the orchard end of the woodlot, the northern one extending into the neighboring property to the north. In winter and spring, water also collected along our line fence at the northeast corner of the old orchard and drained out through a grassy channel that ran parallel to the line fence on its north side before flowing south into our big pasture field and joining another minor waterway that also entered our pasture from the north. This water passed into several acres of swale on the south side of the lower pasture. Except for a few weeks in midsummer, a small stream drained out of this wetland across the southern part of the lower pasture into the night pasture, collecting in a small pool at the fence beside the North Talbot Road

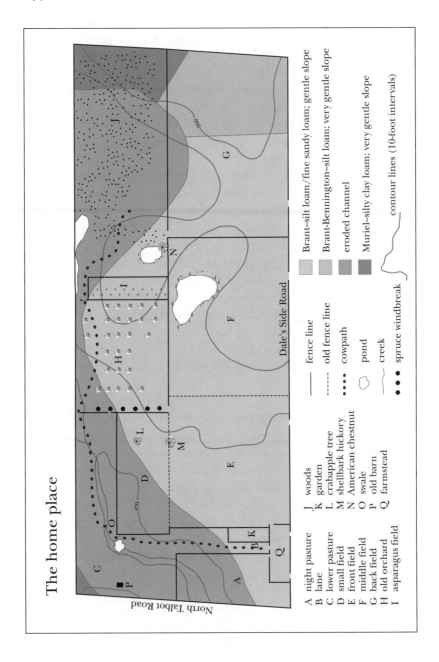

The home place

A night pasture   J woods
B lane   K garden
C lower pasture   L crabapple tree
D small field   M shellbark hickory
E front field   N American chestnut
F middle field   O swale
G back field   P old barn
H old orchard   Q farmstead
I asparagus field

———— fence line
- - - - old fence line
•••• cowpath
◌ pond
⌒ swale
• old barn
•• spruce windbreak

Brant–silt loam/fine sandy loam; gentle slope
Brant-Bennington–silt loam; very gentle slope
eroded channel
Muriel–silty clay loam; very gentle slope
contour lines (10-foot intervals)

North Talbot Road

Dale's Side Road

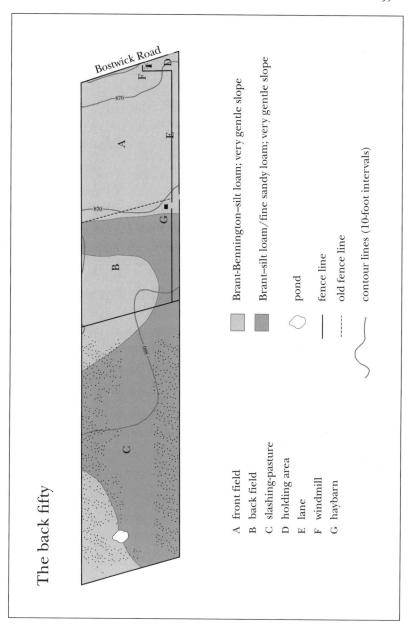

The back fifty

Bostwick Road

A front field
B back field
C slashing-pasture
D holding area
E lane
F windmill
G haybarn

Brant-Bennington–silt loam; very gentle slope

Brant–silt loam/fine sandy loam; very gentle slope

pond

fence line

old fence line

contour lines (10-foot intervals)

and flowing under the road and into the acreage of our neighbors on the northwest corner farm.

The fences on the new farm provided another problem. For the most part they were of large-mesh wire, topped on some stretches by a strand of barbed wire. Most of the fence wire was rusty and sagging between the wooden posts, some of which had rotted at ground level. I am sure that George expected to refence most of the northeast corner farm, but he was able to replace old fencing with new only in stretches along pasture frontage where our livestock showed contempt for the old barrier. Our half of the northern line fence ran through the marshy areas beside the old orchard and at the western edge of the woodlot. Periodically winter ice heaved out some of the posts or separated the fence wires from them. In spring our young cattle then took advantage of the situation by wading through the boundary waters to join the animals in the adjoining pasture. As a result we did our first fence "fixing" of the year by wading into very cold water two or more feet deep—just how cold I discovered when I joined the fence fixing crew. The occasional heifer repeatedly attacked fences head on, and I remember George muttering, "I'll fix her" after he had returned from a search-and-capture mission. This he did by hammering together a four-sided wooden "poke" that the wanderer wore around her neck until we sent her to the back fifty where the fences were in better condition.

Although the farm on the northeast corner needed a good deal of improvement, it was also a farm with much to interest a growing boy. One of the apple trees in the house yard had an ideal limb from which to mount a swing. The others were easily climbed. The basswood tree by the side entrance provided a continual supply of shoots from which I could whittle whistles. The remains of an old pear tree orchard in the night pasture provided another choice of fruit in season, and the small knoll there allowed me to stamp out ice sled runs that provided a slide of seventy-five yards or so, terminating on the ice of the pool beside the North Talbot Road. In spring I used the little stream running into that pool for exercises in dam building or for racing small wooden craft.

Although my interest in wildlife was less keen then than later, the activity of birds and animals around the house and barnyard was diverting. For a number of years, a pair of flickers nested in the remains of an old tree standing close to the light pole in the barnyard. Taking advantage of the fact that the upper half of the horse stable door was usually open from spring until fall, barn swallows built nests above the electric light in the horse stable and one year ventured into the cow stable to nest above the light in front of the milk house door. Pigeons soon staked claims in the upper reaches of the new barn, and a contingent of English sparrows declared itself ready to share any chicken feed available. Robins frequented the house yard, and we saw the occasional Baltimore oriole. Eleta was a flower lover and hummingbirds visited the climbing plants she grew in front of the side verandah. Sitting there on a summer day I could often hear the *bob-white* call of quail or the mournful sound of doves. In autumn we saw cock pheasants strutting between the shocks in the cornfield.

From the age of eleven or twelve I usually fetched the milk cows in the late afternoon when they were on pasture at the home farm rather than at the Bostwick fifty. This was usually the case in the late spring and early summer and again during the fall, when we gave the cows the run of the whole strip of pasturage along the north side of the farm, including both the old orchard and the woodlot, which had a strip of meadow along its south side and occasional grassy stretches elsewhere. Fetching the cows in the late afternoon was a simple task if they had decided to stay in the lower pasture. A ten-foot climb up the windmill brought them into view in that case. But the near side of the old orchard had once been part of a farmstead, and a windbreak similar to that behind our house ran along its western side, hiding most of it from the barnyard. And within the orchard, the ground rose from both the north and south fence lines to a gentle summit, so that much of the orchard was hidden from view even from locations inside it.

Within a year of our occupancy of the northeast corner farm, the milk cows had worn a path down the lane, diagonally across the near end of the lower pasture to the corner of the small field, and thence through the swale and the east end of the pasture to a wire gap where the orchard fence reached the north line fence. From there the cow path continued through the north end of the orchard to a gap in the eastern orchard fence that allowed passage into the woodlot. Once in the orchard I might find the cows almost anywhere in that enclosure, and this was the case in the woodlot as well. When they were at the far end of the woodlot, I had come half a mile before I found them. They usually picked days when I had been delayed at school, it seemed to me, to dally in the farthest reaches of the pasture strip.

At any point in my searches for them, there might be an absorbing distraction. A female killdeer might drag a wing across my path as I emerged from the swale, fearful that I would discover her nest. The red and white chevrons of red-winged blackbirds often drew my eyes to the southern fence line. Muskrats were sometimes visible in the pond just beyond the south orchard fence, woodchucks might scuttle back to burrows on the hillside at the north end of the orchard, or a hawk might float in neutral gear, scanning for snacks below. In season I might come upon morels, common mushrooms, or even a puffball. There was a magnificent cream-colored beech tree standing just inside the tree line halfway along the woodlot and its little nuts were worth a short stop.

During the late summer and early fall, the orchard trees offered a selection of fruits to fortify the cow seeker until suppertime. The King tree was my favorite. It produced a large red apple, crisp and juicy, sweet with just a touch of tartness. I ignored two trees standing next to the gap into the woodlot, although the apples on one were a shiny red and those on the other were huge and elegantly marked with red striping that shaded into white at the blossom end. The scarlet apples on the Ben Davis tree were hard as bullets and sour, and biting into one of the large apples on the Wolf River tree was like taking a mouthful of moist cardboard. "The tree peddler really took in Emerson on those two," George once remarked, referring to one of the previous owners of the place.

The cattle loved apples too. As soon as windfall fruit started to drop, some of the animals rushed ahead when entering the orchard from either the lower pasture or the woodlot, to devour any apples on the ground. This behavior did not enthuse me when I was trying to drive the herd to the barn, because the scrambling of the black and whites among the trees involved me in another roundup before I could persuade the herd out through the gap in the northwestern corner of the orchard and into the lower pasture. When the cattle pastured within the orchard or passed through it on a daily basis, the pickings sufficed only to spice the bovine diet. But if we brought the herd back from the Bostwick fifty after apples had begun to drop, we took care that the cattle not gorge themselves on accumulated windfalls, giving them only a few minutes per day in the orchard until the ground was reasonably clean. During one such period, however, one of the heifers jumped the fence between the old orchard and the lower pasture and spent several happy hours in the orchard. When we brought her out she was tipsy, and when placed in the end stall of the milk row for observation, she was obviously a sick young animal. Soon she began to vomit apples, and for the next twenty-four hours she was miserable. George used the drench bottle to administer a soothing draught, and she recovered.

The farm machinery that George moved across the road to the new farm was unimpressive in amount and quality. There were two single-furrow walking plows, a set of iron harrows, and a disk harrow, spring tooth cultivator, one-horse walking cultivator, roller, mower, hayloader, dump rake, and an old McCormick Deering grain binder. He had a lumber wagon equipped with hay rack and gravel box, a set of bobsleds, a cutter, a buggy, and a very old light wagon, originally fitted with three seats and no top and known as a democrat. This collection of implements and vehicles pales in comparison with that of the farm of year 2000 but if replaced at the retail prices of 1930 would have cost George between fifteen hundred and two thousand dollars, more than 20 percent of the value of the southeast corner farm. The assortment of hand tools included axes, shovels, forks, scoop and stable shovels, a twist-handled scythe, and a fanning mill, and he had a construction jack and a collection of ropes, logging chains, hammers, drills, wrenches, and so on. Apparently the property exchanges and sale of the timber off the Bostwick fifty had left George sufficiently flush to do some upgrading of the machinery inventory. During the first year or two on the northeast corner farm he replaced both the hayloader and farm wagon with new models.

When we began to farm the new place, the cattle herd numbered between twenty and thirty head, all purebred Holstein-Friesian animals. Six horses made the move across the road, each a descendant of George's original team of mares, upgraded in size by the use of Percheron stallions that their owners brought to farms on request. They would drive a horse and buggy with the big stud horse trotting alongside, secured by a rope attached to his halter. Mac and Mae were well advanced in their teens and their youthful iron-gray coats had turned to white. Marg and Pomp were younger animals, still a pronounced gray. Fan was a young mare just recently broken to harness, and Major, the colt that had recovered from joint ill, was almost two years old.

Since we were situated close to a city of more than sixty thousand people, an economist would have predicted that farm operators in our area were concentrating on the production of perishable commodities. To some degree this was true; as producers of milk for bottling, we met the prediction. But the farm operations along our stretch of the North Talbot Road were not carbon copies of one another. His wife and family having left him, Norman (Tink) Bogue farmed with the help of two hired men and a housekeeper. He kept grade dual-purpose Shorthorn cattle and sold young stock for veal or beef and breeding. On the old David Bogue homestead, my Aunt Leila and her second husband, Joe White, kept a few head of cattle and raised a surplus of small grains for sale, but Joe derived much of his income from his position as township assessor. Across the road the Sadlers maintained a herd of Holstein-Friesians and sold fluid milk, either to the cheese factory situated a few miles south of Lambeth or to one of the city dairies. But they also drew significant income from their orchard, which they carefully pruned and sprayed. Next door on the west side of the road, Sam Kilbourne worked in London. Each day in midafternoon his Model T Ford coupe put-putted along our side road as he returned from work. A mature son and a younger adopted lad maintained his small farm operation.

Immediately to the north of the Bogue homesteads lay the Pringle farm, two hundred acres in size and owned by a city businessman who maintained it as a hobby farm. A married manager and herdsman, Clarence Allen, occupied the house, and his brother and another hired man provided additional labor. The Pringle herd of Jerseys included Channel Island stock, and the men exhibited the best animals at the Western Fair in London. The farm income came from the sale of fluid Jersey milk, noted for its high butterfat content, and breeding stock, with perhaps some additional revenue derived from the sale of small grain. Across the road from the Pringle farm, the Bilyea family kept a less distinguished herd of Jersey cattle, processing the milk themselves for sale on a door-to-door route that they maintained in London.

Between the Pringle farm and the southeast corner farm lay a fifty-acre tract that had been owned by an elderly couple whose daughter had married Ed Vanstone, who farmed the southwest corner farm. After the death of the old couple, Fred Merriam purchased the fifty-acre tract. He and his wife were advanced in their thirties, making their first start as owner-operators. They kept a few grade Shorthorn cattle and raised the standard field crops, assisted for a couple of months in the summer by a schoolboy from the city. Across the road the Vanstones also followed a grain and livestock regime but tended their orchard carefully. They usually also grew a cash crop of strawberries each spring and tapped the maple trees in their woodlot for syrup; alone among the farm families on the road between Lambeth and Byron, they did not own an automobile. At certain seasons I was roused from sleep at 4:00 A.M. by the clip-clop of their driving horse on the road, as members of the family set out by horse and buggy for Covent Garden Market in London.

The Vanstone family included four girls and a boy. Two of the girls carried their schooling past the public school level and left home, but two still remained and worked in the fields with their brother and father during haying and grain harvest. Because Ed Vanstone refused to keep a mature bull on his farm, we occasionally saw his son, Millard, leading a Shorthorn cow or heifer along the side road at the end of a ten-foot rope toward John Dale's farm, where the services of a Shorthorn herd sire were available.

When Millard's companion was an inexperienced heifer, this spectacle could be amusing as the animal fought the halter, alternately planting feet and refusing to budge and then trying to spin away to the home pasture. I once made an admiring comment about Millard to Eleta and her face saddened. "Oh, poor Millard," she said. "Why, 'poor Millard'?" I asked. She replied, "Well, the poor fellow's work is paying off the mortgage on that farm, and when his parents die, he will have to buy it again from his sisters." This was my introduction to the practice of equal inheritance.

Fora Cornell occupied the northwest corner farm at the junction of the North Talbot road and our side road. He was not an energetic farmer. With the help of two sons somewhat older than I, he kept a few cattle and a team of horses and grew some field crops and small fruit. In the 1930s he began a small butcher business at his farmstead, slaughtering and dressing out animals brought to him by members of the community. For a time he supervised the central pavilion at Springbank Park, the city recreational facility located at the north end of our stretch of the North Talbot Road. Year by year, however, his butchering business grew.

Mrs. Pack and her sons maintained a dairy farm on the side road beyond Fora Cornell's place and across Dingman's Creek, and she also owned and cultivated the fields in the small holding on the North Talbot Road across from our lower pasture. The barn on that property had long since disintegrated and she rented the house to nonfarmers. The owner of the farm beyond this one committed suicide shortly after we moved to our new location, and his widow followed a number of different strategies in managing her land, sometimes renting her fields and sometimes farming the property herself with the help of three sons. Next came the farm of her brother, Ed Brown, who maintained a general livestock and grain operation but who also did custom corn binding for farmers in the neighborhood. Completing the roster of farms on the west side of the North Talbot Road and south of the second concession road were those of Basil and Stanley Cornell, brothers who concentrated on the production of orchard fruit and berries.

The only active farmer between our place and the second concession road on our side of the North Talbot Road was Andrew McGlaughlin. He was an apiarist as well as a farmer, maintaining colonies of bees in other neighborhoods in addition to those on his farm. His farming practices differed from those of his neighbors in other respects as well. He planted larger acreages of winter wheat than did they, and he used corn silage in fattening a shipment of feeder cattle each year—practices quite different from those on farms like ours, where we emphasized dairying. In growing wheat, McGlaughlin used commercial fertilizer, and although the neighbors accepted the fact that he produced good crops, I heard one of them predicting darkly that he was burning out his soil.

No farmer in our neighborhood was self-sufficient in the use of machinery. No individual operator or small group of farmers owned a threshing rig. Living on the south side of Lambeth, Vic Nichols earned most of his income by providing custom threshing and silo-filling service during the summer, and a second threshing outfit also operated in our neighborhood during most of the 1930s.

We depended upon Ed Brown to cut and bind our corn crop into sheaves. As did the thresher men, he tried to work systematically through the neighborhood, moving from one farm to another nearby, so that he lost little time on the road in moving his machine from job to job. In action, Ed's corn binder required a three-horse hitch, and as part of his agreement with the crop owner, he asked the customer to supply the third horse.

Ed's operation involved me in a traumatic experience while I was a schoolboy at ss 17. During the fall when I was in senior third grade, I was walking home after school along the North Talbot Road one afternoon with Austin, Ed's younger son, a lad who was a year behind me in school. About a quarter of a mile from our corner, we saw a small board lying at the side of the road. It was painted yellow and had several empty bolt holes bored close to its ends. "That came from our corn binder," said Austin, and he picked it up and began to carry it. At this point a large car overtook us, traveling at high speed. As it approached, Austin yielded to one of the sudden and disastrous impulses youngsters sometimes experience; he hurled the board against the car's radiator. I never knew whether he was protesting against drivers who endangered children or whether it was a sudden bit of devilry on the part of a boy usually sober beyond his years. The result was shocking. The driver slammed on his brakes and the car skidded sideways on the gravel road before stopping. He threw open his door, and as he jumped from the vehicle we could see that he was very tall and wearing the brown-and-yellow workday uniform of the Royal Canadian Mounted Police.

The Mountie ordered us into the back seat of his car and demanded our names. Then he asked who had thrown the board. Austin confessed in a weak voice. The RCMP asked us where we lived and started up the car. As we neared our corner, I stammered that I lived in the white house ahead. To my relief the officer stopped the car at the corner and told me to get out and behave myself in the future. Then he pulled away, Austin a subdued figure in the back seat. At school the next day, I asked Austin what had happened after my release. The policeman, he said, had taken him to his house and had told his mother what he had done.

"Did she tell your dad?" I asked. "No," said Austin. Although I had yet to meet a sociologist, I now understood a couple of important social laws: (1) the future is unpredictable, and (2) what can go wrong probably will go wrong.

The cutting boxes used to chop corn and blow the stream of pieces into a silo were less expensive than the thresherman's separator. There was therefore a greater tendency for individual farmers or small groups of them to own these machines, but custom work was common at silo-filling time in our neighborhood. Since we did not have a silo during our eleven years of farming on the northeast corner, I did not become as familiar with the routines of silo filling as with those involved in threshing the small grains, although I did help fill silo at a later date.

When I began to study the history of agriculture in the American and Canadian Midwest, I learned that many of the pioneers had lacked the funds to buy essential equipment, and that this continued to be the case in later generations as well. As inventors increased the kinds and sophistication of farm implements, some useful machinery was too expensive for the average farmer to buy, given the limited amount of use each farmer would have for it. In response to these factors some agriculturists joined with neighbors or relatives to buy expensive machinery, thus spreading the cost across several neighboring farms. As the use of ox- or horse-powered agricultural machinery spread, joint ownership of grain-harvesting machinery was common in the Middle West, and in some areas small groups or rings of farmers purchased threshing rigs to serve their members. The custom operator offered another solution, using his breaking plow to break virgin sod at so much per acre or threshing the farmer's crop of small grains for a fee based on the number of bushels threshed out. On the North Talbot Road of the 1920s and 1930s, almost all our neighbors owned their own harvesting machinery but used the custom provider at threshing and corn-binding times as well as for silo filling. Vic Nichols also owned the equipment necessary to do custom plowing.

Although I was too young to realize it at the time, George and Eleta had disagreed about my brother Len's future. After Len had completed two years of study at Lambeth Continuation School, George announced that he was to stay home and help on the farm. Len was a good student, and Eleta believed that other employment options for him should have been considered. George, an eldest son, had obtained a winter of formal training in business college, and he sent his oldest daughter Myrtle to London to attend secondary school and Normal School. As the end of the 1920s approached, my other sister, Eleanor, was on the same track. But I never heard Len complain about the decision to remove him from school.

Within the family, the two previous generations had helped their children to obtain farms, that assistance provided mainly in the second generation by the process of inheritance. George and his brother Chester ultimately shared David Bogue's land. The biographical sketches of the pioneers printed in the Middlesex county history of 1889 show that the early residents were proud to have established one son or several on farms. Evidently George considered this to be a father's obligation. He planned that the farm he purchased on the Fifth Concession Road would be farmed jointly for the time being and would become Len's when the latter wished to establish his own home.

I never knew the exact financial arrangements under which Len worked on our farm. I do not believe that George paid him set wages, providing him instead with pocket money at irregular intervals. Len's major reimbursement came from profit-making activities that he used farm resources to support. While we lived on the southeast fifty, he maintained a flock of Silver-Gray Dorking chickens, and George gave him a heifer calf, her progeny belonging to Len although George counted the milk from such cattle as his own. When the family moved across the road, Len owned a Percheron mare and her offspring, a younger mare just ready to break to harness, and a number of cattle.

Typically the farmers in our neighborhood derived their income from a mixture of agricultural enterprises. In our case the herd of Holstein-Friesian cattle provided basic continuity in the farm business. We always produced milk or cream, although George's method of marketing these products changed somewhat during the 1920s and 1930s. Livestock sales also contributed to the income from the dairy enterprise. Bull calves were not welcomed with great joy, but they were not summarily knocked on the head, as some dairymen were said to do at an earlier time. During the 1920s the owners of other purebred herds purchased youngsters from George for breeding purposes, and the owners of unpedigreed or grade herds sometimes bought young purebred males in order to improve their stock. This market diminished sharply during the 1930s. In those years we sold some male calves for veal, and purchasers altered others to raise as steers. George did not himself feed steers. Even during the depressed 1930s there was usually a market for surplus females, even if prices were unsatisfactorily low. George sent aged or broken-down cows to the stockyards in Toronto, where they were sold as cutters and canners, their flesh to be used for the cheaper meat products.

Although the dairy herd provided the basic foundation of our farm income, there were supplementary enterprises. The acreage planted to winter wheat was typically large enough to provide a surplus of grain for sale beyond the modest amount needed for chicken feed or seed. During the 1920s the potato patch sometimes provided a market surplus. The orchard produced apples for sale as well as for home use, even though George did not spray for the coddling moth or scab after we moved across the side road. In some years the strawberry patch produced fruit for sale as well as for home consumption in jam, jelly, and preserves. In the barnyard Eleta supervised an active poultry enterprise that yielded eggs, dressed chickens, and geese for sale on the farmers' market at Covent Garden Market in London. This was the type of farm economy that George transferred to the farm on the northeast corner and expected to follow at the farm on the Fifth Concession.

When agricultural depression settled in and Len became ill, George had to resell the Fifth Concession farm at some loss. He then increased the farm acreage by renting on shares the grain and hay fields on the Dale farm, immediately adjacent to our farm on the side road. The owner of this farm was aged, and his son was trying to develop a homestead in the prairie wheat lands. But the arrangement was short-lived; drought and depression on the prairies brought the prairie farmer back to take over the home place.

By this time, however, the purchasers of the Bostwick fifty had found themselves unable to fulfill their purchase agreement and surrendered the tract to George. With this transaction completed, the seventy-five acres on the side road plus the Bostwick fifty comprised our farm unit through 1939. However, in some years George rented pasture for our young cattle and dry cows.

George and Len changed their farming practices somewhat during the mid-1930s. Although the dairy operation continued to be a major part of the farm economy, Len urged that greater emphasis be placed upon market gardening. After several years and Len's marriage and departure to farm in partnership with his father-in-law, our farm operation became less labor intensive, the work force provided only by George, Eleta, and me, with a few days of assistance obtained from my uncle Euart in the summer of 1938. This arrangement ended after three crop years when George, at Eleta's urging, sold the Bostwick fifty and purchased a house in London, where she took in boarders and I lived while going to the University of Western Ontario. George dispersed the livestock from the farm on the North Talbot Road and sold the farm machinery in the late fall of 1939, retaining an apartment in the house and renting out the rest of the rooms as well as some of the crop land. For several years he worked part-time for a small jobs carpenter, spending weekends at the house in town. As a family farm, the unit on the northeast corner had ceased to be.

THREE

Out at the Barn

Our herd of Holstein-Friesian cattle was never among the larger or best in Middlesex County, but Len and I were much more interested in it than in any other aspect of the farm business. During the last years of World War I, George began to replace the grade animals in his milking herd with purebreds. Len later told his son that the process began when George purchased a purebred calf for Len to enter in a club competition. Eleta, however, once explained to me that George laid the foundation of the herd by buying two young heifers and keeping their female increase. The *Herd Book* series of the Holstein-Friesian Association of Canada identifies these animals as Lady Veeman Segis and Madolyn Fayne Segis, born in 1916 and 1917 respectively.

The *Herd Book*s also show that George purchased two and perhaps three other young females during the early 1920s (see also appendix 1 for further discussion of the dairy herd). Of these, Alcartra Pride established a line of descent that was still represented in the herd in 1939 and that included the three animals acknowledged to be mine. But most of the animals in the herd of the early 1930s were descendants of Veeman or Madolyn, to use the stable names of these dairy matrons. My memories of the southeast corner farm include one of a large animal, mostly white in color, occupying the pen in the horse stable section of the barn. This was Fairmont King Korndyke Dutchland, a herd sire that George had purchased from the Arbogast brothers, leading breeders at Sebringville, Ontario.

By the time we moved across the road, George had replaced the first Arbogast herd sire with a young bull from the same source, Hartog Ormsby Fayne. At that time the herd clearly showed the influence of Fairmont King in the number of cows and heifers in it that were predominantly white with minor black markings. Madolyn was white in color for the most part, and this also contributed to the dominance of white in the herd markings.

Veeman, however, was largely black, and most of her descendants carried larger areas of black marking than did the animals in the Madolyn family.

Both cows were good producers, capable of filling a pail at one milking. As examples of breed type, Madolyn was the superior of the two—upstanding, deep barreled, with a large, well-attached udder. The first Veeman had what breeders of the time called a "rough and droopy" rear, with a large bump on her top line between the hip or "hook" bones and the base of the tail and also a pronounced slope from those bones to the "pin" bones at the base of the tail. She too had a large udder but one that was more pendulous than that of her stable mate. Madolyn was a cow of placid and cooperative disposition. When surprised or displeased, Veeman kicked fiercely; George customarily milked her. This foundation cow was gone from the herd by the time we moved to the northeast corner farm, but she and Madolyn added daughters to the herd that displayed some of the same physical characteristics.

To some degree stable names persisted in the herd. When I came to know the cows individually, there was a Veeman, daughter of Old Veeman, in the milking herd and also her daughter, Young Veeman. The original Madolyn survived into the 1930s and her daughter Young Madolyn was a herd stalwart. When breeders entered their stock in the registry of the Holstein-Friesian Association, they could chose names that advertised their herd and also the lineage of the specific animal. When George and Eleta moved to the southeast corner farm, there was a great walnut tree growing between the barn and the house and another just across the side road. George had business stationery printed using the letterhead "Walnut Grove Stock Farm," and for a time he incorporated this farm name into the registered names of some of our stock. When George had completed the paperwork on the heifer calf sired by Fairmont King Korndyke Dutchland and dropped by Madolyn Fayne Segis on May 6, 1926, for instance, she became Dutchland Fayne of Walnut Lodge. Unfortunately breeders could register herd names as well as those of individual animals, and another Holstein breeder had filed a prior claim to "Walnut Lodge." George reluctantly gave up his plan to immortalize our farm in this way.

After Hartog Ormsby Fayne succeeded Fairmont King as herd sire, George used "Ormsby Fayne" as the final two words in the registry name of a number of the calves that he registered with the breed association, these words usually following the animal's stable name. The word *Ormsby* identified a famous line of Holstein-Friesian stock upon which the Arbogast brothers had drawn in building their herd.

Of our family members, Len, particularly, helped in choosing stable names. As I grew older I came to suspect that the female names he suggested were also borne by young women of his acquaintance. When he finally decided that Irene B. was the woman whom he wished to marry and it was announced that she would join the family for a Sunday night supper, George cautioned me that there was to be no mention by name of a young female in the milk row. But Len's imagination was not strictly bounded by his female friends. It was he who suggested that the stable names of twin heifer calves should be Kate and Duplicate. He drew on his knowledge of the entertainment world to name one of his own heifers "Paradise in Person, Helen Peril" and was disgusted to discover that George had used the name "Helen Ormsby Pearl" in filling out the pedigree application. The owners of undistinguished herds like ours found few buyers interested in purchasing herd sires during the depression of the 1930s, and in one year the cows were particularly uncooperative in presenting us with heifer calves. The little fellows soon bore names like Bill Dickey, Tony Lazzeri, and Red Ruffing, as we worked through the lineup of the New York Yankees.

By this time my calf club activity had earned me the right to call a heifer named Ethel my own, and her first contribution to herd growth was a bull calf we named Vernon in honor of the eccentric Yankee pitcher Vernon "Lefty" Gomez. George sent some of these young males to the stockyards and did not bother to register them with the national breed association. Vernon was more fortunate. A local farmer purchased him for service in his purebred herd, and as a result Vernon Alcartra Hartog appears in the *Herd Book* of the Holstein-Friesian Association. In contrast to Len and me, George sometimes sought inspiration in the world news section of the newspaper. During the years 1933–35 young bulls from our herd entered the national registry with names in which "Joe [Stalin]," "De Valera," "King Edward," and "Mussolini" preceded combinations of Ormsby, Hartog, and Fayne.

Work with the milk cows differed depending on the season. From midspring to midfall the cattle spent the night outside, but the livestock were stabled at night and during most of the day in the remaining months. George did not rise at 4:30 A.M. in the summer as some farmers liked to do. He got up at five thirty or six, on the understanding that much of the field work was best done when the dew had dried. If the cows were at the home place, they were secured in the night pasture during the hours of darkness or perhaps left in the lower pasture with the gap closed to the old orchard and woodlot beyond. Since they received grain after being stabled, the cows usually filed willingly through the barnyard to take their places in the stable, shoving their heads into the open stanchions and waiting for them to be closed.

With the last stanchion banged shut, grain was the next order of business, usually "chop" made of ground oats and barley, with oil cake sometimes added. Then milking began. If they were measuring the cow's production in the Record of Performance program of the federal Department of Agriculture, George or Len weighed the milk on a scale hanging from the ceiling on the stable side of the milk house door and recorded the result in the proper column on a many-columned "milk sheet" that George had tacked to wooden backing and hung conveniently on the wall, face inward. Then the milker or I released the cow and hustled her outside through the door at the north end of the stable. The more promptly this was done, the less was the chance that the she would urinate or defecate in the alley behind the cows as she left the stable. That occurrence was messy and odorous in spring and early summer when the cows were pasturing on new grass and their stools were loose. If a cow in those seasons seized the opportunity to relieve herself directly behind one that was being milked, hot brown globules might reach the shirt or cheek or even drop into the pail of the milker, as well as spatter on the whitewashed stable wall. If it was I who had failed to keep bossie in motion, such incidents invariably drew indignant comment from the milker.

When we first moved to the new place, George was selling milk to Silverwood's Dairy in London. Immediately after weighing the milk, the milker poured it through a strainer of clean cotton cloth that was pinned with wooden clothespins over the top compartment of a circular cooler filled with cold water. From there it ran down the outside surface of this cold-water reservoir into a trough that drained via a tap into a waiting milk can. In warm weather the men also set the full cans in a tank of fresh well water. A trucker picked them up each day after breakfast and delivered them to the dairy in London, where technicians graded the milk on the basis of its butterfat content. A couple of years or so after our relocation, George believed that he found a discrepancy between the butterfat estimates of the ROP testers and those reported by the dairy. Given little satisfaction in a confrontation at the creamery office, he decided to buy a cream separator and sell cream rather than fluid milk.

After George had installed a De Laval cream separator in the milk house, the milk handling routine changed. Now George pinned the strainer cloth over the top of the separator's capacious round reservoir and poured the pails of milk through it. To operate the machine, George turned its stubborn

crank until he had worked the separator up to the speed at which the conical
disks revolving within the centrifuge bowl most effectively broke the milk
into cream and skimmed milk. Emitting a growling whine, the separator
did its job both morning and night, the cream issuing from the upper of
two frontal spouts and the skimmed milk from the lower one.

Each morning the calves received their allotment of skim milk immediately after the process was completed. In feeding them, George skimmed
off the froth that had collected on the pails of skim milk as it came
from the separator, because he believed that ingestion of the froth caused
inflammation of the calves' lungs. Meanwhile, in winter, Len gave the stock
their first fodder of the day. After completing these tasks, George and Len
went to the house for breakfast, George carrying the separator's reservoir
with the bowl and the other parts of the separation mechanism inside it, and
Len bringing the milk pails, including one that held whole milk for house
use. Eleta carefully washed the milking equipment later in the morning,
opening the separator bowl so that the stack of disks inside it could be
washed one at a time in soap and water. She did this once a day; in the
evening George merely ran a pail of fresh water through the separator after
he had used it.

Although few farm boys believed that they had it easy, I realized that I was
more fortunate than some. I was never asked to participate in early morning
chores during the school year, as were some of the lads with whom I went to
school. Nor was I enlisted in the round of barn chores on weekday evenings
if there was school the following day. While the milk cows remained on
pasture at the home place, it was my job to bring them up to the vicinity
of the barn after school, but it was understood that during the school year
I would spend the early evening doing my homework. If George came in
from the evening barn chores and found that I was listening to the radio
instead of working on my hated algebra lessons, however, he sometimes
threatened me with barn duty. Such exchanges marvelously renewed my
interest in scholarship. On the weekends, however, I participated in the
late morning chores at the barn and helped with the evening chores there
also, milking one cow initially and a couple in later years. After milking
was finished, I helped to feed the calves their skim milk and to bring down
feed and bedding from the upper-story mows and distribute them to the
barn occupants. During the summer I was the "cow fetcher" but also a
participant in all phases of the evening barn routines. Not until my last
couple of years on the farm, however, was I roused during the summer to
help with the morning milking and choring at the barn.

The animals of the milk herd had their own hierarchy. When I located them in the pasture area on the home farm and started them moving toward the farmstead, they typically fell into rank order behind the same older animal with the rest strung out behind. Once under way they usually moved to the path they had worn down to the bare dirt through repeated usage each year. It ran from the barnyard down the lane, through the lower pasture to the old orchard, and thence well into the woodlot at the back of the farm. While he owned the Bostwick fifty, George kept the milk cows on pasture there during part of the summer, and when they returned to the home barn each animal sought out her old stanchion. Although fastening the cows in their stanchions was basically an orderly process, the animals usually accompanied it with a certain amount of jostling and head tossing and investigation of mangers. A new member of the milking herd that was slow to find her assigned place in the cow line might be unceremoniously butted out of a stall or stanchion that an older animal considered rightfully hers. Stepping in between the cows to close the stanchions called for some care. More than once a hoof supporting twelve hundred pounds plus of dairy matron descended upon my sneaker-shod toes as a cow shifted position.

Both George and Len were skilled milkers. There was a brisk authority in the way that they cleaned off a cow's udder with a damp rag if there was dirt or manure on it, seated themselves on a small box at the right rear of the cow, placed a milk pail between their legs, gently grasped two of the bovine teats, and commenced a rhythmic pull-squeeze that poured two pulsating streams of warm milk into the pail and produced an inch or so of foam upon the rising fluid. That George had small hands and Len had larger ones did not seem to have much effect upon the speed with which they milked. Each could milk a heavy producer in about ten minutes.

In milking most cows the actual process involved three stages. Initially the cow seemed uncooperative; the streams of milk were thin. Then she would "let down" her milk as she got into the spirit of things. After most of a cow's milk was in the pail, the milker entered a "stripping" stage, in which the fluid came more slowly as the internal pressure within the cow's mammary system diminished. At this point technique changed. With the teat held between thumb and index finger, the milker drew his hand down from just below the udder to the tip of the teat to extract a stream of milk. George stressed the importance of continuing the stripping until the udder was empty or virtually so. Like most dairymen of the time, he believed that failure to remove all the milk encouraged a cow to go "dry" prematurely.

Young Veeman, granddaughter of our original kicking Veeman, provided us with a demonstration of a cow's ability to withhold or let down her milk.

Late one summer afternoon I went for the cows on the northeast corner farm and found most of them in the lowland of scrubby timber and swamp grass on the near side of the woodlot. As I drove them out into open pasture before proceeding through the old orchard, I realized that Young Veeman was missing. This third-generation animal in the Veeman line was mostly white in her markings, reflecting the parentage of our first Arbogast bull, and should, I thought, be easy to find. I pushed deeper into the undergrowth until I reached the edge of the remnant of green algae-covered water that had survived along our line fence this late into the summer. There, mired to her stomach in the mud at the edge of the water, was Young Veeman. I shouted at her and threw a stick that splashed water on her; she struggled to free herself and then gave up.

I shouted some more and then decided to go to the house for help. I got the herd started for the barn, but I hated to leave Young Veeman. If she lay down, she would drown. I went back and shouted my loudest at her. She made a tremendous effort to heave herself toward shore, managing to break free and take a couple of strides toward solid ground. More shouts and more heaves eventually had her on solid ground at the edge of the swamp. Her underbelly and udder were plastered with mud, but I thought I saw blood in the caking around her teats. The winter ice in the swamp had lifted the line fence posts free of their moorings to float flat upon the water surface. The connecting fence of wire mesh, topped with a strand of barbed wire, lay treacherously close to the surface. Young Veeman had apparently stepped into this hazard. By the time that we reached the barnyard, the dripping mud and blood indicated that there was a considerable cut at some point at the front of her udder.

When Young Veeman was safely in her stanchion, George began to clean the udder with soap and a bucket of warm water. He soon discovered that the right front teat was sliced open from the tip upward along the milk duct for more than two inches. We were in the depths of the Great Depression and George called the vet only when the situation was desperate. Perhaps he talked to our vet on the phone about Young Veeman and the vet expressed doubts about his ability to effect repair. George decided he would stitch the teat together himself. Eleta produced silk thread and a sturdy needle, and George patted Young Veeman on the flank and started to make the first stitch. Grandmother Veeman's kicking characteristic had diminished in her line, generation by generation; we had always considered Young Veeman to be a model of behavior. But as the needle sank into tortured flesh, she did her grandmother proud and lashed out at George with a powerful hind leg. He jumped back to save himself. There was more soothing and another attempt and then admission of failure. It was clear that cleansing and disinfecting was all Young Veeman would allow.

After we had milked the other cows, George returned to Young Veeman with a milk pail. Since he could not grasp the injured teat to relieve that quarter of her udder, he grasped the uninjured front teat and one of the back ones and started to milk. Within a few moments he could feel Young Veeman let down her milk and milk began to flood from the damaged faucet. Her wound healed in a few weeks, though the duct still gaped open for almost half the length of the teat. We could not milk that quarter of her udder in normal fashion, but Young Veeman continued to cooperate. When the milk let down in the other quarters, it did so from that one as well and flowed unimpeded into the pail of the milker. At the time, Young Veeman was relatively young and no cow buyer had any interest in her thereafter. But she retained her value to us as a milk producer and dam; she was still with us when George sold the cattle in the fall of 1939.

The interior half of the Bostwick fifty consisted partly of open pasture and partly of second-growth trees, undergrowth, and pockets of grass that developed after George logged the sugar bush there at the end of the 1920s. We referred to this ground cover as "slashing." Usually the young cattle and dry females spent the summer there, but the grazing was sometimes good enough to support the milk cows as well for periods during the summer. During these weeks we milked the cows each night and morning in a fenced enclosure just inside the gate opening onto the Bostwick Road. Within this paddock the stubby windmill stood with its adjacent watering trough. Usually we placed pails, a couple of milk cans, and a bag of chop in our Model A Ford, and the milking crew drove over to the "other place" to do the milking. George and Len were the customary milkers, but sometimes I accompanied George and occasionally a hired man during the years when we were most involved in market gardening. George avoided using hired men for milking when possible, not trusting them to strip the cows properly. At times, however, we had a neighbor boy or a man with dairying experience working for us who was pressed into service.

We never owned a truck in our years on the farm. We used the Model A for hauling—calves, loads of grist, produce for market, salt blocks, coils of wire, bags of binder twine, and almost anything else that we could put inside it. Sometimes we removed the front passenger seat, the rear seat, and the surrounding upholstery to provide additional space. At least twice we used the car to carry a blanketed calf to a school fair for exhibition. One evening as we were driving along the Bostwick Road on our way to milk the cows at the other place, a rear wheel spun off and passed us just before the back of the car dropped to the road with a grinding crash. While I ran ahead to retrieve the wheel from the ditch, George picked up the lock nuts from the road, and soon we were on our way again—although not without discussion of the identity of the individual who had last repaired that tire.

When the cows were at the other place and the car was not available, the milkers hitched Len's black standardbred mare, Winnie Mae, to a buggy and drove over to do the milking. Winnie Mae's full cooperation, however, was never assured. One evening when Harold, one of the hired men, drove Winnie Mae to do the evening milking at the other place, she behaved impeccably on the out trip and waited patiently in the enclosure for him to finish the milking. With his task completed and pails and cans stowed away, he drove the buggy onto the road and got down to close the paddock gate, leaving the reins resting on the dashboard. As Harold tugged the heavy wooden gate into place, Winnie Mae decided she was urgently needed at the home place and set off at a spanking trot up the Bostwick Road. Harold ran after her, but despite comparative youth and good health, he could not catch Winnie. About halfway to the junction of the Bostwick Road and Dale's Side Road, Harold realized that Winnie must travel by road, while he could cut his distance by running through the fields along the hypotenuse of the triangle formed by the junction. When he confronted the trotting Winnie at a point several hundred yards up the side road, she stopped with every appearance of good humor and let him climb into the buggy. None dared to ask Harold if he had heard a horse laugh.

During that same summer, Winnie Mae scored again on the hired men. This time the victim was Russ C., a young man from a neighboring farm family who was working for us during the height of our tomato harvest. Russ was a competent milker. George being away on some business relating to the county Holstein-Friesian Association, Len delegated Russ to hitch up Winnie Mae and attend to the milking on the back fifty in company with Harold. Their mission successfully completed, they drove back into the barnyard around suppertime and pulled to a stop beside the milk house. Harold leaped from the buggy and unfastened the harness traces that connected Winnie to the buggy, throwing one of the loose ends over her back with a definite slap. Winnie took that as a signal and leaped forward; Russ, still sitting in the buggy and holding the reins, was taken by surprise and instinctively held on. In the next moment Winnie pulled him from his seat and over the buggy's dashboard to land on the ground headfirst between the buggy shafts she had so recently vacated.

I never approached the level of skill in milking cows by hand that George and Len attained. But by the time I was in my teens I was expected to milk at least one cow at the evening milking during the summer and a couple on Sunday nights when Len went courting. As I have noted, George believed that the dairy's reading of the butterfat content in our milk was dishonestly low. But it was also true that the test results recorded by the ROP testers did not much exceed 3 percent. Len was on good terms with the herdsmen on the Pringle farm, and we arranged to borrow a young Jersey cow from there to fortify our fluid milk shipments to the city dairy. I received the task of milking the Jersey cow in the evening on the grounds that my smaller hands were ideal for grasping the small teats of the young Jersey. That arrangement did not last long. Mr. Pringle's resources were unequal to the demands of a hobby farm in the midst of an agricultural depression. He dispersed the animals in his herd that same fall, our dainty little cow among them.

After George had begun to separate our milk and sell the cream, he usually accumulated cream in the cool basement of the house during the week and sold it on Saturdays as sweet cream to a London creamery that accepted walk-in shipments. Eleta rehabilitated an old tub churn and at times made butter for sale on the farmers' market in London. Sometimes I turned the churn for her, stopping to look through the round glass window in its side for evidence of transformation, although a change in the sound coming from the agitated liquid provided better evidence that the butter was "coming." At that point swishing changed to gentle thumping as the tub continued to turn end over end.

At night as in the morning, George doled out the skim milk for the calves on hand and the occasional hog acquired as part of the second mortgage payout made by the purchaser of the farm on the Fifth Concession Road. When I was at the barn I took the pails of skim milk to the eager customers. Newly born calves suckled the mother for a week or so, the men stripping out the calf's leavings, but after that point we began to pail-feed calves on skim milk. The youngsters were always ready to suck fingers whether milk was involved or not, and teaching them to drink from a pail was easy. One simply guided the small head into the pail while the calf worried one's finger, and it was soon sucking up milk as it sucked at the finger. After a few such experiences the calf needed no guidance when I arrived at the pen, pail in hand.

Len's longtime business arrangement with George, as described, allowed him to keep the female calves dropped by his club calf of years earlier and their calves in turn. George, however, retained the income from the sale of milk or cream from these animals. When Len agreed to join his father-in-law in partnership in 1937, his livestock constituted about half of the herd, and he took these animals with him. George then faced the challenge of building up the herd on the foundation of the animals that he retained. As a result, he and I were still milking only five or six cows during the summer of 1939, none of them heavy producers.

When our cash crop of tomatoes began to ripen, George left for market early on Saturday mornings, taking a load of eleven quart baskets of the fruit to market along with the week's cream. I remained at home to milk the cows and to move ahead with whatever farm job was in process at the time. For much of that summer we saved ourselves the trouble of cleaning the cow stable by milking in the corner of the old orchard nearest to the farm buildings except when it was raining. When George departed for the market at about six thirty on Saturday mornings I hitched Pomp, our gray Percheron gelding, to the stoneboat, placed on it a milk pail, barn pail, milk can, and sack of chopped grain, and proceeded across the front field to the near corner of the old orchard. There the little group of cows was usually still bedded down, perhaps dreaming of the grain rations that I would soon give them. I tied Pomp to the corner fence post, eased the milk can and pails through the adjacent fence gap, placed a halter on Veeman, and led her to another post. After placing half a pail of chop in front of her and cleaning any dirt or grass from her udder, I settled on a stool at her side with the milk pail. With my head tucked into her warm flank, I began the first round of an hour or an hour and a half of milking.

Long before, there had been a house at the west side of the orchard and a windbreak of Norway spruce had been planted along that fence, terminating at the corner gap. Its conifer smell was in my nostrils. The sun was pushing above the eastern horizon but I worked in a fresh coolness, dew still sparkling on the orchard grass. Some fifty yards along the south fence line of the orchard, the pond in our middle front field had shrunk to summer size and was hidden by a border of coarse grass and cattails. A layer of white mist hung above it. The milk streams pinged against the pail bottom for a minute or so and the sound changed to a recurrent sough-sough as the milk level rose and a layer of creamy foam formed on the surface. Killdeers called in the lower pasture and a mixture of other bird songs floated from elsewhere in the orchard and the front field. Sometimes I heard bobwhites reporting to each other. It was too early in the morning for flies to bother the cows and they were placid. It was good to be alive and in that place at that time. My enthusiasm for the Holstein-Friesian was still high, although by this time I knew that my immediate future would involve town life and university. Still, if ever I managed to own the dairy farm of my fantasies, I was determined that it would be equipped with the latest in milking machines.

Whereas in summer the care of the dairy herd was somewhat incidental to the work of growing and harvesting field crops, vegetables, and fruit, the focus of winter work was to a much greater degree centered on the livestock, which were spending most of their time in the stables. The first task of the day involved tidying up the milk cow row by scraping into the gutter any manure that had been dropped on the rear of the stall platform. After the cows received their ration of grain, it was time for milking to begin. That task completed, there was the De Laval separator to be turned and the calves to be fed. While George was attending to those matters, Len used one of the long-handled pitchforks to throw down hay from the mows on the upper floor of the barn, sending it down the central chute into the alley in front of the cow mangers. From there he threw it into the cow and horse mangers and tossed forkfuls into the box stalls occupied by the bull and several of the season's calves. Other youngsters might be tethered in the central feeding alley or penned in the small alleys on either side of the horse stable, and they too received some hay. Then it was time for breakfast.

Winter breakfast for the men was a more leisurely meal than in the other months of the year, and it was nine o'clock or so before they left the house again. On extremely cold days or during blizzard conditions they watered all of the stabled animals in the barn, carrying the water in pails from the pump at the end of the feed alley. (Water bowls were another of the essential fittings in my fantasy dairy barn of the future.) On most winter days, however, one of the men took an axe and shovel, walked down to the small ice-covered tributary of Dingman's Creek that ran through our night pasture, and chopped half a dozen large holes in the ice. Although small and often dry during high summer, this little stream invariably ran during the late fall, winter, and spring. In midmorning the men turned the cows and later the young cattle into the barnyard to make their way into the night pasture and down to the water holes. If the weather was pleasant they were allowed to stay outside for a while and exercise while George or Len cleaned the cow stable. Usually the men led the horses to water after the cows had had their turn. They repeated this watering routine as a final chore in the afternoon before they went in for supper.

Winter was an easy time for the horses and they were inclined to prance and break into a trot when freed from their stalls. I escaped serious injury by little more than an inch when leading a newly acquired young Clydesdale named Prince to water on a sunny winter Saturday morning. Carelessly I had allowed him to move out to the end of the halter shank, putting him some five feet or so ahead of me. Suddenly he reared and kicked out with his hind legs, one hoof whistling close by my ear. Prince was not in the least malicious or unfriendly. He was merely kicking up his heels in the sheer joy of being out of the stable on a beautiful morning. The results, however, were almost serious. The face of my Sunday school teacher in Lambeth reminded me of that morning because one side of Jim's face had been disfigured when a horse kicked him.

As noted, George specified that two large concrete cisterns were to be built adjacent to the stables of the new barn, one at surface level beside the milk house and one in the ground at the north end of the barn. The design of the surface cistern proved faulty, and in the second winter of operation its junction with the barn foundation failed because of the alternation of freezing and thawing temperatures. Water from this cistern began to drain across the floor of the alleyway behind the cows and into the gutter. As a cistern its usefulness was ended, and George disconnected the drainpipe that fed it from the barn eave troughs. Thereafter its walls served merely as part of the concrete foundation over which the approach to the upper barn doors ran. The sunken cistern at the north end of the barn, however, served well. I remember only one summer when the rainfall collected there from the barn roof failed to serve all the needs of the barn residents. At that time we brought in a few loads of water in barrels from Dingman's Creek to supplement our water supply.

None of us liked to clean out the stables, but the job had to be done. Although we could evade it in summer by milking outdoors at the back fifty or in the old orchard during our last years on the farm, cleaning was an inescapable daily task while the cattle were stabled during the winter. A litter carrier that ran on a metal track suspended from the ceiling behind the cows and horses and exiting the barn through the horse stable door was another improvement that George visualized when he built the new barn. That happy future never materialized, and we made do with a wheelbarrow, five-tined dung fork, and stable shovel. George purchased a nicely painted red wheel barrow from a farm machinery outlet to celebrate business in the new barn, but wear and tear took its toll. By the time I reluctantly began to help in cleaning the stables, George had salvaged the wheel and other ironware from the broken-down factory barrow and made a new one out of scantling and rough-milled boards. The box of this contraption sat on a base of two-by-fours that protruded for about thirty inches beyond the rear of the box. George shaped these roughly into handles using a draw knife and plane. This barrow was solid, had considerable capacity, and was a good deal heavier than the factory product.

The stable cleaners started the operation by scraping all the manure and soiled straw bedding from the stall platform onto the manure and urine already lying in the gutter. One of us then wheeled the cumbrous vehicle to one end or the other of the cow-row stalls. We forked and shoveled gutter contents into it, moving the barrow toward the cross alley until there was a full load. At that stage Len or George wheeled it through the cross alley and out of the horse stable door to dump the contents onto a pile at the back of the barn, to be spread on the crop fields later. At the back of the barn there were at times three manure piles. The largest one accumulated outside the horse stable door and smaller ones beside the window of the calf pen and the northeast corner door opening into the herd sire's box stall.

During some winters the men found time to rig a box on the bobsled and haul loads of manure out to the fields where George planned to plant small grains or corn in the following spring, leaving it in small conical heaps to be spread more evenly by fork in the spring. At other times the piles at the barn grew until spring, when the men spent several days hauling wagon loads of manure to the fields. In late August we placed any residue from this operation plus the summer accumulation from the stables and box stalls on the land that was being prepared for winter wheat, a crop that George invariably grew each year.

Instead of cleaning out the box stalls every day, or every few days, we typically threw straw bedding into them every day, which allowed the animals to stay reasonably clean. That practice, however, sometimes resulted in the buildup of an accumulation of a foot or even a foot and a half of well-trodden straw and dung before the floor of the stalls reappeared. At some point during the haying or small grain harvest, a storm would halt operations around noon, and after dinner George would say, "I've got to go to Lambeth [or London] this afternoon. You fellows can clean out the box stalls." The manure in the stalls was always densely packed and highly pungent. For hours after we had completed the task, none needed to ask what we had been doing during that rainy afternoon.

When they first stabled the cattle in the late fall, the men pushed the wheelbarrow loads some thirty or more feet from the barn before dumping them. As time passed the pile crept nearer to the horse stable door. As it encroached there, the men took eight-inch-wide boards and ran them onto the pile, making a viable though springy path for the wheel of the barrow. As time passed they adjusted the boards on top of the growing manure pile. By early spring the pile of manure at the horse stable door had become majestic, and journeys with the loaded wheelbarrow became exercises in skilled navigation. As the spring sun played on the pile and the eave troughs of the barn overflowed and icicles dripped water on it, the mass seethed and bubbled in places. Now a foot slipping off the board path sank deep into a stinking morass of manure. Sometimes the wheel of the barrow slid off its supporting board and the barrow overturned and dumped its load across the throughway, requiring reconstruction of the route.

Following the cleaning of the stables in midmorning during the winter, we brought straw down from one of the mows above or from an outside straw stack standing at the south end of the barn. This we spread under the animals in the stanchion row, and we threw big forkfuls into the box stalls. As soon as the cow stable had received its daily cleanup, we moved on to the horse stable to muck out the stalls and provide fresh bedding. This was a much less messy job, made easier as well by the proximity of the manure pile.

With the stables cleaned and bedding put down, we gave the cattle a feeding of stalk corn, dragging the sheaves into the stable from a pile or sleigh load at the south end of the barn that Len or George had hauled from the previous summer's corn field. Jackknife in hand, one of us dumped the corn sheaves into the mangers, cutting the twine that bound the sheaf and retaining the cut twine as we did so. When the corn went into the mangers there was a great tossing of black and white heads and creaking of stanchions as the cows rooted through the stalks and leaves in search of corn cobs. These they ate first, and one saw two or three cows in a row with heads slightly elevated, cobs projecting from their mouths and even twirling as the animals shelled off the seed corn from the cob or tried to masticate it into chunks appropriate for swallowing. With the cattle fed and the horses issued a ration of hay, the usual winter-morning barn chores were finished. Now the men returned to the house for a break and warm-up and sometimes to look at the morning paper and other mail, which usually reached our box at the crossroads around 10:30 A.M..

George and Len protected themselves against the winter days with some care. Long johns of course were essential, invariably worn under blue denim jeans in Len's case, but sometimes George preferred bib overalls. Around the farmstead, or close to it, both men wore flannel shirts, overlain by sweaters and topped with blue denim jackets. Below the knees, however, preference differed. Len liked to wear two pairs of woolen socks under rubber boots that reached to just below the knees and into which he tucked the lower part of his trousers. In winter George invariably wore heavy outer socks over woolen inner socks, the high tops of the outside pair covering his lower pants to just above the knee. He secured them there with a cord that was stitched into the sock. The Farmer's Co-op in Lambeth kept a supply of these winter farm socks on hand but I never knew their brand name. On his feet George typically wore rubber ankle-high mackinaw boots. Both men preferred green horsehide mittens, finding them warmer than gloves, although they sometimes wore woolen gloves inside the mitts when they were going to take out one of the teams for a considerable time during the winter. On those occasions they also donned overcoats and scarves and replaced the old caps of the farmstead with an ear-flapped hat.

If the weather was at all cold, the men took off their outer socks during the midmorning break and warmed them at the open oven of the big cook stove. Feet too rested for a time on the opened oven door, while a comforting warmth stole back into the toes. After this pause, the men turned to various farmstead tasks. Cows were typically bred at this time, an occurrence I was not allowed to watch until in my mid-teens. Sometimes one of the men groomed the horses with brush and curry comb or applied the same tools to the milk cows. If a louse had dropped on a milker's forearm, George might rub a little powdered sulfur into the top line of the cows. This was an infrequent happening, however. At this time also the men bagged oats, or the mix of oats and barley that George usually sowed as part of the spring grain planting, in preparation for taking a load of grain to the grist mill in the afternoon. If a fresh supply of corn sheaves was to be fetched in the afternoon, they unloaded the remnants of the last load from the bobsled rack and leaned the corn bundles against the barn wall or the fence near the door at the south end of the feed alley. Or they might prepare for hauling a load of hay or straw later in the day from the hay barn on the Bostwick fifty or the Dale place while we rented that farm. To heat the house we used the kitchen range, a large wood- or coal-burning heater in the living room, and a smaller stove in the parlor. Bringing a supply of firewood from the woodlot or the old orchard was also a winter task, and the men might devote the late morning to preparing for an afternoon of woodcutting.

When the major task of the afternoon had been completed at between four and five o'clock, the men turned to the evening barn chores. One of them went down to the water holes in the night pasture to ensure that they were not frozen over and then he let the cattle out for their afternoon watering. Again the men led the horses to the little stream for their second drink of the day and returned them to their stalls. The bull received his second watering by pail from the cistern pump, as did young animals that were not released for a drink. In some years we kept a small overflow of young stock in the basement of the decrepit old barn in the lower pasture, and Len made trips there morning and night to see to their needs for feed and water.

Supper in the winter usually convened at about six, the men returning to the stable immediately afterward, carrying the milk pails and the separator reservoir containing the components of the separation mechanism as well as a clean cotton milk strainer. With the evening graining of cows, milking, milk separation, rinsing of utensils, and calf feeding finished, we gave the livestock a further feeding of fodder, usually hay, although sometimes stalk corn. We raked any manure on the cattle's stall platform into the gutter and scraped any manure in the horse stalls away from the animals. Then we laid down another installment of bedding for all the livestock in the barn, turned off the barn lights, and returned to the house, somewhat after eight o'clock in the evening.

During the summer when the cows were away or in the stable only while being milked, stable management was much simpler than in the winter. A few calves and the herd sire were the only continuous stable residents during these months. The horses too went out to pasture in the evening and were at work in the fields much of the day. In theory we cleaned out the summer accumulation of horse manure in the stable every day, along with anything left by the cows in their stable. In practice there might be a couple of days of accumulation at times of peak work. As the thirties wore on, and particularly after Len joined his father-in-law, stable cleanup became my Saturday-morning obligation. It was not a pleasant assignment, but the barn was warm in spring and fall and cool in summer, and the barn walls did not confine my mind. While forking manure or shoveling residual urine into the wheelbarrow I rehearsed or redelivered arguments for the negative or affirmative on propositions argued by the boys' debating team at London Central Collegiate Institute or once more explained my reasons for placing cattle in a particular rank order at the cattle-judging competitions that were part of the calf-club program.

In later years I have often thought about the reasons underlying the commitment of the purebred stockman. I might have understood them better if I had ever asked George why he decided to keep purebred Holsteins. Family example was surely involved; the chicken-fancy virus had possessed the previous generation of Bogue men. George told stories about youthful experiences when he joined his uncle Dick on the front seat of a democrat, loaded with prime specimens of fowl, and trotted off to agricultural fairs in the area. He particularly remembered one incident when they arrived late on the evening before fair day in Ridgetown and found accommodations in a run-down boarding house. Sharing a double bed, they soon realized they were not its sole occupants, and they spent a good deal of time on fair day scratching numerous bites. Despite misadventures, George had obviously enjoyed these breaks from farm routines. The pleasant excitement of competition, the prize ribbons, and the small premiums dimmed the memory of failures or of times when manifestly inferior competitors carried off the top prizes.

The members of the board of directors of the local farmers' co-op considered themselves progressive farmers, and several were dairymen on a larger scale than George. At board meetings they discussed the interesting things they were doing on their farms and provided examples for him to emulate. The Ontario Department of Agriculture's county representative, the "ag rep," also encouraged interest in purebred stock. He probably suggested that the Middlesex County Holstein-Friesian Breeders' Association be organized, and its board of directors usually met in his office just off the Covent Garden Market in London during my years of awareness. George held office in that organization from the late 1920s, usually serving as secretary, although he was president for a couple of years during the mid-1930s. Such influences may have encouraged him to maintain a herd of purebred Holsteins.

Economic motivation was in play as well and was perhaps the controlling factor. Men like George kept purebred stock because they believed that such animals were better producers of milk and butterfat than were grade animals. The offspring of cows that had impressive "records" of milk and butterfat production "on ROP" could be expected to bring good prices as breeding stock. But involved with such motivation were elements of local prestige, camaraderie, and friendly competition. I do not believe that any of his children saw George as an ideal parent, but in giving both Len and me herd foundation calves and encouraging us to participate in competition, he made farm life much more attractive than it would otherwise have been.

Dairying was of course hard work. Committed to his milking tasks night and morning, the dairyman was tied to the farm to a degree unknown to the grain farmers then trying to develop the agriculture of the prairie provinces or in other types of farming in southwestern Ontario. The dairy farmer who entrusted his herd to hired men would pay, George and his friends believed, in calves lost at birth and fresh cows suffering from milk fever, also known as garget—sometimes induced, they understood, by irregular or incomplete milking. One of George's friends reported firing a hired man because he found him inserting straws in teats so that the milk ran out voluntarily, a trick that produced infection as well as lessening production.

George preached constant vigilance. If I was ever alone and a cow showed signs of bloating, he told me, I must put a small cup of coal oil in a drench bottle and administer it immediately. Left in charge of the place on a misty fall day in 1938 and told to allow the cows two hours in the grain-field stubble at the end of the afternoon with a final few minutes in a stand of twice-cut alfalfa, I lost myself in my Latin authors reader. When I next looked at the cattle, they were in the alfalfa field. Damp green alfalfa in quantity, George had warned, could cause bloat. I stanchioned the cows in the barn and discovered that Veeman's middle was bulging ominously. Beside myself with worry, I found the coal oil can and charged the old Scotch bottle that we used for drenching. Veeman did not suffer fools gladly; although she was secure in the stanchion I knew that she might give me only one chance. So, with the drenching bottle in my left hand, I walked up from the rear on her left side and stationed myself in the manger in front of her stanchion, pressing into the warm neck. Then with my right hand I reached over her neck and grasped her jaw just below her mouth. Quickly raising her head until her muzzle pointed to the ceiling, I slipped the neck of the bottle into her mouth behind her front row of teeth, pushing it as far into her throat as possible. Veeman tried to wrench her head away and gave a bovine sputter but did not cough out any of the coal oil. I managed to hold onto the bottle. After fifteen minutes the large indentation that one normally sees between the upper ribcage and the hip or hook bone of cattle had reappeared in Veeman's side, to my considerable relief. Whew!

In addition to the necessity of constant skilled attendance and the unending rounds of cleaning stables that were involved in dairying, the bovine personality could be annoying. Some cows perversely lay down and dangled their switches in the urine standing in the gutter behind them. Brought to her feet in preparation for milking, such a cow might then slap the unwary milker across the face with her tail as he settled into the task of milking. No one can understand the nadir to which relations with a cow can sink who has not experienced the exquisite agony of a thousand wet and wiry threads stinging the face; smarting, pungent urine flooding the eyes; and feces-filled liquid dripping down one's chin to stain one's shirt.

Always within our herd there were some animals that were particularly quick to take advantage of gates or fence gaps that had been left open or that would methodically test the fences separating pasture from attractive alfalfa in an adjacent hay field. Others, as already described, tried to break away from the herd in search of windfall apples while being driven from the woodlot through the old orchard. One summer, my pretty young cow Ethel earned a permanent place in Eleta's black book. Eleta maintained a bed of annuals beside the fence dividing our lawn from the night pasture. Her indignation overflowed one evening when she observed this animal lean a black and white shoulder against the mesh fence, stretch it lawnward to the utmost, and then reach over to harvest the blooms from a handsome stand of zinnias. Young cattle that penetrated line fences to join those in the fields of neighbors could be a particular irritation because when being rounded up, they often tried to break away to go back to their newfound friends and sometimes tried immediately to test the repaired fence. We had no juvenile delinquents as determined as the heifer for which George made a poke, but once through an open gate or fence gap, a Holstein yearling could accelerate remarkably. The committed dairyman dismissed such minor irritations as part of the game, even speaking admiringly of his more mischievous charges.

FOUR

The Ormsby Faynes and Other Friends

During my growing up years on the farm I had no playmates of the same age. Because of my social clumsiness, the occasional interaction with younger or older neighbor children seldom worked well. It was natural, therefore, that I aped my brother's interests and enthusiasms despite the difference in our ages. Thirteen years my senior, Len was six feet, three inches in height and slim but also well muscled. He had his mother's gray-blue eyes and a nose more generously proportioned than hers. He was a great reader, even bringing a book or magazine to the dinner and supper table. I, too, became an enthusiastic bookworm but, alas, Eleta did not allow me to read during family meals. "Unfair!" I complained. I was unhappier yet when she ruled that there would be no books from the Lambeth Library for a week because she discovered I was leaving volumes face down in order to save my place and thus endangering their spines. More relevant to this account, however, Len transmitted his enthusiasm for Holstein-Friesian cattle to me. When I was in the stable during milking and still too young to chore, I usually positioned myself opposite his stool in the alleyway behind the cows. (Actually the milkers usually sat on empty wooden packing boxes that George bought for a nickel or a dime apiece at the Farmer's Co-op.)

Len first showed me that if one stood beside the manger of one of the more docile cows and stroked her neck just below the end of the jaw bone, her head would slowly elevate until the underneck shaped a straight line from brisket to jaw tip and her mouth opened a little in pleasure, showing the incisors on the lower jaw and the bald upper gum above them. Cows usually grazed into the wind, he told me, because the inclined stalks of grass were more easily pulled into their mouths and across their teeth when approached from that direction. I was amazed to learn that cows rechewed their food, and he set me to watching how cows lying at rest assumed an introspective expression that was followed by a contraction of the neck muscles, soon in turn followed by a satisfied look and a methodical chewing action of the jaws.

"Have you ever seen a cow's cud?" I once heard Len ask Gordie T. "I'll bet that you can't make one of the cows give you one." Gordie spent the next quarter of an hour trying to extract a specimen cud from Arabell, who stood beside the passageway through the milk row and usually was a most cooperative animal. She, however, would have none of it. When Gordie managed to insert a hand into her mouth, it was empty. Arabell had decided to postpone rumination until human foolishness ceased.

Len showed me how to teach calves to drink and told me to stick my mittens deep into my pockets when standing beside the calf pen to prevent inquisitive youngsters from pulling them into the box stall. When I was in my teens, it was he who first asked my help in delivering a calf from a cow that was slow in dropping it.

In our first years on the northeast corner, George subscribed to *Holstein-Friesian World*, the official publication of the Holstein breeders' association in the United States. Each year that organization distributed a large wall calendar picturing the Holstein-Friesians that had most distinguished themselves in the various classes at major cattle shows during the previous twelve months. Len ordered a number of these All-American calendars, and during our first years on the northeast corner, two of them hung in the upstairs bedroom that we shared. The mature bull honored on one of them was Johanna Rag Apple Pabst. In the calendar of the next year Sir Fobes Ormsby Hengerveld replaced him.

We felt a special interest in the first of these animals because a wealthy insurance magnate, T. B. Macaulay, had purchased him to head the Macaulay herd in Quebec, where the bull made a great contribution to the breed, improving both its butterfat production and physical conformation. We could not know the long-term significance of this Yankee migrant (all Americans were Yankees to us), but we agreed that he was a magnificent animal. Spurred by the pictures on the calendars, when I was confined to bed with pleurisy I spent much of my time cutting out images of prize animals from issues of the *World* and combining them in fantasy herds that took all the first prizes, both male and female, and of course the grand championship, at the London Fair, at the great Royal Winter Fair in Toronto, which ended the year's show season in Canada, and even at the famed Dairy Cattle Congress in Waterloo, Iowa.

The development that sparked my enthusiasm more creatively began on a Saturday evening in the spring of 1932. George had returned home from the city in the late afternoon, after attending a meeting of the board of directors of the Middlesex County Holstein-Friesian Breeders' Association. After such trips he often relayed local and area news to us at supper. That evening his report involved me.

W. K. Riddell, the county ag rep, he said, was organizing a Holstein-Friesian calf club. "The boys in it are supposed to be twelve years of age but he wants one more lad to make up the minimum number needed. I told him that Allan would join to help him out, although he is just eleven." This was the first I had heard about the formation of a calf club.

Turning to me, he continued, "I am going to give you a heifer calf to start you off as a livestock owner, and remember, you are going to have to look after her and show her in the fall."

I do not remember much about my first year as a calf club member. George took me to a meeting of the new club, where I met the ag rep, a vigorous, stocky man in his late thirties or early forties. He welcomed us all into the club and explained our obligations as members. These involved the daily care of my calf and the preparation and submission of a monthly report in which I summarized the kinds and amounts of feed she was getting. He handed out cardboard-covered books of tear-out forms for use in preparing the reports. He explained the mechanics of choosing a club president and we selected one of the older lads at the meeting to fill that role.

I did not meet my obligations as a club member very faithfully in the club's first year. I named my calf Clarabelle, and on summer evenings I gave her a pail of skim milk with a helping of calf meal stirred into it and threw straw and hay into her box stall. But in the mornings I slept on while Len and George fed Clarabelle along with the other cattle. Nor was I faithful in sending in my reports. As the summer moved along and the fall show at which the calf club members exhibited their calves approached, Len helped me to make a halter out of light rope and he coached me on the proper way to show an animal. Holding the halter shank coiled in left hand and standing at Clarabelle's head on her left side, I should, Len told me, walk backward while in the ring so that I could position her squarely on all four legs when we were told to halt. If she persisted in standing at sixes and sevens, I must nudge her feet with my foot to make her square up. And I must train her to be sufficiently docile to stand motionless while the judge ran his hands over her in testing the pliability of her skin and evaluating her bone structure and general condition.

I did not practice much, and Clarabelle and I did not achieve true rapport. In our show ring maneuvers we never reached the point of moving together as a team. Indeed Clarabelle never learned that the team leader was at my end of the halter shank rather than at the heifer end. In our outings she periodically lowered her head and tried to twist away from me so that she could return to the stable. I dimly recall the judging of the calf club class that year at the fall show of the Middlesex County Holstein-Friesian Breeders' Association. By that time, Clarabelle's adult appearance was predictable and her hindquarters were not the kind that judges of Holstein-Friesian cattle preferred. Nor had I adequately blanketed and groomed her during the summer to the point where her coat was flat, smooth, and shiny.

The judging ring was encircled with red snow fence, and when we entered it, I had difficulty convincing Clarabelle that we should stay there. Somehow we reached a compromise and managed to stay in place as the entrants circled the judge, who leaned on his cane while making a first evaluation of the calves. When he began to point to one calf and then another for them to be brought into a stationary line, it took a long time before he acknowledged that Clarabelle and I were present. At the judge's signal, I managed to steer her to the end of the line and struggled to keep her there while the judge surveyed us all. Then he sent us out to the ring perimeter for another walk-around and switched the positions of several calves when he brought us back into line. Clarabelle and I successfully defended the end of the line. My first experience with club work was daunting, but it made me the full-fledged owner of a registered Holstein-Friesian.

I stayed in the Middlesex County Holstein-Friesian Calf Club through my last year of high school. I did not, however, receive a new heifer calf each year. Clarabelle was mine, but henceforth I showed a "loaner," the calf that we considered most promising in terms of Holstein type from the small annual crop of heifer calves on the farm. Sometimes these calves were the progeny of George's cows and sometimes they were the daughters of cows among the growing number that Len owned. In the year following my misadventures with Clarabelle, my club experience was one of rags to riches. I owed this change of fortune to Donabelle Ormsby Fayne.

Donabelle was a member of the Madolyn line and beautifully marked in a pattern similar to that of the breed's true type female, an animal portrayed in miniature on the cover of the *World*. In June 1933, the county Holstein-Friesian breeders held a Black and White Day in Springbank Park, near Byron. To this combined field day and picnic and other such occasions, nearby breeders brought a few representative animals to use in a judging competition or as illustrative material for a lecture by the regional field man of the national Holstein-Friesian Association or some other dignitary. We took Donabelle to this gathering and she drew many admiring comments.

Both Len and George believed she was the best heifer calf our stock had thus far produced.

The leaders in the county Holstein-Friesian Breeders' Association tried to stimulate interest in the breed and in its improvement by staging a fall show, the Black and White Show, and also by having representative breeders exhibit stock at the Western Fair in London, where there was a class for county herds. Donabelle, we were told, should certainly go to this exhibition. Handling the calf in the open class at a show against national competition was clearly beyond my abilities; that was to be Len's responsibility. But George allowed me to use Donabelle as my calf club entrant, and I tackled my club duties that summer with enthusiasm. We gave Donabelle sole possession of the calf pen and I made a blanket for her by slitting a large feed sack and fashioning ties of binder twine that ran under neck and tail and others that anchored the covering around her back legs. This made Donabelle's hair lie flat and sleek. Both Len and I exercised her on halter so that she became very manageable, and I brought her out of the barn for the inspection of visitors who were interested and some, I am sure, who were not. Having finished the morning chores one Saturday when Eleta and George were in the city, Len and I decided to allow Donabelle to see how the two-leggeds lived. I led her up the path to the house, up the step to the porch, and from there into the living room and the kitchen. Donabelle was cooperative and looked around the kitchen with some interest, although perhaps disappointed that there was neither hay nor grain on the kitchen table. At this point we realized some of the complications that might occur in this experiment, and I hastily guided Donabelle outside.

She continued to thrive during the summer and in September came the fall fair season crowned by the London Fair. Here the animals were on exhibition for several days, and some of the exhibitors came from other Canadian provinces. In those days, according to Len, a dairyman or firm with outstanding stock could send a show herd on circuit to begin exhibition at Calgary in early July, move east to other fairs in the prairie provinces and midwestern American states, check in at the Canadian National Exhibition in Toronto in late summer, and thence move on to London for the Western Exhibition, ending their year on circuit with an appearance at the Canadian Royal in Toronto as winter was about to begin. If there were enough outstanding animals in such a herd, the show premiums defrayed a good deal of the cost of the venture, although such exhibitors derived their major payoff from the enhanced reputation of their herds and the higher prices that they obtained for breeding stock as a result of showing their animals.

For the most part, the outstanding show herds of those years represented large dairying or breeding operations or hobby herds. However, one that included the London Fair in its travels for several years during the mid-1930s came from the Canadian Maritimes and included a good share of the owner's cattle. In the year when I learned the most about this herd, the son in charge had been absent from home for a couple of months and expected to remain on the road for some considerable time yet. Show herds such as these traveled by railroad car; a spur track ran directly behind the cattle barns at the London Fair Grounds.

One of our local truckers took Len and Donabelle to the fair and Len slept there for several nights, bunking in a couple of comforters on a bed of straw close to the calf. I was allowed to skip school on show day and traveled into London with George and Eleta after the morning chores were finished. We found Len and Donabelle in fine fettle. Len had given her a thorough brushing and a bath on the previous day, soaping her thoroughly and then putting bluing in a final rinse to make her coat a dazzling contrast of black and white. After giving her some time to dry, he had blanketed her for the night. He had cleaned her black hoofs and scraped them with glass and emery paper and had used the latter also to smooth the emerging black knobs above her ears.

In the morning he gave her the regular ration of grain and hay and fed her a pail of soaked beet pulp and as much tasty new hay as she wanted at around eleven o'clock, a couple of hours before exhibition time in the early afternoon. As ring time approached, he allowed her to drink more water. This feeding strategy, we hoped, would present the judge with an animal showing a capacious barrel that could be expected to support a generous milk flow two years hence. An hour before show time, Len slipped away to a lavatory and emerged in the white duck slacks, white cotton shirt, and black oxfords he would wear in the ring. Now he unfastened the braids that had confined Donabelle's switch since her bath and combed the long tail hairs into a puffy white cloud. Half an hour before ring time he roused Donabelle, by now extremely full and content. Standing behind her, he pulled off the blanket, drawing it to him so that her hair lay flat. He replaced the rope stable halter with one made of shiny brown leather and with an under-the-chin draw chain to which the leather lead strap was attached. Then while George held Donabelle, Len used a fly sprayer to cover her with a mist of oil-based fly spray, rubbing off the excess with a rag. Now she really shone. Len shoved the rag into his rear pocket and the little entourage of Donabelle and Len with George and me trailing in attendance set off for the judging arena, which stood a couple of buildings away from the cattle barn where we had quartered her.

The show ring of that time in the arena of the London Fair complex was oval and floored with tan bark during livestock events. It was large enough to enclose comfortably the layout of obstacles used in the evening equestrian competitions during the fair or to allow several different types of livestock to be judged at the same time. A walkway ran completely around the ring, separated from it by a chest-high white wooden fence. Beyond this concrete pathway rose tiers of wooden bleachers. An entrance at the end of the building gave access to the ring gates. A second set of gates, midway up the side of the ring, opened into a covered passageway that led into the swine and sheep barn. Leaving Len and Donabelle to muster their courage outside the arena while waiting for the heifer calf class to be called into the ring, George and I entered the building, he to take his place beside one of his friends from the county organization along the ring railing and I to climb the short stairs into the bleachers where Eleta was already sitting.

Soon the last exhibitor from the previous class left the ring, the Holstein-Friesian judge and his ring steward or assistant withdrew to their table in the center of the ring, and black and white calves began to enter. Since the rules of the time specified that calves were animals born after July 1 of the previous year and we were now in the month of September, many of the calves were more than twelve months of age and of substantial size. But there were much younger adversaries in the class as well and into the ring now all came, some mostly black, some mostly white, and some, like Donabelle, more or less balancing the two colors in their markings. When they stopped coming through the ring gate and the judge moved to the middle of the circle of black and white calves and gestured with his cane to start them moving at a walk around him, there were more than thirty entrants in the ring.

After a while the judge held up his hand to stop them and began to move from animal to animal, pausing for a moment as he approached each posed animal to consider her, then running his hands over her to check the pliability of the hide, the bone placement, and the general condition of the calf. He bent over briefly to see that four teats were squarely placed on the undeveloped udder between the hind legs. Then with a final look of consideration, he moved to the next animal in the circle. After a few minutes of this the tension became too much for me; I left Eleta, followed the alleyway to the entrance of the adjacent building, and began to tour the sheep and hog pens. After what seemed a considerable time I looked through the outside door of this building and saw a flood of black and white leaving the arena. It was over, I thought. I started to rejoin Eleta, only to see from the arena entrance that the judge was still at work. He had merely winnowed the class to a more manageable size, and Len and Donabelle were still in contention. I turned back to the sheep and swine pens.

When I finally returned to the arena I found the judge and his assistant preparing to record the numbers on the white cards the showmen wore across the back of their white shirts as they held a dozen or so calves in line. Len and Donabelle were standing second in line and about to accept the blue ribbon that at Canadian shows signified that placement. The entry of Hays and Company of Calgary, Alberta, was in first place. But to us, second prize, placing Donabelle above the entries of some of the best herds in Canada, was beyond our greatest expectations. Jubilation ruled in the Bogue family that day.

Donabelle returned home to cut a swath of triumph in the little show circuit where we exhibited her and a few of our other cattle during the next few weeks. She took first prize at the fair of the Westminster Township Agricultural Society in Lambeth and at the fall show sponsored by the Middlesex County Holstein-Friesian Breeders' Association. In the calf club class there she allowed me to exhibit her without any challenge to my leadership, and the red ribbon was ours. By this time Donabelle had become so accustomed to being exhibited that she chewed cud while we stood in line. I was allowed to take her to school one afternoon, perhaps the largest show-and-tell object in school history. Success with Donabelle turned me into an avid competitor, and the fall fair season was my favorite time of year during the remainder of my life on the farm.

I remember most of my club calves with affection. With Donabelle's successes behind them, George and Len had great hopes for the calves of the following year. Several new heifer calves arrived during the late summer months while we were fitting Donabelle for the fall shows, and one of these, we hoped, would be a worthy successor. Two of these youngsters carried the predominantly white markings of the Madolyn line, but Donabelle's full sister was predominantly black in color. One of the white calves developed a respiratory infection and died, despite a barn call by the vet. George decreed that the black youngster should be named Bonnie Bell, and the surviving white youngster was one of the growing number of animals in the herd that Len owned.

By early summer both calves were developing well, but Len and George disagreed as to their relative merit for the show ring. When Bob Holtby, the Holstein-Friesian field man, dropped by one evening after the milking, George seized the opportunity to put the issue before an independent arbiter. Holtby was a stocky little man whose Vandyke beard was streaked with gray and who usually wore a black bowler hat on his bald head. George had high respect for his judgment. Leon and I put halters on the two calves and led them out of the box stall they were sharing. We posed them under one of the two lights in the empty cow stable. After the mandatory physical examinations and several minutes of stepping around and stepping back for views from the middle range, Holtby said, "Well, if they were showing today I think that the white calf would have it." George did his best to hide his chagrin and Len looked somewhat smug.

Len named his white calf Helen Peril, and she continued to develop into a growthy young heifer with the desired straight top line. She lacked Donabelle's "barrel" and flashiness, however. Helen also went to London Fair, and because George misunderstood the judging schedule, I was not present when her class was called in the late afternoon of the day before the one on which I had hoped to attend the show. Alas, Helen won no ribbon. George returned from the show in a vile temper and scolded me aggressively for having failed to bring the cows home from the Bostwick fifty in preparation for milking. Eleta intervened, telling him to stop and to remember that I had not known whether he wished to milk there or in the home stable.

The county breed association was now calling its annual show the Black and White Show and holding it in conjunction with the fall fair at Strathroy. There Helen was more successful, placing high in the open calf class. She also garnered a red ribbon for me in her role as club calf. When a milking heifer in her first lactation, Helen taught me a lesson in the practical mechanics of bovine structure. Confident in my abilities as a bareback horseman, I accepted a dare from one of the hired men and jumped on Helen's back as she left the stable after milking. But I discovered no comfortable natural saddle on Helen's back of the kind that horses offer. As the affronted young matron accelerated, I found myself at the apex of a vibrating white hump, Helen's white coat sloping steeply away from me at both front and rear. I did not remain in place long, coming to earth beside the manure pile outside the chicken pen.

The year Helen served as my club calf was the last one in which members were allowed to show senior calves. Until this time, we had been showing calves born in the previous summer or fall and destined for open competition in the hands of other family members. Henceforth we must work with calves that had been born after January 1 of the year in which we exhibited them. I remember my next two calves only dimly. One was only a few months old when I showed her, and as in the days of Clarabelle, we were waved to the end of the line. With my next I was somewhere in midline. By this time, however, I was a more conscientious young cattleman than I had been at first. I now faithfully tied the hay ration of my club calf into a bundle with light rope and hung it from the hook of the milk scale so that I could fill out my monthly report form accurately.

The ag rep ensured that the club members received instruction on judging techniques in informal classes at the Black and White Day show and at meetings held at dairy farms in various parts of the county. Each year he took a team of older club members to the Agricultural College at Guelph for a provincial judging competition and spent a day in prepping his team by visiting various farms where the owners had consented to provide a class of four cows for the students to judge. On a couple of occasions he included our farm in this process, and I was all ears to the discussion that followed team members' efforts to rank the cows in order of quality. Once Byron Jenvey, Bob Holtby's replacement as regional field man, accompanied the group and lectured us on the qualities one should look for in the productive dairy cow, including that elusive quality "dairy temperament."

Standing beside one of the cows, he began his talk, saying something like this: "My dad used to say that you could hang your hat on the hook bone of a good Holstein cow, pull up the stool, and go to work without any more ceremony." I never understood whether this little anecdote was a tribute to the protruding hip bones of some early Holsteins, was a bow to the fact that the productive dairy matron was not as fat as the typical beef-breed cow, or merely acknowledged the no-nonsense personality of the typical Holstein female.

At some point in the late fall or early winter the members of the county Holstein-Friesian Breeders' Association held their annual banquet. There was always a parade of speakers, and the ag rep W. K. Riddle invariably said a few words. He usually prefaced his remarks with a quip or two. Typical was the evening when he described such occasions as gatherings where people came together to eat turkey stuffed with sages and to listen to sages stuffed with turkey. On these occasions also, he announced the overall rankings of the calf club competition. Show placement was involved in these results, but exhibiting the best calf at the Black and White Show and being judged best showman were not enough to place one at the top. Attendance at meetings, the monthly reports on the amount of feed dispensed, and the general quality of care observed when Riddle or his assistant dropped by during the summer were also involved.

In the early spring of 1937 Len separated his animals from the herd and drove them south on the North Talbot Road to the farm of his father-in-law at Tempo, where the two farmed in partnership for a number of years. Now the number of cattle on our farm fell far short of a full barn and there was no club calf in the offing for me. George solved that problem by buying a couple of young heifer calves, one of them from a herd that had recently purchased from us a bull for breeding purposes. The most promising of the two little heifers became my club calf for the year. Hannah was a growthy youngster, and with Len now departed, I gave her more attention than any of her predecessors. I blanketed her in the early summer to make sure that her coat was flat and sleek and worked her on halter sufficiently often that she handled well. By this time the junior exhibitor division of the Western Exhibition was sponsoring competition between representatives of the calf clubs in the counties of southwestern Ontario. Riddle and his assistant selected Hannah and me to be members of the Middlesex team.

The Western Exhibition was a week-long fair, and George arranged for a trucker who was taking other cattle to the fair grounds to pick Hannah up on Monday, the day when exhibitors arrived and established themselves. We followed in the car and our program leader, Riddle's assistant, was on hand to meet us and guide us to the stalls reserved for club calves in one of the cattle barns. There were some three dozen boys in the group of club teams, and we used an area under the bleachers of the arena as a dormitory. We assembled there at mealtimes to follow our leader to one of the restaurants that church groups managed under the main grandstand, skirting along the back of the midway shows and passing the stands of a medicine man, a guess-your-weight operator, an armless man who did amazing things with his feet and toes, and various other pitch folk eager to take our money.

As an officer in the Middlesex County Holstein-Friesian Breeders' Association, George had helped to select animals for the "county herd" that was to compete with those of other counties. Each day he dropped by on business related to that effort. Eleta and I went to the grandstand performance one evening, and on another night I attended the equestrian jumping events in the arena. "Doc" Bovaird, the Ontario Department of Agriculture veterinarian who administered the TB test to our cattle each year, was a horseman and I saw him ride his famous jumper Cash and Carry to victory.

Victory, however, was not to be our lot in the club competition. I had carefully used our animal hair clippers on Hannah on the day before we came to the show, running them over her head and neck and back to the rear edge of the shoulders. I had clipped from the base of her tail down to the beginning of her switch and taken a bit of hair from the top of the bump that was beginning to show between the hook and pin bones. On the day before exhibition I gave her a bath beside the show barn, using lots of soap and giving her a final rinse in which I put some bluing. I left her switch in braids overnight, to be fluffed out just before ring time, and used emery paper on her hooves. On show day I fed her to repletion. When I gave her a final slicking down with a rag soaked in olive oil and we departed for the judging ring, she was as full as a tick. Artifice could do no more.

As I feared, however, Hannah did not win the judge's favor. Her chine did not sit atop the shoulder blades but instead rested between them; her skin did not have the thin pliability that dairy experts look for, and her hindquarters were beginning to suggest to some that she would be "droopy" when mature. In the eyes of the expert, Hannah was somewhat coarse and lacking in dairy temperament. After conducting the initial walk around and individual inspection, the judge waved us with other discards to the sideline. We watched him continue his examination of the dozen or so survivors that he finally lined up in order of merit. Then we rejects were called back into the group to be judged on the basis of our showmanship. Here too we achieved no distinction, and I was thoroughly depressed when Len arrived later in the afternoon with his trailer to take us home. But the experience had been an exciting one; it was the first time in my life that I had been out of the sight of family members for more than a few hours at a time. And there had been some amusing incidents. We were served shepherd's pie one evening, and the boy sitting next to me discovered a button in his portion. In the flurry of ensuing repartee someone wondered: "Were we also eating the shepherd?"

When Len withdrew his cattle from our herd, besides reducing the number of calves from which I could select a club calf, he also took with him some of the cows that adhered most closely in appearance to the Holstein ideal type and that might perhaps produce a high flyer. Veeman, daughter of Old Veeman and dam of Young Veeman, was deep-barreled and already at an age when most milk cows had begun to fail in their production but still a good producer. In type Veeman's front end and barrel were quite acceptable, although she was a drooper and her udder was pendulous rather than square and solidly attached. However, she freshened in early 1938, successfully delivering a heifer calf. Hannah had proven that the future of purchased calves was uncertain. Having bought a new herd sire, George pled poverty to the suggestion that we buy another calf, and I decided to gamble on Veeman's young daughter, Meg.

As summer drew on Meg developed well. Predominantly black, she had inherited her mother's appetite and substantial midsection, and unlike her dam, she promised to remain reasonably square in the hindquarters. The assistant ag rep visited us in the summer and was impressed. In late August we learned that Meg and I would be among the club representatives at the London Fair. I approached the event more philosophically this time; we would do our best and not hope for too much. As it turned out, we had some success. Meg was a flashy calf and she had cooperated when I trained her to accept the halter, to follow my lead smoothly and stand squarely on all four legs when halted. During the last several years of my membership in the calf club the ag rep negotiated a sponsorship agreement with the London Kiwanis Club, and my Kiwanis Club sponsor dropped by to say hello and to admire Meg. I described her fine points with pride, although I doubt it did much to lessen the gap between city and country that this institutional arrangement was meant to address.

In evaluating the calves on the basis of conformation, the judge did not place Meg and me at the head of the line, but we did, I believe, finish in fifth or sixth place. After this assessment of the class as examples of the breed, the judge tested our showmanship. As we circled him, I sensed that he was attentively watching us. Then he signaled us all into line and watched us position our calves as we halted. Following this maneuver, he sent us once more to move around the ring perimeter. Now he signaled another boy and calf into line, then us, then a number of others, and then with a wave of the cane he dismissed the remainder. But he was not yet satisfied. He came back to the head of the line, cogitated, and then signaled for calf one and calf two to do a small circle and return to the line. Meg did not settle quite squarely on all four feet. I used my foot to nudge her near back foot a couple of inches backward. The judge smiled and said, "Too much fussing." We settled for the blue ribbon.

By the time of the county Black and White Show several weeks later Meg had reached peak condition. It was a sunny day, and when we went into the show ring for the club competition her coat glistened and her white trim made a dazzling contrast. As we circled the ring for the first time, Len leaned over the fence and said softly, "You've got it." And so it proved.

My next show calf marked a new era in the history of our cattle, one in which for me the joy of competition was mixed with sadness. I would again show a calf that was truly mine, but I would be denied the pleasure of seeing it grow to maturity. After the second bull purchased from the Arbogast brothers had serviced our herd for several years, he had reached the point when he would have been breeding his daughters if we had kept him. George and Len were unwilling to accept that degree of inbreeding, preferring to linebreed or even to outbreed if an exceptional animal was available. As he aged, this Arbogast bull had grown increasingly bad-tempered, challenging those who passed his box stall with muted bellowing sounds that came as close to growling as the male bovine can achieve. He had begun to use his horns to butt the vertical hollow iron pipes that formed the siding of the bull pen and its interior door, loosening some of the pipes in their cement footing. George shipped him to the Toronto stockyards for sale to a meat-packing firm, and here, according to the trucker, he sent an employee scrambling over the fence of the holding pen.

By this time Ontario farmers were mired in the Great Depression of the 1930s and the illness, hospitalization, and death of my sister Eleanor must have depleted George's finances further. He did not believe he could afford to purchase a new herd sire. Instead he began to use a young bull from Old Madolyn, the "typiest" cow of her generation in the herd, and sired by the second Arbogast bull. Such breeding did not mate father to daughter in breeding but half brother to sister. Unfortunately the results of such breeding practice can be unpredictable. In this case some of the calves were the closest in appearance to the Holstein-Friesian ideal type that we had produced, but none of the heifers equaled their dams in milk production.

By the time that Len withdrew his animals, this homegrown herd sire had become a fully mature animal, and his temper promised to be even worse than that of his father. At an early age he began to batter the walls and outside door of his box stall. Several times he managed to force the door open. The first herd sires that I knew had no stable name; they were simply "the bull." Some prim farm wives preferred that their male animal be known in farm conversation as "the beast," or "the animal," but everyone in our family preferred to call a spade a spade. And the cry "The bull's out, the bull's out!" was the most frightening warning I knew. Both times that it happened when I was present, Len raced to fill a pail with grain and lured the bull to him, slipping his hand into the pail beside the black and white muzzle to seize the animal's nose ring and then leading him back to his box stall. I watched the engagements from a safe distance. When the pen door was slammed shut and reinforced with a plank, one end firmly anchored in the ground and the other set under the door handle, I discovered on one occasion that my nails had left imprints deep in the palm of my hand.

The pump for the cistern at the north end of the stable stood in the central alley beside the bull's pen. He shoved a couple of the upright iron posts in the pen wall apart by battering them with his horns so that he could stick his big muzzle into the corridor just behind the pump. We had a number of hired men during the summer of 1936 and they were reluctant to fetch water from the pump, with good reason. One started to carry a club when he went to the pump, and we suspected that he used it without need. When George and Len took the bull out to service a cow, they customarily snapped two ropes into his nose ring and exercised control by positioning themselves on either side of him. But this process became increasingly difficult. Len took the softball bat from the house and leaned it against the adjacent barn wall while he and George supervised unions of bull and cow. On one occasion George slipped, releasing his rope, and the bull charged Len. He had to use the softball bat.

Clearly it was time for a change, but for the time being George did not have funds for a new herd sire from the kind of Holstein-Friesian line that he believed would upgrade the herd. For some months he and Len again resorted to using a young male from our own stock. After Len's departure George decided to use some of the profits from the partnership year of 1936 to purchase a new bull to head what remained of the herd.

He consulted Byron Jenvey and one of the ROP testers whose work took him to the best herds in southwestern Ontario. Probably George consulted with friends among the local breeders as well. Who was producing outstanding breeding stock, he inquired, but not yet so established in reputation that they asked extremely high prices for young bulls? On the basis of the answers, particularly from Jenvey, George purchased a young bull from a herd owned by J. J. Fox, a breeder who lived several counties to the east of Middlesex.

George used the trailer to bring the young fellow home, and I was in the barnyard when he drove in. We brought the new arrival down the chute from the trailer with care. When George pulled off the blanket placed on the animal for the trip, I was impressed. Len and I had come to believe that we were better judges of Holsteins than was George, and perhaps it was true. But I had to admit that this time George had not made a mistake. Dixie Posch Hartog 6th was nicely marked with a bit more white than black showing in his coat. He had good shoulders, a deep barrel, and smooth square hindquarters. George had brought back an animal that at least in Middlesex County was a show animal. We proved that to be the case several months later when Dixie took the red ribbon in the yearling class at the Black and White Show in Strathroy. He was the sire of my last successful show calf, Joan Ormsby Fayne.

Joan's maternal ancestry linked back to Clarabelle in a peculiar way. George had told me that Clarabelle was to be mine, a gift intended to reward my cooperation in his effort to assist the ag rep in establishing a calf club in the county as well as to increase my interest in the farm. But when Clarabelle was two years old and "springing" with calf, George announced that he was going to trade a younger animal to me for my old club calf. A buyer had made an offer for my foundation animal. I protested vigorously, having expected soon to be the owner of a second animal. Len—somewhat duplicitously, I have thought in retrospect—calmed me. He explained that Ethel, the heifer I was to receive in exchange, was a far superior animal to Clarabelle. George, he also said, needed money. All this was true enough, but my hopes for expanding my livestock holding received a setback because Ethel was almost two years younger than Clarabelle.

In breeder's terms Ethel was indeed a better animal than Clarabelle. We had not fitted her for show as a youngster because her birth date would have required her to compete against considerably older animals. Her first offspring was a bull calf and a disappointment to me since, like milk, male calves fell to George. Ethel's second breeding was to the new bull, and in the early fall of 1938 she was nearing the end of her first lactation and beginning to show definite signs that her offspring was developing well.

Seeking to enlarge its water supply, the Public Utility Commission of the City of London had drilled a number of wells on properties adjacent to the North Talbot Road in our neighborhood. One, located on the side road in our middle field, did not produce enough to be used by the city. Another, at the northwest corner of Dale's Side Road and the North Talbot Road, produced adequate volume and was being given an extended pump-out. The water from this well ran westward down the side-road ditch into the same little tributary of Dingman's Creek that wandered through our pastures and crossed from our night pasture into the northwest corner farm. Its flow through our fields was not sufficiently great to satisfy our livestock in this season, and since our windmill was not working well, George had obtained permission to set a water trough in the ditch beside the city well and to divert the pump's stream through it. For several weeks we drove our stock to this trough in the morning and late afternoon. This was the background of near tragedy in my career as stockman.

In the course of digging the well and installing the pipe of the city water line, workmen had dug out a deep trench near the location of our trough and refilled it with gravel after they had completed their work. Water soaked into this fill and turned it into a quagmire some four feet deep. After drinking at the trough one evening, Ethel stepped into this trap and sank so deeply that her forequarters were engulfed above her elbows. As she struggled, she seemed to sink deeper. To urge her was hopeless. I ran for George, who had the team hitched to the wagon in the barnyard.

He quickly slipped the draw bolt out of the wagon tongue, leaving the team attached to the double tree, told me to bring a logging chain from the garage, and hustled the horses out to the corner. He looped one end of the chain around Ethel's horns and fastened the other to a clevis in the center of the double tree. Then he gently urged the team forward. The chain tightened. Ethel's body moved forward, one foot emerged onto solid ground, a second, and then her hind legs. She scrambled to her feet.

I was beside myself with fear that as a result of her accident Ethel would throw the calf she was carrying. But she did not. By November she was an extremely large young animal. It would be a big calf, predicted George, or perhaps twins. Twins might not be good news. A few years earlier the sexes had been split in a set of twins that one of our cows had dropped. In such births the heifer was almost invariably a freemartin, an unbreedable animal. But when I returned from school one afternoon in mid-November 1938, George greeted me in great good humor—there were two little heifer calves in the barn, he said. I was now the owner of three purebred Holsteins.

Registration of calves with the Holstein-Friesian Association of Canada required that the breeder fill out a registration form and on it sketch the markings of the animal, using the blank outline of a male or female animal that appeared on the application. By the late 1930s the association allowed breeders to paste a photo of the live animal over the sketch outline, but we continued to do the artwork by hand. The breed organization did not accept applications for animals that had black switches, were all white or all black, were solid black at the hoof on all four legs, or were red and white. The twins, although predominantly white, had some black marking on the shoulder and neck area. Neither possessed any of the forbidden patterns, and as I sat on a box in their pen one morning that summer and outlined their markings on the registration blanks, I was a happy young man. Both Joan Ormsby Fayne and her sister Jane developed that summer into promising calves, although Joan was flashier than her sister.

I was not a member of the club contingent to the Western Exhibition in London in 1939. Given her date of birth, Joan was not eligible for that level of competition. Veeman had belatedly provided me with a youngster of an age that put her at considerable disadvantage in the calf club class. Joan faced a similar handicap in the open class, but circumstances nevertheless gave me the opportunity to take her to the London Fair. That summer George and other officers of the Middlesex County association spent a couple of days recruiting animals for a county herd to be shown at this fair in competition with the Holstein breeders of other southwestern Ontario counties. The only Middlesex breeder who could muster a significant number of show animals from his herd at the time was Hardy Shore of Glanworth. George and his colleagues persuaded other breeders to bring in one animal or several to round out a competitive county herd, promising that someone would be available to help look after the animals during the slack time of the show and also to help with their preparation the day before exhibition. George volunteered my services for this role in 1939. We also entered Joan in the open calf class, where she would compete against calves that might be several months older than she.

I enjoyed my few days in the exhibition cow barns in London in 1939. The professional herdsmen in charge of show herds that competed at a number of major exhibitions usually fashioned small headquarters at one end of their strings, setting up cots in little alcoves made of bales of hay or straw, their tack trunks, and other equipment. I had placed Joan at one end of the Middlesex cattle and at night unrolled a couple of quilts on a bed of straw a few feet from her. In the middle of one such night a large and handsome black bull from Elgin County broke away from his moorings across the aisle from my sleeping spot and started to tour the premises. An exciting few minutes followed.

The day before exhibition I took the lead in washing two dozen Holsteins in preparation for competition; it was hard work but I did not mind it. W. K. Riddle organized a junior farmer judging competition on one morning and I amazed myself by winning it. George appeared on the morning of show day with some fresh-cut field corn to tempt Joan to a particularly hearty meal, and that afternoon I led her into the arena to compete in a class of several dozen calves, most of them some months her senior. One of the members of the famous Innes family from Oxford County was the judge, and to my surprise we were the sixth entry to be waved into the final lineup of the class.

By this time George had decided that there was to be a dispersal sale of our livestock and farm equipment in midfall, and we agreed that a few ribbons won at the Black and White Show might give the auctioneer a talking point. When it took place several weeks after the London Fair, we took Ethel, Joan and her twin sister Jane, and Dixie there as well as my calf club calf. During the afternoon of the day before the truck's arrival to transport our stock to Strathroy I washed the twins and the new bull in preparation for their ring appearances, planning to do the same for Ethel when we brought the cows to the barn later. The calves of course gave me no trouble. The new bull, now three years old and almost full grown, was an impressive animal that had thus far shown none of the ill temper of his predecessors. I moved him from his stall into the cow stable and fastened the strap attached to his nose ring to one of the posts embedded in the cow mangers. When the first wave of water hit Dixie, he jerked backward and the ring in his nose broke in two. I had left the doors at the end of the cow stable open to provide ventilation. Dixie trotted out while I searched for a halter. George had elected to bring the cows up from the old orchard and they were approaching the barnyard via the lane when Dixie erupted into the barnyard. He met the cows at the top of the lane and immediately looked for romance. None of the cows was interested. Ethel, with a strong sense of every animal's proper place, met his advances by charging him and knocking him into one of the posts supporting the wire-mesh fencing at the side of the lane. The post broke and Dixie floundered in the fallen fence. With two herdsmen on hand, we were able to herd him and the cows into the stable, and with the doors closed, we put a halter on Dixie and returned him to his usual stall. George kept an additional bull ring, which he slipped into Dixie's nose. Now I could continue with the preparations for the fair.

The Strathroy Fair of 1939 was the last one at which I showed cattle of our own breeding. At London, Joan had placed well above other county entrants in her class. The judge at Strathroy, however, placed several larger calves above her, giving the first prize to a calf that had placed twelfth at London. Such were the fortunes of war and fall fairs. A month or so later, George held the dispersal sale, one of his friends from the county organization adding enough animals to the sale circular to make the offerings respectable in terms of number of animals offered. Now Dixie, Ethel, Joan, Jane, and the other cattle went to new homes. I wanted no part of the sale and did not attend, although I knew the several hundred dollars that went to my bank account from the proceeds would pay my tuition costs for the year at the university with something over for future years. Still later that fall, I borrowed the family car and drove out to the farm. I parked it at the crest of the gentle hill on Dale's Side Road and looked across at the old orchard and down at the empty barn in the farmstead. I cried.

FIVE

Horse-Power Days

During the 1930s the farmers on the North Talbot Road were living in the final years of the age of horse-powered agricultural technology. When we moved to the farm on the northeast corner there were no farmers in our neighborhood who owned tractors. By 1939 several did, but none of them had completely dispensed with horse power. After Len removed his livestock from our farm in 1937 we farmed with one team of horses. Pomp and Prince went to new owners when George held his dispersal sale in the fall of 1939. George never expressed interest in buying a tractor.

I first saw a tractor at work on the North Talbot Road in the summer of 1929 or 1930. Bill Topping and his sons were trying to farm both the southeast corner farm and the adjacent farm to the east on Dale's Side Road, where only the blackened foundations of their former barn and house remained. Falling behind in their work, they hired the custom thresher and machine operator from Lambeth, Vic Nichols, to plow a field in preparation for sowing winter wheat. One early afternoon in the first days of August, we saw Nichols's Case tractor go along the side road, pulling a plow capable of plowing three furrows at once and running in the flat bottom of the ditch to spare the road surface from the chiseling of the triangular steel lugs attached to the rims of the tractor's big rear wheels. Soon the operator was at work in Topping's second field back, turning over alfalfa sod at a rate of speed that no team of horses could match for more than a matter of minutes. By suppertime the tractor man had turned over an acreage that a plowman and team might have taken a couple of days to complete. We had glimpsed the future, but none of us sensed the full implications of that Case tractor chugging back along the side road. Local solons soon refused to allow their roads to be chopped up by the chisel-lugged wheels on the tractors of custom operators and local farmers. They declared that operating such machines on the roads was illegal, giving farmers incentive to buy tractors equipped with rubber tires. But the tractor did not take our section of the North Talbot Road by storm. At the end of the 1930s the farm operators there who had tractors were still in the minority. The rural prosperity accompanying World War II allowed almost all of them to move into the tractor age. I gained my experience in doing field work with a tractor on the farms of my brother and brother-in-law during the 1940s on the seats of flashy green John Deere machines rather than the more conservatively hued Case tractors.

At the time of his marriage George owned a team of mares he had named Doll and Fan. Until the mid-1930s our horses were all descendants of those two animals. I remember seeing a faded snapshot of this team in harness in the yard of the southeast corner farm. George maintained that they were exceptionally intelligent and durable animals. In the snapshot they appeared to be rather ordinary, middle-sized horses, probably brown in color. George bred them to Percheron stallions brought through our district, and the coats of the offspring were bluish brown in youth, fading to white as the animals aged. Our horses of the early 1930s were not of show quality, but they were handsome animals and somewhat larger than the average workhorse in the neighborhood.

When we moved across the road we took with us an older team, their coats already pure white, the mare Mae twelve or thirteen years of age and her partner Mac several years older and blind. Len owned a mare, Fan, which was driven in team with Pomp, a gelding about six years of age. He also owned Fan's daughter Marg, broken to harness in the first year of our residence on the northeast corner. With the other horses came Mae's colt, Major, the yearling that had survived joint ill and was apparently developing into a fine young animal. In our first or second summer on the northeast corner Mac became entangled in the line fence at the point where one of the tributaries of the brook in our lower pasture entered our property. The poor old fellow drowned in a few inches of water. But with the young horses coming along, there were still more horses on the farm than were needed for the two teams that George liked to have available. So he sold Mae to a farmer on the Third Concession. She was still prospering several years later in the hands of her new owners.

Mac's accident and death was not the only misfortune that our horses suffered during the thirties. In the early summer of 1934 Len's mare Fan was carrying a colt that proved to be misplaced in the womb. The vet's help at the time of delivery was insufficient to save either the colt or Fan. Len was desolate at the loss of the mare he had owned since she was a colt. He believed he might have overworked her in drawing out manure to the fields that spring. In the space of several years we moved from a situation in which the farm was oversupplied with horse power to having only Pomp, Marg, and Major available for field work. Times had become tight, and we needed a fourth horse. Len solved the problem for the time being by attending a farm sale on the Second Concession Road and purchasing a black standardbred mare with a narrow white blaze on her face. Wiley Post and his airplane the Winnie Mae being much in the news that summer, Len named the newcomer Winnie Mae. She was of indeterminate age but, Len admitted, no spring chicken, and by nature she was capricious and touchy. Periodically she showed that she did not consider herself a common workhorse and that she resented being placed in team with any companion of that sort.

During the mid-1930s the horses provided still another disaster. Major had matured into a fine steady animal and we usually paired him with Pomp. On a Saturday in the late summer of 1935 George noticed that Major was standing in the lane with his head down, making no effort to graze or to seek shade. He brought the horse into the stable and called the vet. The latter administered an enema and Major remained in the stable. On Sunday evening George and I were doing the evening chores and he was milking the last cow while I sat on a stool in the gutter alley talking to him and ready to usher the animal into the night pasture when George had stripped her dry. Suddenly there was a great crash in the horse stable. Major had collapsed, carrying part of his stall wall down with him. We rushed to the horse stable. Major lay dead, the other horses shifting nervously in their stalls and whinnying softly. George hitched up Pomp and Marg while I ran to the garage and fetched a logging chain. This we attached to the center clevis of the team's double tree to haul Major from the stable.

Customarily when we disposed of a dead animal we called a London rendering plant, which sent a truck to take away the body. However, one of George's friends from co-op days, Will H., was now raising foxes for their pelts, and he was willing to butcher dead farm animals for their meat and bury the offal at the site. Will agreed to take away Major. In doing so he performed a kind of layman's autopsy and found a great accumulation of parasites in Major's intestines. Botflies had been prevalent that summer, and although George tried to destroy the eggs that they planted on the leg feathers of the horses by applying coal oil, he had apparently been unsuccessful in Major's case. But it was also possible that Major's bout with joint ill as a colt had left his heart impaired. So died a fine young horse while apparently in his prime.

Now George needed another horse, and he purchased a young Clydesdale that we called Prince. In contrast to the early years, our work stock was now a mixture—two Percherons, one Clydesdale, and one standardbred. Usually Pomp and Marg worked together as our number one team, and Prince and Winnie Mae did lighter work. After the departure of Len and Marg, Pomp assumed the task of converting Prince into a reliable working partner.

George was a good horseman. He kept his animals in fine condition and grained them with rolled oats during the seasons when we used them most. He was careful about the quality of hay that he fed them and would not allow us to water them until they had cooled down after coming in from the road or field. He examined their shoulders daily when they were being worked and kept a tin of blue salve in one of the barn windows to apply when shoulders chafed or developed sores under the sweat pads that we used under their collars. He watched for botfly eggs and tried to destroy them. Such care did not avert our loss of animals during the 1930s, years when the prices of farm products were low and when we suffered one year (1934) of dry weather that greatly affected the yield of the field crops. But none of us on the farm, I think, regarded the horses as mere animals. They were participants in the enterprise, their good qualities a matter of pride; they received friendly pats as the harnesses came off and when we released them into the night pasture.

Even so, I never developed the rapport with the horses that I did with my club calves or even with some of the cows. I learned to ride bareback, of course, but never rode with the élan that Len displayed. I remember a spectacular parting from Marg when we jumped the swollen creek in the lower pasture one spring. My landing thoroughly wet my corduroy school pants and earned some derisory comments from Len, who had successfully led the way on Pomp. Although I have described how close I came to being seriously hurt by Prince's youthful exuberance, he became sedate faster than did the Percherons. He would allow me to approach him in the pasture without the aid of the grain bucket that the gray horses expected. But in his third year with us, Prince once again proved that you could not take farm animals for granted. Bringing him in from the lower pasture one summer afternoon, I was able to put on his halter without any problem. Expecting to lead him in, I had not bothered to bring the usual rope halter shank. But we were a good distance from the barn. Why not ride? I thought. I climbed on without any sign of rebellion from Prince, and we set off for the stable. Leaning up over Prince's neck to twitch the halter, however, did not prove to be an effective way of steering him. Our desired course was south and a little west. Prince preferred true west and a little north. At this

point the experiment should have ended with a dismount, my return to
Prince's head, and a hand in his halter. Instead I removed my straw hat and
leaned up over Prince's neck to place it over his right eye as a suggestion
that he veer south. Prince's veer was straight up. I grabbed for his mane,
missed, and flew off, rolling to escape flying hooves. As I sat up, Prince was
departing at a sedate Clydesdale canter.

Since Winnie Mae was a light horse, it seemed reasonable that she should
also be a riding horse. We did not own a saddle, but that did not deter us.
On occasion I rode Winnie Mae to herd cattle to or from the Bostwick
fifty and on errands around the neighborhood. Occasionally neighbor lads
came to visit Len, and Winnie's exhilarating potential was clear to them as
well. Winnie never bucked off a rider, but she unseated several innocent
visitors with a maneuver that she used whenever given the chance. If the
rider tried to change Winnie's direction when she was moving at a good
trot or light canter, she spun quickly in the suggested direction, so quickly
that the unwary rider continued on the original course. Len and I survived
Winnie's first efforts to demonstrate this maneuver, although I had to grab
a handful of black mane in order to do so. Thereafter we watched for her
trick, shifting our weight inward as the black ears pivoted in front of us.
When neighborhood lads dropped in accompanied by townie friends, Len
sometimes asked them if they would like a ride on his black mare. More
than once Winnie returned to the barnyard without her rider.

On one occasion Winnie clearly got the better of me. I was not tall
enough or athletic enough to mount Winnie without standing on some sort
of elevation. George had used some large glacial boulders in the foundation
of the outer portion of the barn approach. One of these protruded from
the side of the approach beside the milk house, and I used it in mounting
Winnie or the other horses. Among the neighborhood ponds where we
skated and played hockey or shinny on winter evenings and weekends, one
at the junction of the North Talbot Road and the Second Concession was
a particular favorite during my high school years. On a winter afternoon
during a school break I decided to ride Winnie Mae to the pond and practice
my stick handling. Encumbered with my hockey stick, skates tied together
by their laces and looped around its crook, I mounted Winnie successfully
at the barn and we trotted off.

Once at the pond I tied her to the fence, put on my skates, took the puck
out of my pocket, and for an hour did my best to imitate the stick handling
finesse of Joe Primeau, the center of the Toronto Maple Leafs' celebrated
"Kid Line." It was a mild day but Winnie Mae stamped, fidgeted, and
built up frustration. When I tried to remount by using the middle strand

of the road fence as launch pad, she refused to cooperate, dancing away just as I tried to leap from the fence to her back. The hockey stick and skates hindered me, and Winnie professed great fear that I would hit her over the head, rolling her eyes to show the whites and snorting. I leaned my burden against the fence and mounted successfully, but she refused to let me lean from her back to pick up the gear, shying whenever I got close. I dismounted and once more tried to mount with stick and skates in hand. Winnie kept prancing and coyly withdrawing. Half a mile away, I knew, Eleta was well advanced in preparing supper, and the day's radio adventure of "Jack Armstrong, the All-American Boy" was about to begin. I surrendered, slipped the looped riding reins over Winnie's head, and with these in one hand and hockey stick and skates in the other, I trudged home. Len was finishing late afternoon chores at the barn and he saw me slink through the gate with Winnie quickstepping triumphantly behind. "Got tired of riding did you? Winnie too much for you, eh?" I was mortified.

Eleta and her friend Verna C. at the fruit farm exchanged magazines. I cannot remember the exact terms of trade, but they swapped the *Ladies Home Journal, Woman's Home Companion, Chatelaine, Saturday Evening Post,* and *Good Housekeeping.* Since I was the most avid reader of such literature in our house, I sometimes volunteered to use Winnie to take an installment of magazines up to Verna's and bring back her accumulation. I never dismounted on these trips, fearing that Winnie would embarrass me utterly.

Being in school, I was never much involved in the spring field work that prepared the fall plowing for sowing oats and the mixture of oats and barley that George liked to include in the small grain seeding or for the corn planting that occurred several weeks later. But I was available on Saturdays and during spring vacation and did not completely escape the field work of this season. I remember riding the roller on a back field of the Dale farm—bundled up in overcoat and scarf to protect myself against the sharp west wind that blew in the faces of horses and boy as we crossed the field toward our line fence—and other experiences aboard the disk harrow and spring-tooth cultivator. Preparation of the ground for winter wheat came in mid- or late summer, and in this I was more involved, particularly after Len left us in 1937. It was then that I helped haul and spread manure on the field we were preparing for planting winter wheat. It was then also that I first went behind the single-furrow walking plows we used for all our plowing because George believed that riding plows asked too much of the horses.

I learned the basics of plowing one August afternoon in the second field back, with George presiding and Pomp and Prince providing the power. The physical mechanics of plowing with a walking plow were not highly complicated. You knotted the two reins from the horses together so that they would hold snug at your waist when you stood immediately behind the plow handles. Then you slipped them over your head, maneuvered the plow to the point where the furrow was to start, leveled the plow as it sat on the ground, and clucked or shouted "get up" to the team. As the horses stepped into their harnesses, the tugs tightened, and the double tree rose to a position parallel with the ground, you pulled the handles up slightly, pointing the plow point downward as the rig began to move forward.

At a depth of five or six inches you leveled the plow bottom and stepped forward in the furrow as the slice of sod rode up the curved silver side of the mold board and dropped bottom-up beside the furrow. Once across the field, you pressed down on the handles to bring the plow point out of the ground and tipped the handles to the right as the plowshare emerged, so that the plow skidded on its side as you moved one or both of your hands to the lines to turn the team at right angles to the line of the furrow. Then you drove across an unplowed strip, or headland, at the end of the field to your start point for the return furrow, which traced out the "land" on which you and the team would concentrate until it was all turned over. With the land established, Prince would now walk in the old furrow, and the plowman would concentrate on making a furrow slice that was of uniform width and thickness across the field, thus plowing a straight furrow.

All this is simple in theory and telling, but the initial experience was a different matter. Although frost brought occasional small rocks to the surface in our cultivated fields, they were not much of a problem in plowing. The horses were well mannered. Even though Prince was a comparative novice, he was a willing worker and somewhat intimidated by Pomp's tendency to bite him on the neck if he did not walk in the furrow. One day early in my plowing career we were working in a field that had initially held a good catch of alfalfa. Some of it had been winter killed the previous year, but live alfalfa roots were plentiful in the sod, and these were a challenge. The collision of plow point with tough alfalfa root could throw the plow out of the ground, and in the process the plow handles would give the plowman a breath-exploding knock on the ribs. Then team and plow had to be pulled around to pick up the furrow where it stopped. I quickly learned to hold tightly to the plow handles to avoid this problem.

I discovered that finishing lands was also a challenge because the team and I confronted a narrow strip of sod with furrows on both sides, and it was difficult to keep the plow properly engaged. Aside from these hazards, I did not find plowing difficult. Still, I was cheered by George's suggestion that the furrows should run parallel to the road fence, rather than at right angles. No neighbor could criticize the straightness of my furrow.

I learned the different sounds and feel in motion of the spring-tooth cultivator, the disk harrow, and the roller as I rode them back and forth across our fields. The overriding recollections of such work in the spring are of cold winds and of the hardness of the molded cast-iron seats on these implements. Most of the seats were studded with a pattern of holes so that spring winds played directly on the driver's bottom unless he took precautions. The men often put some straw in a burlap sack to make a cushion, but I sometimes forgot to do so or found that the cushion in place had been soaked by spring rains. In the latter case the cushion must be removed and the seat wiped dry with whatever I was using as a handkerchief. But the surfaces of all the seats were rough with rust so that no amount of wiping dried them completely, and the seat of one's pants became unpleasantly damp after one or two trips across the field. Even without padding, the seats of the cultivation implements were more comfortable than that of the rake, which in haying season left impressions on both body and mind because its iron tines banged against the seat while releasing every dump. That one, a hired man said, was a "real ass-breaker."

Our set of harrows had four sections of iron teeth set in iron frames and attached at the front to a ten-foot wooden scantling that held the clevis of the team's double tree. Usually we used the disk or spring-tooth cultivator—sometimes both—to work up the plowed fields, then the roller followed by the harrows before we began to plant seed with the grain drill. Sometimes George omitted harrowing in the sequence if the ground was well pulverized. But we always followed the drill with the harrows to cover grain lying uncovered in the small trenches left by the shoes of the grain drill. Harrowing was a much livelier operation than was riding the other tillage implements. The horses found the harrows a light draw and we walked along smartly; my blood circulated briskly. But if the ground was dry, dust puffed up with every step of horses and driver, clogging the throat, penetrating shoes and socks and lower trousers, and leaving the lower legs coated with soil.

When plowing was under way, blackbirds and crows inspected the work, seeking worms or insect larvae in the turned sod, and sometimes robins or less common birds joined them. The first two constituencies usually appeared as well when the grain drill was in use, hoping to find exposed seed grain after the machine had passed. George became concerned if large numbers of crows were at hand at corn planting because he feared that these canny birds would later pull up the little plants for the kernel still attached to the roots when the rows of tentative green shoots first appeared above ground. At the time I was more impressed by George's concern than inspired by these visitors to inquire into the wonders of nature. Once or twice George made a scarecrow consisting of a stake some five feet in height with a shingle attached at the top by several feet of doubled binder twine. The shingle revolved and flapped in the wind and, George hoped, would make the crows so suspicious of foul play as to avoid our cornfield.

If he planned for a hay crop to follow in the year after a crop of oats, or oats and barley, George returned to the field a few days after seeding to broadcast either alfalfa seed or a mixture of alsike and red clover plus timothy grass seed. For this job he used a shoulder-carried seeder consisting of a canvas sack and shoulder strap attached to a hand-cranked broadcast mechanism.

The first round of haying fell between the completion of corn planting and the harvest of the small grains. Into these weeks as well we usually worked a round of cultivation in the corn rows with the one-horse cultivator. We hoed the corn as soon as we could after this operation, cutting out any weeds that the cultivator shovels had missed. As I grew into my teens I came to believe that George planned the first cutting of hay to coincide with the date in early June when my summer holidays began. At this time also George visited the co-op store and bought me a pair of bib overalls or jeans, a wide-brimmed straw hat, and a pair of sneakers. These clothed me for the summer work ahead. There might also be a visit to the blacksmith's shop, one establishment down from the co-op store on Highway 4, to have a broken section replaced in the knife of the hay mower or to have all of these units sharpened. Sometimes George or Len performed the latter task at home, using the hand-cranked grindstone wheel in the garage or a hand file and a stick of emery stone. That done, the knife was slipped into its channel in the cutter bar of the riding mower and attached to the pitman rod, which in turn was linked to the drive wheel by an eccentric wheel and gearing. With driver aboard in the hay field, the team in motion in front of him, and the cutting bar down to his right, the knife chattered metallically as it whickered back and forth.

The dogs must be confined, George or Eleta reminded us, while we were operating the hay mower or grain binder. During our first years on the northeast corner, Len or George once forgot that rule. Hunting mice in the hay field, or attracted by the team in motion, Bob's successor, Lufra, was badly cut on one front leg and died of infection or loss of blood some days later. After poor Lufra's death we always locked his successors in the barn when we were cutting hay or the small grains.

Driving the mower was a dangerous job and I was well into my teens before I was allowed to ride that piece of machinery. When I did, I found the experience to be rather pleasant. The clovers were in bloom at the time, and they and fresh-cut timothy grass perfumed the air. Meadowlarks sang and bobolinks performed acrobatics. There was the occasional flash of yellow as a goldfinch—wild canary, to us—flew toward one of the fencerows. The team and I were perhaps interfering with their domestic arrangements, but that did not trouble me in those years.

My usual jobs in haying while Len was living at home involved driving the team on the hay rake, on the wagon in the field, and at the end of the hay rope while unloading the wagon at the barn. When raking the hay into windrows we used an old dump rake. Its original tongue long since broken, George had made a substitute from two green saplings, flattened on one end to take the bolts that held them to the rake's frame. At the other end they were squared, cut down, and cross-bolted so that the end was small enough to fit into the dangling metal ring of the wooden neck yoke that ran between the breast straps of the two horses in the team. We always tried to make our windrows run the length of the field, and so I drove the rake back and forth at right angles to the long sides of the hay field.

Starting at one corner of the field, I lowered the tines of the rake and clucked to the horses. When the tines had filled with hay, I pressed a metal lever positioned beside my right foot. The rake teeth rose, disengaging from the accumulated hay, and then fell to fill with hay once more as the horses and rake moved forward. Thus driver, team, and rake proceeded across the hay field, leaving behind a series of dumps of hay. On the return trip, I was expected to drop my accumulations in line with the first set, leaving behind the twenty-foot beginnings of straight windrows of hay. If dumps were out of line the hay loader would later miss the outliers, and George and Len became sarcastic.

Raking was light duty for the horses and inspired them to walk faster than usual. This increased the difficulty of tripping the rake at exactly the right spot. In the mid-1930s year Winnie Mae and young Prince made up the rake team, and the black mare was more interested in biting the young Clydesdale than in walking a straight line across the field. Restrained, she would try to break into a trot. Her diversions were distracting. The faster the team walked, the harder the rake's teeth clanged against my metallic foundation. On our way to the Bostwick fifty we drove by the old Topping place, now rented by the Bilyeas, and there I could see the lovely small straight windrows left by their side delivery rake. But George pointed out that their crew took longer to put a load on their hay wagon than we did. Despite the neatness of the side-delivery windrow, he added, the Bilyeas still needed to rake the field a second time to collect all of their hay, just as we did in using our antiquated dump rake.

At some point during the first cutting of hay and its curing in the field, George and Len rigged the barn for unloading the hay. Close under the peak of the roof and suspended there by short iron rods, a wooden track ran the full length of the barn. Mounted on this was a metal hay car, its wheels seated on top of the track, its other working parts suspended below. Now, carrying a tin of axle grease, someone must climb the rickety ladder nailed to the inside of the barn's south end beams, bring the car to that end of the track, and grease its working parts. If the big hay rope had been removed from the car during the winter for some reason, it must be reinstalled in the car, one end terminating at the car and held from pulling away by a big knot, the other end fed through a pulley on the hay fork attachment and then threaded through the other end of the car. From here the rope ran to a pulley in the barn peak at the end of the track. Thence it dropped down to the ground outside the end of the barn, was led through another pulley attached to the bottom of the adjacent gatepost, and was there fastened to the double tree to which the team was hitched when we were unloading hay or grain sheaves.

We did not start bringing wagon loads of cured hay into the barn at 7:30 A.M. First the dew must dry from the windrows of cured hay, and as a result we seldom rattled out of the barnyard before 9:30 in the morning. Most of our hay went into the barn mows in the afternoon. Soon after we moved across the road, George purchased a new lumber wagon, or farm truck, as agricultural implement catalogues described it, and Len built for it a hay rack several feet longer than those in general use in the neighborhood. To make a front endpiece he nailed five cross boards at intervals to two-by-four scantlings, making a kind of ladder, up which I climbed while driving the team in the field as the level of hay behind me dictated. To accommodate the mechanical hay loader, he made the tailpiece of the rack much smaller than the front end, using only two cross boards.

When our hay loaders were in use, the sturdy curved metal fingers on a rotating, open-sided cylinder picked the hay off the ground and deposited it on a rotating elevator belt. Controlled by cogwheels working in the links of flat metal chains on each side of the machine, this belt consisted of wooden cross slats held in place by light ropes running lengthwise from slat to slat. When we attached the loader to the rear of the wagon and drove along a windrow, a continuous stream of hay moved upward on the belt and dropped over the machine's projecting snout onto the rear end of the hay rack. Since the rear wheels of the hay loader generated the power to turn the cylinder and to move the endless belt of the loader, they were large and had knobs on the rims to provide better traction. Two smaller wheels supported the front end of the loader, and running forward from them were connector rods that joined to terminate in a spring lock. This we snapped into an iron ring bolted to the rear end of the wagon's reach, the connecting wooden bar that joined the front and rear sets of wagon wheels. Viewed with a little imagination at a distance in the evening as it sat at one end of the hay field, the loader looked like a huge bird hunched down and resting for the night.

Our haying crew through the mid-1930s usually consisted of Len, George, and me, and in the field the division of labor placed Len in the rear, "taking away" from the loader. George built the front end and I drove the team while standing on the boards of the front panel of the rack. My first test as driver came when we arrived in the hay field and neared the hay loader. Approaching from its rear, I was expected to drive the team and wagon close beside the loader and then swing in front of it, to stop some eight or ten feet beyond its front wheels. From there I must back the team so that the ring on the end of the reach came close enough to the loader's tow rods for Len to lift them and attach the spring lock to the ring. Clumsiness in performing this wagon maneuver provoked humorous comments from the loaders or, worse, foot-by-foot instruction as to how to swing the team and wagon tongue. Len, however, was usually helpful, sometimes tugging the loader forward or turning its front wheels so that the connection could still be made when I missed my target.

The harpoon hay fork that we used in unloading was a relatively large one, and the men constructed the loads in the field to facilitate its use. As the team walked along the windrow and hay spewed from the hay loader, Len built a dump that covered the back half of the hay rack, spreading the hay evenly and tramping it in place until he was working some four to five feet above the floor of the wagon. With that accomplished, he began to pitch hay to George, who filled the front half of the rack to the same height. When the lower front dump was complete, Len built up the back end of the load by another four feet or so. From that height he again pitched hay forward to George, who built the fourth and final dump of hay at the front of the wagon. Then Len threw a few large pitches onto the middle of the load to round it off and to bind the two top dumps. That accomplished, he slid down one side of the load to the ground in order to unhook the hay loader from the wagon. During most of the 1930s George then took over the lines and I became a passenger, sitting at midpoint on top of the load.

"Taking away" from the hay loader was the most demanding of the jobs involved in loading the hay wagon. The hay came from the loader in a continuous stream, and the fork man at the back had to distribute it evenly and tramp it down while building the back dumps. His job was less challenging while he was pitching forward to the front of the wagon, but even then he must pay strict attention to the job. If the rake driver had fashioned windrows that were too thick, the hay came from the loader in large chunks, threatening to overwhelm the rear worker. If the wagon driver allowed the team to step out too briskly, the result was the same. And if the rear loader reached too far back with his pitchfork in facing a heavy stream of hay, he might thrust it over the steel axle at the tip of the hay loader's projecting beak and into the moving belt of ropes and wooden cross slats carrying the flow of hay. When that happened, a rising slat promptly pinned the fork handle against the axle, and cross slats began to break against the fork handle with loud cracking sounds. Although errant forks were hastily withdrawn a number of times, the worst case scenario happened only once in my experience. On that occasion everyone on the wagon shouted "whoa," but a number of slats and the fork handle broke before I managed to stop the team. It was our first year on the northeast corner, and the men "toggled up" the old hay loader to finish the season, but this accident was the last in a series of breakdowns that made the old machine undependable. George purchased a new loader at the beginning of the next year's haying season.

My usual job as wagon driver was not onerous, and I knew that I could stay in the good graces of the loaders if I drove the team at a moderate pace and did not threaten an overturn by cutting corners too sharply at the headlands or by driving diagonally through the furrows that ran across some of the hay fields, reminders that the plowman had completed a land at that point. Windy days, however, made the driver's task unpleasant. A following wind gave additional force to the pitches thrown to the front dump by the rear loader, and flying chaff caromed off the back of my neck and tumbled inside my shirt, covering my back with irritating bits of leaf and plant stem. When we rented the Dale farm, we discovered that the hay fields there also boasted a healthy stand of Canada thistle; dried thistle stalks and prickled leaves assaulted my neck and arms. Yellow sweet clover dominated in one of the Dale hay fields, many of its overripe stems reaching

Patriarch at rest. The gravestones of John and Elizabeth Bogue in the Brick Street Cemetery, London, Ontario.

The newlyweds: George and Eleta Britton Bogue with maid of honor, edith Britton, and best man, Chester Bogue.

(*Above*) The young family: George and Eleta with children Myrtle, Leonard, and Eleanor, ca. 1915.

(*Above right*) Covent Garden Market Square, 1909. Courtesy of the J. J. Talman Regional Collection, The D. B. Weldon Library, The University of Western Ontario.

(*Below right*) Covent Garden Market Square, 1936. Our trailer appears in upper center. Courtesy of the J. J. Talman Regional Collection, The D. B. Weldon Library, The University of Western Ontario.

(*Opposite left*) Leonard and Irene Barney Bogue, 1935.

Eleta holding Leonard and Irene's son Arthur in 1937, with the author, Leonard, and George in the back row.

Eleta and the young farm Collie, Bingo, 1938.

Following the Ormsby Faynes. Members of the milking herd on Arthur and Irene's farm, ca. 1980.

The author (*right*) in front of the Bren gun carrier that he drove in a parade through Brockville, Ontario, in 1944.

several feet in length. While George was building the front-end dumps on the wagon, these stalks flew forward like little javelins.

Under a full load of hay the wagon and team rumbled along with a peculiar combination of sounds made by the horses' clopping hooves and the burdened steel wheel rims turning on hard sod or the gravel surface of the side road. We steered carefully in the fields and on the road, knowing that dropping one wheel of a fully loaded hay wagon into a depression might jar a corner of the load into slipping off and creating a tumbled mass of hay that had to be pitched laboriously back onto the wagon. In turning from the side road into our barnyard we passed through a shallow ditch, and here the driver needed to take special care to square up the front wheels before starting to cross it. When we reached the barnyard George swung wide to line up with the approach and then gave an extra cluck or shout to the horses so that we hit the incline with a good head of speed. Then the load tilted upward and after a few moments, the hooves of the team pounded on the planks of the drive floor, and George and I ducked to avoid the lintel of the big second-story doors as we entered the barn.

The horses stopped with their noses a few feet from the half doors on the other side of the barn floor, and we climbed down over their backs to unhitch them and send them outside, one at a time, to be hitched together again on the approach behind the load of hay. Typically our loads of hay seemed to fill the barn floor completely, but the horses pushed out between the load and the adjacent mow. Pomp was particularly adept at snatching one or two mouthfuls of fragrant hay from the wagon as he passed it. He would then stand contentedly chewing while we put the team back together before driving the horses down to the double tree lying at the end of the big hay rope that snaked down from the barn peak.

There were times when ominous clouds gathered in the west as an afternoon in haying season moved along, and we headed out for a last load of hay knowing that bringing it in without workers and hay getting soaked was touch and go. And what a sense of triumph we felt when the team's hooves drummed on the drive floor just as the first salvo of rain rattled on the metal roof of the barn.

Unloading was most effectively done by three people. One man, usually George, loaded the harpoon hay fork, first dragging it to the middle of the upper front dump, thrusting it deep into the load, and then jumping on top of it to send it down into the hay as far as possible. Then he engaged the lever and catch that turned the points of the tines inward and fastened them in that position, moved back to the center of the upper rear dump, and with trip rope in hand shouted, "Take it away!" Outside at the end of the barn, I responded with "get up" and the horses threw themselves into their collars and surged forward. As the slack in the big hay rope was taken up, the ground-level pulley snapped outward from its anchor post to the extent that there was slack in the chain fastening it to the gatepost, and the rope and double tree lifted off the ground, the pulleys squeaked, and the whole set up creaked and groaned. Inside the barn, a big dump of hay separated from the wagon and rose straight up until the snout of the hay-fork pulley engaged in the hay car and it began to run along the track toward my end of the barn. At the proper moment George pulled the trip rope, and the dump dropped with a loud swish into one of the mows. Outside the barn, the hay rope went slack and I grabbed it just behind the double tree and drove the team back to the starting place. Meanwhile George used the trip rope to pull the hay car and fork back to the track stop and lowered the big prongs to the wagon to remove another quarter load of hay, removal being in the reverse order from how the men had built the load in the field.

Meanwhile Len was in the mow. As soon as the dump of hay dropped, he went to work with his pitchfork, spreading hay evenly across the surface of the mow. As the hay level rose, he sometimes used a pole or his pitchfork to swing the dump to one side or the other just before George pulled the trip rope, saving some of the labor involved in spreading the hay. Usually the mow man had a bucket of salt with him, thinly spreading handfuls of it on the new hay after he had mowed away every load. Most neighbors believed that spontaneous combustion had caused Topping's barn to burn, and almost every summer we read in the newspaper of barn fires attributed to that cause. Of course, spontaneous combustion was most effectively avoided by placing only well cured hay in the mows, so that heating did not proceed to the point of ignition. But George believed that the salt provided additional insurance. I also remember a few occasions when, with rain threatening, we brought into the barn hay that George believed should have been allowed to dry longer in the field. After it had been in mow a day or two, George and Len pitched it into an adjacent empty mow to ensure that it would dry out without being compressed under additional loads of hay.

Eleta worried constantly when I began to drive the team in the unloading process and cautioned me to walk well to the side of the horses when I was "driving off." Should a piece of harness or a whiffletree break, the double tree might fly back with terrific force. She knew that youngsters had been severely injured or killed in such accidents. In our last years on the farm Eleta sometimes came out from the house to drive the team while I was on the load or in the mow during the unloading process. At other times George and I handled the work alone, sometimes letting the dump hang from the track while I left the horses and came into the barn to trip the dump as George climbed into the mow to swing it in the direction in which we wished it to fall, two workers doing what was more effectively done by three.

With the wagon unloaded and the team standing safely at the end of the barn, two of us lifted the tongue and shoved the wagon backward off the barn floor and onto the approach. When the rear wheels were several feet beyond the barn floor, the slope of the bridge took control, with George guiding the wagon by its tongue until it was midway down to the level of the barnyard. Then he twisted the tongue to one side, causing the wagon to swing out into the center of the barnyard with a considerable clatter. Now I brought the horses over to the wagon and hitched up in preparation for another trip to the hay field. If the load had been our second in the afternoon, there might be a short break at this point while we adjourned to the kitchen for a cool drink. In those years Eleta made raspberry vinegar, and a mixture of that liquid and cold water made a drink well worth the walk to the house.

After we had pulled the hay loader along all of the original windrows, we did a final cleanup of the field. It was usually my task to drive the dump rake once more over the field, picking up hay we had missed or that had fallen from the wagon during loading, and making one or two new windrows. This second operation never yielded more than a good partial load, but it left the field looking tidy and even a half load was not to be wasted.

When the Bostwick fifty was part of our farm operation, one of the fields was usually in hay. There was a small dirt-floored hay barn there, which had a drive-through and one mow. We took the hay wagon, mower, rake, and hay loader over to the "back place," but since there was no track for a hay car in the little barn, we pitched the loads of hay into the mow one forkful at a time, one of us working in the mow to keep it leveled off. On a beautiful afternoon in the summer of 1936 we were at work there and all had gone well until the level of new fodder in the mow reached the height of the upper framing beams that marked the transition from siding to roof. George and I were on the nearly empty wagon and Len was beginning to spread hay into the back corners under the roof. Suddenly Len whooped, ran to the front of the mow, and leaped out and down, to land with a bang on the hay rack. He was waving his straw hat around his head, and as George and I looked over in amazement, he shouted, "Yellow jackets!"

We all sprang to the ground and dashed outside. Looking back, we could see flashing yellow-brown dots in aerial maneuvers above the wagon. Moderation was in order since we could not counterattack and burn the nest without endangering the winter's feed supply. We allowed the little hornets to calm themselves and, after a few minutes, threw the rest of that load of hay into the mow without spreading it in yellow-jacket corner. Standing outside the barn, the horses had not been attacked and may have enjoyed the incident. When we returned with another load of hay, we declared one corner of the mow to be out of bounds and pitched no more hay into it. Len got his revenge by destroying the nest that winter while hauling loads of hay home from the barn on the back fifty.

We did most of our haying in June and early July. But usually a third of our hay acreage was planted to alfalfa, and this marvelous legume always gave us a second cutting in mid- or late August. We all shared a good feeling if the late summer crop topped off the three mows in the barn to the point that there was no room for more. We knew that if the corn crop was also good, the livestock would do well in the winter to come.

When all the hay was in mow, George or Len detached the hay fork from the big ropes and pulled them over to the west end of the beam that paralleled the drive floor on its north side at eave-trough level. By pulling on the length of rope that ran through the hay car and along the track to the barn peak and thence outside, we drew this section into the barn, gathering the excess in a heap on the hay beside the mow beam. Now three lengths of the big rope ran diagonally from this pile to the hay car, still positioned at its stop on the track above the middle of the drive floor. One end of the hay rope now terminated at the hay car, still threaded through a channel at one end of the car and held in place by a large knot to prevent it from pulling back through the car. The farm hand with time on his hands could pull this section of rope to the center of the mow, along with ample slack, and swing across the barn floor to land on the matching beam on the other side. Leaping into space some fifteen feet above the floor to sweep first down and then upward to make a scrabbling landing on the far side was thrilling—and somewhat dangerous, as George pointed out.

One winter Sunday evening while the Toppings were still our neighbors on the southeast corner farm, George and Eleta departed shortly after supper to attend a church meeting, leaving Len and me to finish the barn chores. As we were nearing the point in our tasks at which we climbed the ladder in front of the middle horse stalls to throw down hay and straw for the animals' final installment of feed and bedding, Gordie T. and one of his younger brothers dropped in for a visit. They accompanied us on our mission to the hay and straw mows, and when the proper amounts had disappeared down the chutes, conversation turned to mow swinging. By this time of the year much of the hay had disappeared from the north mow adjacent to the drive floor, and the pile of hay fork rope had subsided along with the surface of the hay. Now the upper beam at the side of the drive floor ran high above the remaining hay in this mow, but the hay fork ropes were still looped across it at the point where the barn roof pitch began. One of the group averred that he would not want to swing across the barn floor from bare beam to bare beam, but Len said there would be nothing to it. He clambered up the barn framing along one wall to emerge on the upper beam, and the rest of us followed, to perch on it as he pulled to the center of the barn the length of rope secured at the hay car and dragged out sufficient slack from the pile of rope to allow a free swing across the chasm.

Taking a firm hold of the rope running down from the center of the hay track, he said, "Here's how it's done." He leaped into space. We watched in awe as he arced downward and, with some eight or nine feet still below him, began to swing upward toward the beam on the other side of the drive floor. But then came disaster. Rope and Len fell to the floor with a thump that seemed to shake the whole barn. In the dry atmosphere of the upper barn, the knot in the end of Len's length of rope had apparently shrunk sufficiently to pull through its channel in the hay car when the full force of Len's weight on a downward trajectory was applied to it. We spectators scrambled down from our perch and ran to Len, who was moving gingerly and testing his limbs by the time we reached him. A thick layer of chaff on the barn floor had apparently cushioned his fall enough to prevent injury.

When we started down the ladder into the stable sections of the barn, we found that we were descending into blackness. George did not always keep a bulb in the electrical socket in the horse stable, and that night we were depending for light on the two set in the ceiling above the gutter alley in the cow stable. Len's landing had jarred both of these bulbs free from their contact with the Ontario Hydro Electric Power Commission. Stumbling in the darkness of the stable, we found a milk stool by dint of shin contact, and Len stood upon it to give a twist to the light bulb hanging in front of the milk house door. "Thank goodness!" Light to work by. At this point the Topping boys decided that they ought to be getting on home. Len and I fed the livestock their last ration of hay for the day, distributed fresh bedding, and departed for the house, quietly agreeing not to mention the evening's adventure to Eleta or George.

SIX

Harvests of Field and Wood

As we worked on the first cutting of our hay crop we could see the field of winter wheat changing color day by day. Shiny dark green changed to light green, shimmering into ever changing patterns of lighter and darker as the wind played with varying force upon the canopy of seed heads or highlighted undulations of the ground below. Next the light green began to show yellow tints and then the field was all yellow, deepening finally into a rich gold. In the last days of haying George began to prepare for cutting wheat. We had taken an old McCormick Deering binder to the northeast corner farm and now wheeled it off the drive floor of the old barn that stood across the creek in the lower pasture. George thoroughly oiled or greased its moving parts. The sickle or knife of this machine was a foot or so longer than that used in the mowing machine. He sharpened the cutting edges of its triangular sections and checked to ensure that the rivets holding them to the knife bar allowed no play.

George usually stored the binder's canvases in the granary during the winter. We now brought them out to inspect them for tears or mouse damage and to check that their reinforcing wooden slats were intact. The canvases were the most vulnerable parts of the binder; these carried the cut stalks of grain from the flat table below the rotating reel and elevated them above the machine's massive drive wheel, where they dropped into the cog-driven battery of elongated packing fingers. The fingers and cord-carrying needle shaped the sheaf, encircled it with binder twine, knotted and cut the cord, and then kicked the sheaf outward to drop on the ground or upon a sheaf carrier. If the carrier was attached to the side of the binder and operational, the driver accumulated enough sheaves on it to make a shock, or a good beginning of one, and dropped them in a pile or cluster. From these deposits, the field workers built stooks or shocks, the butt ends of the sheaves set on the ground, the grain ends leaned together and bound, perhaps with a final sheaf laid across them parallel to the ground to protect the grain below from rain.

In the first years of our stay on the northeast corner farm I was young enough to enjoy clambering onto the high seat of the binder and to pretend I was driving a three-horse hitch that pulled it, reaching over occasionally to the socket that held the whip when the horses were at work. As whips went, it was not fearsome—a slender tree shoot some seven or eight feet in length with a length of doubled binder twine attached to a foot or so of discarded driving rein at the top end. Our horses were willing workers, and with Len or George in the driver's seat, the whip was used only occasionally to startle the third or outer horse into walking abreast of the inner two that carried the massive binder tongue, its outer end resting in the ring of the neck yoke between them. George made it a rule that the tongue must be dropped on the ground when the driver stopped for repairs or to clean a plug of weeds from the sickle channel. That done, startled horses could not run the machine over anyone who was trying to make repairs from in front or from underneath it.

George had purchased this binder in 1904 or 1905, shortly after he began farming. Because he had never had adequate storage sheds for the farm implements and machinery, it had stood outside in some winters. Rust and wear had proceeded year by year, and in the spring of 1939 George pronounced it beyond redemption. Evidently McCormick Deering agents were particularly active in the neighborhood during the first years of the century; our neighbor on the northwest corner, Fora Cornell, owned a binder of the same age and model. Fora had not farmed actively for some years, and George believed that his binder was probably less dilapidated than ours. Investigation confirmed suspicion and George struck a bargain with Fora. George would combine the two binders, and we would cut a large field of oats that was Fora's only crop of small grain. During the previous two years our team of Pomp and Prince had pulled the binder without the aid of the usual third horse. It was asking too much of the horses. George proposed that Fora allow us to use one of his horses to make up a three-horse hitch while we were cutting our grain, and in return we would provide an additional horse to work with Fora's team while cutting his oats. The bargain struck, George spent a day or so salvaging working parts from our binder and using them to replace broken or missing equivalents on Fora's machine.

Our seven or eight acres of wheat that year were planted on the Bostwick fifty. After George had completed his mechanical merger, we shifted the binder tongue to the grain-table end of the binder and installed the small wheels that allowed us to move the binder to the back fifty on the road. There a fine example of the benefits of commercial fertilizers awaited us. Short of cash at seeding time in the previous year, George had fertilized only about half of the crop, although he had put a thin scattering of manure on some of the rest of the acreage. This area he had planted to a variety of winter Russian Wheat. The fertilized wheat was an Ontario variety popular in the district at the time. As I drove the team and binder up the lane of the back fifty, I looked at the fertilized wheat across an intervening stretch of land previously mown for hay.

The wheat stalks stood tall and thick, the heads shimmering bronze in the sun and almost as level as a table top. In George's view his winter wheat crop produced well if it surpassed twenty-five bushels to the acre, and his oats or barley acres were a success if yielding about forty bushels per acre. As I drove the binder through the tract of fertilized wheat, it seemed to me that I had hardly tripped the sheaf carrier before I needed to do it again. When we shocked the wheat a few days later, the shocks stood closer together in their rows than I had ever seen, and George admitted that he had seen only one comparable crop during his years of farming. Threshing day verified our judgment that this was an unusual crop. The fertilized acres yielded grain at the rate of fifty bushels per acre. The unfertilized did not reach twenty. Commercial fertilizers were no new thing in our neighborhood. Yet some farmers in the community viewed them with skepticism.

I had thought it fun to ride the binder in my imagination during our first years on the northeast corner farm. In the summer of 1939 reality replaced fantasy; for the most part that year I drove it in harvesting our small grains as well as a few acres of timothy grass grown for seed. The binder had long since lost any charm for George. He was happy to serve as machine tender and shocker, sensing, I am sure, that driving the binder was both challenge and thrill for me. His attempt to combine the two old machines into a functional one was successful. In the fields of the back fifty and on the home place it performed without complaint. When we moved into our neighbor's oat field we met our first trouble of the season. A few rounds into the crop we came upon a large rock embedded in the sandy soil, only a small portion of it protruding above the ground. But the ground fell away at one side of it so that the binder's drive wheel was lowered when it reached this unobtrusive obstacle, dropping the power train to the cutter bar much closer to the surface than if on level ground—so close that there was a loud crack when we passed over the innocuous looking rock. The sickle stopped its whickering, the oat stalks ceased falling on the table, and I shouted "whoa" to the team. George came running from the end of the field, and together we dropped the tongue from the neck yoke and assessed damages.

"Broken pitman," said George.

On this model of McCormick Deering binder, the binder knife or sickle ran in a protective sheath of projecting metal fingers along the leading edge of the binder table and was attached to the end of a wooden pitman rod some three feet in length. The other end of this rod was attached to a small revolving wheel, powered from the binder's main drive wheel by gearing. With the binder in motion and in gear, the rapid rotation of the small wheel gave the cutting knife its rapid back-and-forth motion. We did not repair broken pitman rods; they had to be replaced. Thus on a beautiful summer afternoon I was left with the task of removing the two ends of the broken rod from their connections. With that done I spent three quarters of an hour sitting in the shade of the binder while the horses lazily stamped and occasionally switched their tails. Finally George returned from town with a new pitman. This essential machine part had round holes bored at each end designed to fit over spool-like projections on the eccentric wheel and at the end of the cutting bar. Cotter pins inserted at the outer edge of the spools held the pitman in place. But as we examined the new pitman, we could not decide which end should be attached to the knife and which to the eccentric wheel. We made our best guess—perhaps it did not matter. We slipped the end of the tongue into the dangling middle ring of the neck yoke, checked to see that none of the horses had stepped over its tugs during their rest period, and I once more mounted to the binder seat.

I braced my feet against the foot rest, evened the slight slack in all three reins, shouted, "Get up boys; let's go," and we were off. But not for long. The sickle began its usual whicker. The slats of the reel began to trace their circle and knock the cut grain stalks back onto the moving canvases, and a mat of yellow stalks moved across the binder bed and rose between the elevating canvases below and in front of my feet. But once the knotter mechanism was reached, that device did not accumulate the stalks into a bundle encircled with twine or knot and sever the twine so that the resulting sheaf fell into the carrier. Instead the packer arms began to rotate without stopping, and uncut twine flagged out behind the machine.

"Stop, stop!" shouted George. "Whoa, whoa!" I echoed. The binder groaned to a halt. "I've seen this happen before," said George. "We put the pitman in wrong end to."

And so we dropped the tongue again. I wriggled under the front end of the binder with the pliers and extracted the cotter pins so that we could remove the pitman and reverse it. Once more we lifted the tongue and prepared to start up. This time all went well and the binder clattered around the field without need to stop. With a third of the job unfinished, supper and milking times arrived, and we decided to break off work with the binder for the day. That decision paved the way for some high drama the next morning.

While cutting our own grain we had used our neighbor's horse Tom as third horse in the three-horse hitch. Tom was a small sturdy bay that often irritated Fora or his sons by balking at crucial times while they were driving him. George was circumspect in handling Tom. He did not like the way the horse rolled his eyes when we were close to him and cautioned me to be careful when hitching Tom up. Tom was a balker, not a kicker, but there could always be a first time. Throughout the binder work at our place, however, Tom had been a model horse. Our sturdy and sensible Pomp and Prince carried the binder tongue, and perhaps Tom felt that working as outside horse in the hitch was a pleasant change from the boredom of pasture and stable at home. There for a number of years he had been teamed with a placid older horse that had died a few months earlier. His new partner, Ringo, was a light but rangy bay with a narrow white blaze on forehead and nose. Our neighbor had bought Ringo from an Indian owner on the nearby Oneida reservation, and some of the Native American lads had tested their jockey skills upon him. Driven in team earlier in the season by our neighbor, Tom and Ringo had run away while hitched to the hay wagon and left unwatched. Placed on the tongue with Pomp on the outside during the previous afternoon, they had worked without complaint, although not enthusiastically. After we had breakfasted and I had harnessed Pomp, George departed for the village on an errand. Pomp and I walked over to our neighbor's farmstead, where his son Bill had Tom and Ringo harnessed and ready for the binder.

We walked the team back along the side road to the oat field, where I oiled the binder and hitched up while Bill prepared to set yesterday's sheaves into shocks. I started cutting from the southeast corner of the uncut grain, proceeding north along the edge of the uncut grain, and the first round went well until we reached the southwest corner. From here the field sloped moderately upward toward my starting point. To cut a square corner with the binder I drove it straight through the standing grain and then swung the team around to the left, so that the binder pivoted backward to give the cutting knife a straight shot at the grain as we started on our new course across the side or end of the field. At the southwest corner this meant that the team must start the binder up the little incline from a dead stop. This was too much for Tom; perhaps he had begun to feel that pulling a binder was heavy work. At the get-up he balked. I swung the whip and struck him on the rump with the short piece of driving rein attached to the end of the whip rod. Whether Ringo's old bridle allowed him to see the whip or the light *splat* of the leather leader against Tom's rump reminded him of the start of races on the reservation we cannot know. Ringo leaped forward and one of his tugs broke, allowing him to run free between a willing Tom and helpless Pomp. We careened across the field in full runaway, the kicker arms of the binding mechanism going around and around. I clung to the lines and tried to steer the team away from the line of black hydro-electric poles that ran diagonally across the end of the field.

In most haying and harvesting seasons our newspaper carried at least one story of a runaway team and a driver or wagon riders who had been fatally injured. Eleta repeatedly urged caution lest such an accident befall our family. Now I was in the midst of a runaway. Stopping the team seemed impossible, no matter how hard I pulled on the reins. When Tom balked, George was walking into the field, carrying a fresh ball of binder twine. He rushed into our path, waving his arms and shouting, "Whoa, whoa." We thundered right at him and he scurried out of the way. I tried to steer toward the overgrown fencerow and dilapidated barbed wire fence that divided the oat field from Fora's cornfield. As we neared this barrier the team started to hold back, but the machine still pushed them forward. Luckily the tongue struck a fence post, at which point Ringo half leaped the fence into the cornfield, and his companions stopped.

George puffed up and we inspected the damage. It proved to be remarkably little. Tom had a small cut on his chest. The other horses were unscathed, although Ringo's harness was broken. That afternoon the work continued with Pomp and Prince on the tongue and the despicable Tom relegated to third horse. I was content to let George ride the binder for the final few hours of work. Eleta thought George excessively critical of his children, but he did not complain about the way I had handled the team. As we began to check out team and machine, young Bill Cornell remarked, "If I had just had a long pole with a hook on the end I could have caught a bridle and stopped you." "Oh sure, Bill, oh sure."

When cutting grain, we tried to follow the binder as soon as possible to place the bound sheaves in what we called shocks but my grandmother called stooks. This step was important because rain-soaked sheaves remaining on the ground retained water, which encouraged the grain kernels to sprout, reducing both their nutritional value as feed and the salability of the grain. We always built round shocks, forming an interior tripod with the first three sheaves and then leaning another six or seven around them.

Some farmers preferred a sheaf arrangement in which pairs of sheaves stood in a row side by side with a single sheaf at each end, making a narrow shock rather than the round one that was favored by most of the neighborhood farmers. We seldom capped our shocks with a final sheaf, although farmers who preferred the long, skinny shock often did so.

During the early 1930s George and most of our neighbors began to change their threshing practices. Until this time, after allowing the crop to stand in shock for some days in order to dry thoroughly, they had hauled their small grain crops to the barnyard. There they stacked them or filled barn mows with them to wait for the threshing machine. Probably influenced by the example of the farmers in the prairie provinces, who threshed their small grains out of the shock, some of the local farmers began to thresh from the field. This system eliminated days of labor spent in loading the hay wagon with sheaves and then unloading them again in the barn or nearby. On the other hand, farmers who changed to stook threshing ran the risk that rain would cause the grain to sprout in the shock before the threshers arrived. Adopting stook threshing also resulted in a somewhat different kind of labor exchange within the local threshing rings. Whereas barn or stack threshing required neighbors or their hired men to come bringing only a pitchfork, several of them were now expected to provide a team, wagon, and driver. Although stook threshing reduced the hauling that teams did at home in preparation for barn threshing, the horses probably hauled as much grain as formerly since they were now used at several threshings.

The savings involved in the changeover occurred mainly in the labor output of the family work force. Stook threshing took about the same length of time as barn threshing but eliminated time spent in mowing or stacking the crop at the barnyard preliminary to threshing day. Put differently, the change eliminated one step in the process of bringing the grain sheaves from shock to separator. Threshing from the field was also a cleaner process than was barn threshing, in which clouds of dust rose from the dry sheaves as they were handled in the mow, and even more billowed up from the separator where it sat on the drive floor. The half doors at the front of the drive floor in our renovated barn allowed breezes from the west to blow much of the dust outside, but in some of the barns of neighbors it was trapped in the building so that the mow pitchers worked in a fog of flying particles of chaff, weed stalk fragments, grain smut, and perhaps also the irritating spikes of barley or bearded wheat.

In the first several years of our lives on the northeast corner farm, George and Len continued to haul the sheaves of grain to the barn preparatory to threshing. As at haying time, I was the team driver in the field, steering the team up and down the rows of shocks and stopping at every shock or couple of shocks while Len pitched from the ground and George built the load. In the year we rented the Dale place, I remember helping one sunny summer afternoon with the loads of oats and barley we were hauling into the barn there. There were two orchards on the Dale place, one very old and going to wrack and a younger one that was now in abundant bearing. We passed the end of the old orchard on our way to and from one of the grain fields. Our rental agreement gave us no right to the fruit in the orchards, but there was a Yellow Transparent tree in the old orchard that was well loaded and had begun to litter the ground with windfalls. In midafternoon Len asked George to stop the team at the old orchard as we were returning to the field for another load. After a few minutes Len jumped back onto the wagon carrying a small feast of ripe yellow apples in his straw hat. How good they tasted!

The ripe stalks of the small grains were slippery, not intermingled and twisted together as in the stream of hay that dropped from the beak of the hay loader. Sheaves were separate entities. If the teamster drove carelessly over uneven ground or turned rapidly through the ditch between the field gate and the side road, a load of sheaves was more likely to break up before we reached the barnyard than was a load of hay. As the pitcher on the ground forked them onto the wagon, the man on the load arranged them so that there was a row on each side of the wagon rack with the butts pointed outward. Then he bound them in place with sheaves running at right angles along the center of the wagon rack, stamping them into place with his feet. This done, he started new rows along the outer edges of the load, binding them in as before, until the load was complete. The good field pitcher gave the loader ample time to put the sheaves in position and helped him by forking up the sheaves with the grain end first if the loader were working on the near side of the load and butt first if the wagon man was building the other side of the load.

Despite the best efforts of the loader, a load occasionally began to show signs of collapse, the sheaves on one corner bulging out and threatening to slide to the ground if the wagon gave a sudden lurch. We used a stubby endpiece at the back of our hay rack that would fit beneath the nose of the hay loader, and Len and George did not bother to make a high rear-end gate for the grain harvest, as some neighbors did. When we hauled small grain bundles, we built the back end of the loads to a point some four or five feet above the end gate, depending upon gravity and the skill of the loader to hold them together. Len sometimes drove in loads of oats from the fields while standing far out on one front corner of the load to balance the other side where the top rows of sheaves had slipped well out beyond the foundation sheaves below. Sometimes he deployed me at a particular spot on the top of load so that my weight reinforced the loader's arrangement of bundles. Occasionally the back end gave way while the horses were pulling a load of sheaves up the barn approach, leaving a tumbled pile of grain halfway up the incline. At such times, we had to attack the tangled mass on the approach after we had cleared the rack of its remaining load, carrying the sheaves up to the barn floor one or two at a time and forking them up into the mow.

When unloading grain sheaves we used sling ropes. These light ropes came in sets of two, four sets in all. They were long enough to surround a quarter of a load of sheaves and had small loops on each end. The loader carefully laid the first set on the rear floor of the rack, parallel to its sides and several feet in from the outer edges, the back rope ends dangling over the rear rack and the front ends extended to the front of the wagon for the time being. When he had built up a sizable rear section of sheaves George folded the loose ends over the top of this dump and repeated the process in the front of the wagon. With that completed, he laid out sets of sling ropes on top of the bottom half of the load and built the upper rear and front dumps upon them. In unloading, George found the ends of the set of sling ropes around the front top dump of sheaves and slipped the loops onto a hook that replaced the harpoon hay fork used for unloading hay. Then unloading proceeded as at haying time, the sheaves in the dump tumbling into the mow when George pulled the trip rope.

For farm kids threshing was always a great time. I do not remember much about the process while we were on the southeast corner farm. But one memory is clear. Perhaps in our last year on that place I was stationed in the granary, using a scoop shovel to move the wheat and oats to the back of the granary bins as men hustled in carrying burlap bags full of grain on their shoulders, fresh from the separator grain spouts, and emptied them over the board fronts into the bins.

None of the farmers in our neighborhood owned a threshing rig. We threshed our first year of crops on the northeast corner farm by using Vic Nichols's rig from Lambeth. He was still using a steam engine that year. The outfit arrived in the early evening and stood overnight in our driveway—a black steam engine; a silvery colored separator, streaked here and there with golden chaff or darker dust where machine oil or grease allowed particles to adhere; and a four-wheeled water tank, its red painted sides faded and chipping. A member of the crew drove a small truck that Vic used to carry coal and to haul the water tank to Dingman's Creek for refilling. A year later this threshing crew was using a big Case tractor to provide power—a major change in threshing practice—and the half-ton truck now carried fuel cans in the back along with a can of lubricating oil and a tub of grease for the grease cups on the separator.

Throughout the decade Nichols employed a veteran thresherman named Joe Redman to handle the rig. Joe was red-haired with great brown freckles on face and forearms. Year by year his hair grew whiter, but he remained a master in the art of setting up a threshing rig for action. There would be a short conference with George about the most convenient place to set up the separator. Placement depended upon whether we had the sheaves in mows in the barn or stacked them in the barnyard or planned instead to haul them directly to the separator from the grain fields. As noted, threshing from the stook or shock became increasingly common in our neighborhood during the 1930s—the second major change in threshing practice during these years.

Once the location for the separator was decided, Joe stood at the steering wheel of engine or tractor, his hand on the spinner knob of the steering wheel, and engaged the throttle and gears. At frightening speed, it seemed to me, he swung the separator in a circle so that its back end pointed toward the setup location. Then he and his helper attached a push pole to the short tongue of the separator, fitted the other end to the front end of the engine or tractor, and pushed the separator exactly into place, Joe's helper handling the short tongue of the separator. If the separator was to sit on the drive floor between the mows, setting up involved pushing the separator up the narrow bridge to the second-story barn doors, and the width of the approach allowed little margin for error. But under Joe's direction the separator never strayed from its proper path by so much as an inch. Although George liked Joe and the Nichols crew, he did not always use them during the 1930s. A threshing crew based to the north also did satisfactory work, and in some years George found that he could get our threshing done at a more convenient time by employing their rig. A pair of personable brothers ran this outfit, pleasant and efficient men if less memorable than Joe.

When the separator sat on the barn floor, the positioning of the platform of planks that supported the men pitching into the mouth of the machine varied, depending on whether the sheaves were to come from the south mow or the north end of the barn. There was also a question about the destination of the straw. Was it to be blown into an empty mow or would the separator's wind blower poke through the doors on the far side of the barn floor and deliver the straw to a stack to be built outside? One year the separator stood on the north side of the barnyard, and the separator man directed its straw into a north mow through an opening George created by removing two boards from the barn siding.

In moving the separator from job to job, the operators folded the self-feeder conveyor back against the front of the separator. This they now extended and locked in place, ready to pass sheaves forward into the knives and arms of the band cutters and the self-feeder, which would thrust the stalks of grain between the whirling teeth of the cylinder and the interlocking stationary teeth of the concave. Beside and slightly in front of the sheaf conveyor they used a tubular iron frame to construct a "table" of planks on which the spike pitcher would stand. The "separator man" cranked the straw blower or wind stacker into position. In the last stages of preparation this man scurried around his machine filling grease cups from a small pail of grease and oil ports from a long-spouted oil can. Now the tractor boss laid out a massive rubberized belt between engine or tractor and separator and then slipped the ends over the belt wheel of the power source and that of the separator, sometimes backing the tractor slightly to attain the proper tension. During all this neighbors or their hired men were quietly assembling, leaning on their pitchforks and chatting as they watched the ongoing preparations, or perhaps jumping immediately on a wagon headed for the grain fields if it was to be a day of stook threshing. Meanwhile George had produced a pile of grain sacks—a small one if the grain was to be dumped in the granary, a larger one if he wanted to reserve some of the sacked grain for immediate sale. He placed these bags near the separator's delivery pipe, which had twin spouts so that one sack could be filling while the grain tenders were removing a full bag from the other spout and replacing it with an empty.

When all preparations were complete at a barn threshing, the mow pitchers clambered into the mow and the slow put-putting of the tractor quickened into a louder steady hammer beat. If Redman was in charge, the tin can that he used to place on top of the exhaust stack of his tractors began to jump up and down, the great belt began to rotate with one twist in the middle, and the separator gave a moan as it roared into life. Its smaller external belts began to move, and the spike pitcher on the table began to feed sheaves onto the conveyor as the men in the mow tossed them down in front of him. In the last years of barn threshing on our farm I found little to do, aside from carrying out a bucket of drinking water and dipper to be passed up into the mow and seeing to it that the wood box in the kitchen was kept filled while Eleta worked at preparing the one or two meals that we would provide for the threshermen and the work ring of neighbors. When we switched to stook threshing, however, I drove the team in the field for Len, who took charge of our wagon at threshings as long as he remained on the home farm. By the summer of 1939 I was in command of our wagon when we threshed at home and on the back fifty and also when the neighbors who sent wagons to our place did their threshing.

Four teams and wagons bringing in loads of grain to the separator was about the right number for the threshing outfits that served our neighborhood during the 1930s. I remember one instance when there were only three wagons involved, and the threshers sometimes had to wait for a loaded wagon to reach the separator. Unless we were hauling from the back fields of the farms, a four-team rotation sometimes gave the incoming driver a few minutes of rest, but George at times put a spike pitcher on the incoming load to help the driver with the unloading and to make his work a little easier.

Drawing on his experience, Len told me that there were good field pitchers and also bad ones, wisdom I would verify when I graduated to loading the wagon. Good pitchers forked up the sheaves one at a time and always gave them to you with heads first, or butts first, or even sideways, as you might need them while building particular sections of your load. "Old Mr. Vanstone," well into his seventies and stooped but still spry, virtually built the load for the wagon man, understanding exactly what was needed on the load at any particular time and placing sheaves on the side of the load at exactly the right place. But there were some young smart alecks who wanted to load a wagon as fast as possible so that they could sit down for a rest or a smoke before pitching to the next driver. Usually the field pitchers worked in pairs, and when two hurry-up boys got together they might rush at a shock from each side and, with a simultaneous heave, dump most of it higgledy-piggledy in the middle of the rack. Then as one cleaned up what was left of the shock, the other trotted to the horses' heads and led them forward to the next shock, which he prepared to throw aboard before the poor loader had finished his housekeeping. This game was harder to play as the height of the load rose, but the finished load might not reach the separator if the bottom tiers of sheaves were badly set. The driver who lost a load found himself in a most embarrassing situation, subject to the gibes of the pitchers who helped him reload. Usually there was a mixture of old and young heads in the field-pitcher brigade and good manners prevailed, but a recent middle-aged addition to the threshing ring, a city man turned farmer, was as inconsiderate as the occasional younger man.

In our last year on the farm I drove the wagon for our threshing at home and on the back fifty and took our team and wagon to the McGlaughlin and Coleman farms for the threshings there. A neighboring widow had planted her own acreage that year after a period in which she rented her land, and she asked us to provide a field pitcher. I worked that day in company with Ed B., our custom corn cutter, and greatly enjoyed it. Some days later, I rode my bike four miles to work in the field when Len and his father-in-law threshed their grain. Long-handled pitchfork in hand, I also attended two barn threshings and one in a barnyard that summer.

Some of the fields on the McGlaughlin farm were quite hilly, and Len had told me of an experience he had while threshing there. Another wagon driver topped off his load at the bottom end of the field, but his team balked when he tried to drive up the hill to reach the farm lane on his way to the threshing machine in the farmyard. Leon hitched our team to the stalled wagon, and Pomp and Fan pulled the load up the hill into the lane without difficulty. That outcome demonstrated the quality of our horses to the neighbors and, I suppose, also reflected the competitive spirit that Len and I shared. It also made me apprehensive as I drove team and wagon up the North Talbot Road to Andy McGlaughlin's farm on the morning of the threshing there. Quite apart from the danger of overloading in hilly fields, building a load while on a slope was tricky. But the team and I met the challenge without serious difficulty, although I once arrived at the separator standing on the extreme left front of the load while the other front corner bulged alarmingly. The field pitchers all cooperated that day. At day's end I had the satisfaction of knowing that the half load of sheaves sitting in a ragged pile where the farm lane curved down into Andy's barnyard had dropped from the wagon of his hired man, Gordie T., rather than from mine. That day I also met a neighborhood character for the first time. With his twin brother Billy, who sometimes served as township reeve, Walter B. farmed on a side road between the Second Concession and Byron and was a famous swearer.

When Walter and his partner approached my empty wagon beside the first row of wheat shocks, they were arguing about food. Walter looked up at me and said, "Don't you think that a damn big plate of roast beef is the best God-damned thing that a cook can put on the damned table?" Not above a little deviling, I replied, "Gee, I don't eat meat." And Walter boomed, "Well Jesus Christ, what kind of a God-damned feeble answer is that?" Serving in the Royal Canadian Armoured Corps a few years later, I learned that Walter was neither very inventive nor even dirty mouthed by military standards, but the language used on our farm and on most of those of the neighborhood was usually free of profanity, and Walter was a change. He was a good pitcher, however.

I incurred George's wrath for a breach of threshing etiquette while we were threshing on the Bostwick fifty. When we began to thresh out the wheat field there, I brought in a big first load from the great crop on the fertilized acreage. The wheat stalks in the sheaves were exceptionally long in the stem as well as heavy with grain. As the separator groaned to life, I began to toss sheaves onto the conveyer and promptly plugged up the cylinder, forcing the threshers to shut down while they cleared the blockage. George was incensed that the home outfit should show such carelessness. But the yield of grain soon put him in better mood.

In taking a team to a stook threshing one assumed a good deal of responsibility. The team was our source of field power, and an accident could jeopardize the whole farm operation. But one worked in excellent conditions in an atmosphere of some sociability. Field pitching was pleasant also unless one's companion was uncongenial. When the grain sheaves were mowed in the barn or stacked at the barnyard, however, conditions might be less attractive. In 1939 two of our immediate neighbors to the south had mowed their small grain crop and a third had stacked the sheaves adjacent to his small barn. In the latter case threshing day was sunny but cool, with a light breeze that blew the separator's dust and chaff away from those of us working on the stack. The conditions were ideal. That was not the case at the barn threshings. The separator stood on the barn floor and we pitched the sheaves out of the mows onto the spike pitcher's table, positioned beside the separator's self-feeder. On neither day was there a sufficient breeze blowing to carry away the cloud of dust and chaff that rose from the machine. In one barn the separator man cranked back the blower to send straw into the mow on the other side of the separator, and a back draft carried some of it back over the separator and into the grain mows. Accustomed to this kind of threshing, older hands sometimes wore big bandanna kerchiefs that they raised from around their necks to cover the nose and mouth. I was too inexperienced to take that precaution but also too proud to do anything less than my full share of the work in the mow, where pitchers at the back threw sheaves forward to others who formed a kind of chain, moving the bundles to the outer edge of the mow to be pitched to the spike pitcher. Sometimes the dust became so heavy in the mows that the pitchers on the interior end of the chain could not see the spike pitcher at the separator.

Given the amount and direction of the wind, building a straw stack adjacent to the barn could be one of the dirtiest of the jobs at a barn threshing. Local threshing custom held that a member of the home-farm work force took this job, whether owner, son, or hired man. Perhaps ignorant of such practice, a new neighbor placed me on his stack in my first year as a threshing hand. George was considerably annoyed. After that experience and work in the mows during our last year of farming, I spat out phlegm loaded with black dust and bits of chaff for a day or so.

At the same adjacent farm in 1939, I saw a threshing accident that almost produced serious injury. The farmers in our immediate locality did not contract with Vic Nichols of Lambeth that year but instead used the outfit of a longtime Strathroy thresherman, who owned two threshing rigs and who lined up jobs for the crews and kept them supplied with fuel and other necessities. Two brothers, Ron and Mike, ran the outfit that came into our district, the former handling the tractor and general setup duties and the latter attending to the separator. The threshed grain emerged at the bottom of their separator, as it left the battery of vibrating sieves in the machine's interior, and was elevated to the deck of the separator in the cups of a conveyor belt running within a protective housing on the side of the machine opposite the big belt attachment. From there the grain dropped into a metal worm, rotating inside a metal tube, that propelled it across the top of the separator to enter the down pipe to the baggers. A small exterior belt on that side of the separator powered the worm.

We had been at work only a few minutes when this belt flew off and grain began to back up at the point where the worm received the grain from the conveyor belt. Thinking that a piece of milkweed or Canada thistle stalk had jammed the worm, Mike climbed to the top of the separator, removed the cover at the junction point between the belt conveyor and the worm, and shoved his hand into the worm channel to pull out the obstruction. At that moment, with the big drive belt still turning between separator and tractor, Ron came to investigate. Ignorant of his brother's location, Ron slipped the dangling side belt back onto its drive wheel. The worm screw began to turn, pulling Mike's hand into the grain channel beneath its revolving edge. He screamed, the small belt flew off, and the worm stopped turning, but Mike's hand was firmly wedged between it and the interior surface of the grain tube.

Now Ron ran for tools to use in taking apart the worm mechanism, but this was difficult. He could not find the right wrenches at first. Meanwhile, his brother was slumped over the grain tube, face gray beneath its tan and dust, neither he nor anyone else knowing the extent of his injury. Finally Ron and the bagmen loosened the worm to the point where Mike could withdraw his hand and clench it around a towel. Someone drove him off to the doctor's office in Lambeth and Ron reset the conveyor screw in its tube. An hour later Mike returned with his hand bandaged, and work resumed. He had a cut across the bottom of all four fingers on his right hand, but the damage was not serious. Had the side belt stayed on its drive wheel for a few additional seconds, Mike might have lost his fingers and perhaps part of the hand as well. While Mike was away at the doctor's office, Archie, the outfit's owner, arrived and learned of the accident. At the end of the account, he shook his head and said, "I warn my boys to be careful but sometimes they forget. Carelessness causes accidents." At this point one of the work crew noticed that Archie's right index finger was missing. "What happened to your finger, Archie?" he said. "Carelessness," Archie replied. Archie was one of many old threshermen who had missing fingers. Unshielded belts, conveyors, cogwheels, band cutters and other sharp edges made the work of custom machine operators hazardous and endangered their clients as well.

Some accounts of threshing emphasize the cooperative aspects and neighborhood bonding involved in the work of the threshing work ring. In our neighborhood the interchange of labor at threshing time went smoothly. I never heard of anyone complaining of being asked to contribute more than a fair share of labor. It was not a time, however, when a group of neighboring farm operators talked over matters of common interest. For the most part the threshing workers were the farmers' sons or were hired men, with the occasional farm owner mixed in. Cordiality usually ruled, although I once saw a neighbor's son exchange harsh words with Vic Nichols's son about the shortcomings of the Lambeth threshing rig crew. That exchange stopped short of blows when the thresherman turned his back and walked away.

Since the crew used their truck to go home in the evening, Eleta was never required to put them up overnight in the years spanned by my memory. But if the outfit had been set up on the previous day she served breakfast to the crew members. Contrary to the accounts of some threshing historians, the wives of the ring members in our neighborhood did not help each other in preparing and serving the threshing dinners to any great degree. Eleta carried out all the preliminary preparations by herself, and on threshing day my eldest sister and occasionally a hired girl from the village assisted her. I vaguely remember my grandmother coming to give a hand sometimes when I was younger. The situation was much the same at our neighbors' farms, where a sister or mother-in-law and children usually aided their mother, although in one instance I remember a neighbor wife assisting another housewife in the work ring. On the evening before threshing day or early that morning, George brought home a "threshing roast" of beef from the Farmer's Co-op. Eleta served this with new potatoes and at least a couple of vegetables. There would be fresh cabbage slaw and applesauce, sometimes Jell-O salad, and at least two kinds of pie. She prepared all of these major ingredients of a threshing dinner and served them in large quantities. Bread and butter were on the table, of course, but were not highly popular. As Andy McGlaughlin's hired man Gordie T. said to my sister when she offered to bring the bread dish from farther down the table, "Why eat bread when there is all this other good stuff?" An evening threshing meal at our place was much the same as the noonday spread, but Eleta served cold roast beef and usually accompanied it with sliced ham. She sometimes supplemented the pies with cake or cookies at supper. My philosophy on threshing meals was much the same as Gordie's, and my appetite in 1939 was sharpened because Eleta was already established in London, and George's cooking was both basic and bad. When the threshers reached our farm, Eleta arranged to come and prepare the meals, helped by my sister Myrtle. They set up a table on the lawn and served the food there, not having time to give the house the kind of cleaning it needed now that it had become a bachelors' hall.

For the couple of weeks that the threshing rig was in our neighborhood that year I "lived high on the hog," as George said, and he attributed a small boil on my arm to the excessive amounts of pie that I ate at the threshing dinners. More likely the eruption was attributable to the communal wash basins that stood on a table or box at the back door of most of the neighborhood houses on threshing days. Bachelors like Walter B. enjoyed threshing the most, given the socializing opportunities and good food it provided. At the McGlaughlin farm in 1939, Frank Duncan, another bachelor, provided an unforgettable gastronomic memory. Eleta was a good friend of Frank's sister Jessie, whose father owned the last working farm on the North Talbot Road before it took its big dip down to Springbank Park in the valley of the Thames River. Jessie kept house for her father and brother for a number of years after her mother had died but then married and moved to Delaware, leaving brother and father to "bach it." In his own way Frank was as much of a character as Walter, outgoing and given to joking. Mrs. McGlaughlin was a wonderful cook. George believed she served the best threshing meals in the neighborhood, in part because she always placed honey in the comb on the table. Her lemon meringue pie was a triumph, delicious yellow filling topped by thick meringue, lightly browned on top and speckled with brown beads of sugar syrup. Because I had to stable and feed our team when the machine shut down, I came to the dinner table after Frank and other field pitchers had begun to eat. I was busily attacking a heaping plate when I heard one of the other men shout, "Frank, what are you doing? Good God man!"

Everyone's eyes swung to Frank. He had put a slice of lemon meringue pie on his plate and was carefully ladling thick pork gravy from a bowl onto the pie.

"Adds to the taste," he laughed. Luckily Mrs. McG. was in the kitchen.

Cutting the field corn provided the final harvest of animal fodder on the farm. The hybrid corn breeders had not yet developed varieties of Indian corn that ripened sufficiently early to be harvested as a cash grain crop in southwestern Ontario. Almost all the farmers in our neighborhood used their field corn as dry fodder or ensilage for the farm livestock. We planted our acreage with the grain drill, closing off enough of the seed outlets so that the corn rows allowed a one-horse cultivator to pass between them without damage to the young corn. Weather permitting, George cultivated the corn as soon as the seedlings were tall enough that the wave of dirt generated by the outer shovels of the cultivator did not bury them.

Then we took down the hoes hanging on the inside wall of the garage. Unfortunately there were three of them, giving me no excuse for avoiding hoe duty, and it was sufficiently light labor that I could not beg off because the work was too much for my young muscles. After sharpening the blades with a file or emery stick we set to work in the cornfield, cutting out the shoots of grass and thistles that were sprouting between and around the young corn blades. Since the corn was ready for the hoe at about the same time as we made the first cutting of hay, hoeing was often done on drizzly days or after storms, when the hay fields were too wet to allow work. George liked to get through the cornfield with cultivator and hoe a couple of times before the crop was laid by in early July, but this was not always achieved. On the other hand he never allowed our crop to be swamped by quack grass, foxtail, and other weeds, as we sometimes saw happening in fields we passed on our way to London. Hoeing with Len or George or one of the hired help was a companionable sort of job that allowed conversation about all manner of things, from the latest escapade of my fox terrier, Jiggs, to Len's trip to see the Detroit Tigers play baseball. I hated hoeing, however, when I was sent out by myself while the men were working elsewhere.

Most of the local farmers had silos and converted their corn crop to ensilage. George also used a silo on the southeast corner place. The silo that he envisioned for the northeast corner farm was never built, so we shocked our corn and fed it in the winter from the bundle, as did a few other farmers along the road. One nearby neighbor managed his corn crop differently from us and the silo owners. A man from a farming family who was in his mid-thirties before he had accumulated resources sufficient to marry and to purchase a fifty-acre farm to the south of us, he followed what might be called intensive general farming. After shocking his corn and letting it stand for a few weeks in shock to dry, he sat beside each shock and husked out the grain into little mounds, where it dried still further. Then he cribbed it and later fed it to his hogs, reserving the corn stalks for his small herd of Shorthorn cattle. The occasional old corn crib on neighboring farms suggested that this practice had once been more general. But in our years on the northeast corner farm, George preferred to let the cattle obtain part of their grain ration from the corn fodder.

I always found the cornfield a wonderful place as the corn stretched up and sprouted tassels and then great green-wrapped cobs. As the stalks grew to be seven feet or so in height, the intervening spaces became private and shaded, and all around there was the pungent smell of growing corn. Although the ripening oat and wheat crops were not devoid of odors, these were muted, often scarcely perceptible. But when the corn pollen was drifting from the tassels, the cobs were extending their silks, and little deposits of rainwater were evaporating from the joints between stalk and leaf, the cornfield generated a powerful sweet perfume that also carried a slight acid bite, an acidic sweet sourness that became more pronounced when ensilage cured in the silo.

Corn cutting always took place in September after I had returned to school. Ed Brown, a neighbor who lived several places up the North Talbot Road toward Byron, had developed custom corn cutting as a profitable enterprise. He cut our corn for us during all of the 1930s and that of almost all the other farmers in the neighborhood. Here was an instance in which the local farmers were convinced that custom service was more economical than investing in their own machines. Adherence to this practice perhaps also reflected the fact that there was less urgency involved in cutting the corn at a particular stage of ripening than was true of the small grains, although George wanted his crop to have some sap in the leaves and stalk when cut, and so did the silo owners.

As the corn crop was approaching full growth, George contacted Ed and they agreed upon a tentative cutting date, understanding that it might be postponed a few days if rain delayed the latter's work elsewhere. Ed usually dropped in on the day before he proposed to bring his corn binder to our farm, or perhaps rang George on the telephone, to ensure that a harnessed horse would be waiting when he and his team drove in on the binder, its gears disengaged for road travel. In the field our horse took the outside position in a three-horse hitch. It was on one of these transfers from farm to farm that Ed's binder had lost the board that placed his son Austin and me in the hands of the Royal Canadian Mounted Police.

As I grew into my teens I sometimes shocked corn on Saturday afternoons with Len or George, and this was hard work. Ed's binder left the cut corn in big twine-bound bundles, and if the corn had been tall and was still somewhat green, these were heavy. Although the men sometimes used pitchforks in carrying the corn sheaves to the shock, I found it easier to carry the bundles in my arms. Since the binder twine would burn or even cut one's hand and the occasional Canada thistle had succeeded in reaching full growth after the last hoeing, we wore unlined green horsehide gloves for protection. We started the shocks by propping three corn sheaves together to make a leafy tripod and then stacked additional bundles around this center, bringing in enough bundles from the rows left by Ed's binder to make a substantial shock. To secure it, we encircled it with a light rope that had a metal ring at one end. Feeding the other end through the ring, we pulled the rope as tight as we possibly could and tied it at the ring. Then we tightly bound a double thickness of binder twine around the compressed shock, removed the ring rope, and moved forward to where we would plant the next shock in the row. Once in shock, the corn cured and waited for the wagon or sleigh that carried it to the barnyard for feeding during the later fall and winter months.

Prior to his departure from the farm, Len spent many a winter afternoon hauling in loads of corn sheaves to the barn on the bobsled. He usually leaned the first loads against the fence adjacent to the south end of the barn. Occasionally he stored several loads on the barn floor or in an empty hay mow. This practice was unsatisfactory if the corn was left there for any length of time; the warmer temperatures in the barn encouraged the cobs to mold. One winter the men stationed a portable corn cutter on the barn floor and powered it with a gasoline engine to chop the corn into ensilage-sized bits. Although this stopped the cows from leaving stripped corn stalks in their mangers, the men thought it too much trouble to continue in succeeding winters.

Almost always, my smooth-coated black and white fox terrier, Jiggs, accompanied Len to the cornfield. Purchased as a pet for his daughter by George's cousin Edgar, Jiggs had rebelled against the town life of a house dog in Strathroy. He repeatedly jilted our cousins in favor of living with a disreputable old soak who allowed Jiggs to sleep on his bed. Working on the principle that he would like to obtain some return on the twenty-five dollars he had paid for a purebred pup, Cousin Edgar "traded" him to me for a kitten—a kind of livestock that was often in surplus on our farm. The kitten left us to enjoy a lifetime of pampering. Jiggs joined us as self-appointed rodent destroyer and busybody. His introduction to our family was memorable. As soon as Edgar placed Jiggs down on our kitchen floor, two large tomcats leaped from the couch in the kitchen and fled into the living room with the little dog in hot pursuit. The chase ended in the parlor, where each cat scaled a curtain and perched on the window valance, cursing the black and white invader barking and dancing below.

Accommodation ensued during the next few days, and Jiggs took to farm life like a duck to water. He roamed the farm on hunting expeditions for groundhogs and muskrats and anything else he could stir up but always checked in at the house in time to have meals with the family. Jiggs once dived into the middle-field pond and pulled a muskrat to shore, where he had dispatched it before Len arrived. It was summer, and each day thereafter Jiggs besought Len's admiration by bringing him the decomposing trophy. Finally the stench was too much, and Len ruled that show and tell must stop. One winter Jiggs surprised a neighbor's tough old tomcat on the drive floor of the barn and dashed to the attack. Fighting back, the cat bit Jiggs deeply at the junction of front leg and chest. Jiggs three-legged it for the rest of the winter but gradually recovered use of the limb as spring advanced.

Jiggs regarded winter trips to the cornfield as part of his particular duties, running in the sleigh tracks when the snow was too deep for free movement or begging his way aboard, where he stood in the middle of the rack floor, his legs braced and his sharp little nose cocked for any interesting smell. In the field he scrambled off and retreated a few yards to supervise while Len forked the first few bundles of corn onto the sleigh rack. As the number of corn sheaves in the shock dwindled, Jiggs moved in closer, his nose twitching in anticipation. Sometimes, as a bundle was forked up and onto the sleigh, a fat brown field mouse broke cover and tried to dash for the next shock. At this Jiggs leaped forward. A quick crunch and sometimes an upward toss indicated a failed escape. With only five or six bundles left standing, mice tried to escape with every removal, running in all directions, and Jiggs was then in his element, darting here and there, snapping and barking. Initially he might eat a few mice, but soon hunter's blood lust was in command. None escaped him, from the wiliest and fattest elders inching surreptitiously into a clump of grass or weeds to the smallest babies tumbling from a nest of shredded corn leaves. Corn-hauling day was the highlight of Jiggs's winter week.

Every winter the men devoted several weeks of afternoons to preparing a supply of firewood for home consumption during the year. Although we had a large coal-burning stove in the living room, we sometimes burned wood in it and invariably burned that fuel in the kitchen range and in a small tubular heater in the parlor. Often the stoves in the living room and parlor were used only at night in the winter, and the fire in the kitchen range was usually allowed to die during those hours. In sum the fireboxes of these stoves consumed a substantial pile of wood each year. Sometimes George and Len cut down large dead or dying trees from along the fence lines—a number of hard maples died in those locations during the 1930s— and some of the trees in the old orchard split or were blown down as well. But most of our firewood came from the woodlot in the northeast corner of the farm. These acres of "bush" had never been cleared for the plow and contained a mixture of some very old trees, mainly maples with some beech trees, standing amid growth that had gained most of its size since a "Great Cycloon" (George's words) had swept across the acreage in the 1890s. This younger stuff included many sugar maples large enough to merit one sap bucket in the spring. Great numbers of young hickory, oak, ironwood, and ash trees four to eight inches in diameter grew around the maples. In the early 1930s there were a few American chestnut trees as well in the lot, but these sickened with the blight that was killing that great tree throughout the northeastern United States and southwestern Ontario. I remember Len knocking chestnut burrs from the upper limbs of a chestnut tree on the southern edge of the woodlot in the tree's last year of life. A few stumplings continued to sprout from the dead tree's roots for some years, but none survived to bearing age.

When the men planned to work in the old orchard or woodlot on a winter afternoon, they usually spent some time before the noon meal in readying their tools. George sharpened the teeth of our crosscut saw with a triangular file or perhaps with the narrow side of the eight-inch file that was an indispensable farm tool. This completed, he used a "set" tool that resembled a small bolt with a square head set about half an inch from one end. There was an aperture in this protuberance that George slipped over the sharpened end of a saw tooth. Then he tapped the tool with a hammer to bring the tooth of the saw into its most effective alignment with the neighboring teeth. Meanwhile Len was sharpening the axes, using a file or emery stick, until he had removed all the nicks from the cutting edges and they were, as he said, "sharp enough to shave with." If a wooden handle was loose in the sleeve of the axe head, he split that end with a chisel and drove a small wedge of wood into the gap to make it fit tightly. Eleta often reminded the men that more than one farmer had died in his woodlot when the axe head flew off the shaft of a companion. Sometimes they stood the axes in a bucket of warm water during dinner to allow the handle heads to swell and bind more tightly within the axe sleeves. On several occasions George made new axe handles out of green hickory wood, although Len and I much preferred the ones that Indian craftsmen sold at the farmers' market in London.

In early afternoon George and Len carried their axes and the saw back to the old orchard or the woodlot, where they began to fell and cut up trees. When working in the bush area they tried to take out all dead wood and to thin out the younger trees. They had some mild disagreements about the best trees to retain, but the results of their cutting were usually a mixture of long poles of young stuff some four to six inches in diameter and larger trunks and limbs from older trees that had died or appeared to be dying. On days sufficiently warm to allow the horses to stand out in the orchard or woods while the felling and cutting up was under way, the men brought a sleigh load of wood with them when they returned to the farmstead. Otherwise they simply threw it into piles to await good hauling conditions when they were able to bring several loads from the woods in the course of an afternoon. When working on larger trees George and Len sometimes used the crosscut saw to cut the trunks into stove-length cross sections that they later split into smaller pieces with the axe in the farmyard. But in general they preferred to reserve most of that work for the circular saw because it cut up the lengths of wood much faster than they could with the crosscut saw.

As with most farm jobs, wood cutting had a dangerous side. George's younger brother Chester had died in the woods on the home place when he failed to retreat far enough from a falling tree that he had helped to cut down. As a result, George was cautious, always giving a cautionary shout when a tree began to topple. He and Len tried to run a considerable distance from the falling trunk. When I was in the vicinity, George usually gave me an additional warning somewhat earlier. Cutting wood in winter posed additional hazards because one or two feet of snow at a tree's base made rapid movement difficult, and the snow became slippery when packed down. When an axeman slipped in the midst of an axe stroke, the razor-sharp cutting edge might end in foot or limb. I once saw Len slice off the outside layer of a four-buckle galosh and peel a shaving of leather from the sole of his work boot.

After some weeks of such work, George and Len decided they had cut enough wood for the coming year; now it must be hauled to the barnyard to be cut into stove-length pieces in a session with the circular saw provided by Vic Nichols, which we referred to as a buzz saw. In preparation for hauling wood from the old orchard or woodlot, the men inserted four-foot side stakes in the outer frame of the bobsled rack, and in loading they piled the ten- to fifteen-foot lengths of wood lengthwise between the stakes. Always eager to finish a job as soon as possible, Len usually rounded up his loads above the stakes. Also as usual, George preached caution, but he did not always go to the woods on these trips, and when he did, he usually walked to the farmstead after loading rather than riding, for reasons of both safety and comfort. Len continued to haul big loads and on one occasion there were unfortunate consequences.

The usual route of the sleigh led from the woodlot across the old orchard to a gap at its southwest corner, from where team and sleigh came across the first field to the barnyard. During the last fifty yards through the orchard, the packed snow of the sleigh trail descended a gentle slope, inviting the winter-fat and frisky team to break into a trot. In the winter of 1933–34 Len was bringing up a big load of wood, standing as usual in precarious balance on top. Also as usual, the horses broke into a trot as they approached the orchard gap. When Len drove through it, a projecting log in the load struck the fence post at one side of the gap. Their progress suddenly checked, the horses swung sideways and tipped the bobsled on its side, its load of small logs and saplings sliding to the ground and spilling onto the adjacent orchard fence. So suddenly did disaster strike that Len lost his balance before he could leap clear. His effort to do so did take him beyond most of the load, but as he lit in the snow an ironwood sapling struck him in the ribs.

One-handed, Len managed to unhitch the team and walk them to the barn. At the house Len and Eleta probed his ribs and decided that the injury involved more than a bruise. "Three cracked ribs," reported the doctor later, before strapping great swatches of adhesive tape around Len's torso. Our doctor was a man of stern remedies. His parting words were: "Take a couple of aspirin at six-hour intervals." Len suffered through some days of pain and even more of itching as his skin rebelled at the adhesive tape. But he was soon back at work and even hauled some loads of wood to the big pile accumulating on the house side of the barnyard. I doubt, however, that the lengths of saw wood on the sleigh were heaped as high as before the accident.

Sometimes the old woodpile gave out before George and Len were ready to bring in the buzz saw operator, and they prepared some of the newly cut lengths on a day-to-day basis for use in our stoves. This occurred in the first

two years in which I went to the Lambeth Continuation School. During
the school year my only daily duty involved filling all the woodboxes after
I returned from Lambeth. When the men were cutting stove wood each
day, I usually reached home at about the time that George and Len had
returned from the woods and finished watering the cattle and horses. As I
trudged up the drive and across the crunching snow to the back door, my
mind focused on glasses of milk and cookies or the dessert left over at lunch
time, George would appear at the south barn door and shout: "Come on
out and give us a hand with the house wood."

With a mouthful of cookie, I walked to the barn, where I found that the
men had piled a number of lengths of tree trunk or limb at the junction
of the milking alley and the cross alley to the horse stable. As one walked
through the cross alley from the milking alley, one passed first between the
tubular steel endpieces that kept the cows in their places on either side,
then past the ends of their concrete mangers, and then into the central feed
alley. As I shrugged out of my lumber jacket, Len rested a length of sapling
on the cement ends of the mangers so that it ran across the passageway and
projected on either side into the manger area, running below the throat
and brisket of Wooley, the first cow in the northern section of the cow
row, and that of her neighbor to the south, Arabell. Wooley was a big,
rough, dehorned cow, nicknamed for her tendency to grow a shaggy coat
in winter, and she was a great scratcher. Periodically she decided that the
wood-sawing operation was a concession to her comfort, and she would
begin to rub her chin and throat vigorously on the small log, threatening to
tip it off the opposite manger and into hers. To forestall this, Len, stationed
on the feed alley side of the cross passage, would quickly install the stick
of wood in place, give Wooley a light cuff with one hand, place a lifted
foot on the wood to pin it in place against the metal post of the stanchion
frame, and extend an end of our crosscut saw to me where I stood in the
passage between the cows.

Now Len and I made a succession of crosscuts on the stick of wood at
intervals that would produce lengths to fit the firebox of the kitchen stove
but taking care to pull out the saw when an inch or so of wood remained
uncut. Had we cut completely through the stick, it would soon have become
too short to reach from manger to manger. But once we had made saw cuts
along its whole length, a few blows with the axe would separate the stove-
length pieces. Back and forth went the shiny brownish blade of the saw—
push-pull, push-pull, push-pull, *pheet-pheut, pheet-pheut, pheet-pheut*—a
somewhat deeper tone sounding when Len brought the saw toward him.
There was a kind of hypnotic quality in this alternation of effort, and I

found that my French teacher's phrase "peut-être que oui, peut-être que non" fit this exchange of labor between Len and myself. Push: "peut-être que oui;" PULL: "PEUT-ÊTRE QUE NON". But as I succumbed to this trance-inducing formula, Len would suddenly break the spell: "Al, you're riding the saw. Wake up!"

When we had used the saw on all the wood and George had broken it into stove-length firewood with the axe, I began my evening task of filling the various woodboxes in the house. Whether I was carrying stove wood from the barn or, more usually, from a woodpile at the house side of the barnyard, I usually tried to persuade George and Len also to carry an armload of stove fuel to the house when they went in for supper. The number of times that George declined on the grounds that he was carrying something else was quite surprising. Len was occasionally cooperative but more often took the position that filling the woodboxes was my job. If I had been late from school or was detained at the barn, I would make the last trips at a jolting trot to avoid missing that day's installment of "Jack Armstrong, the All-American Boy" on our Philco radio. Undue haste, or a slip on the icy path, sometimes led me to drop my load and then pick up the faggots from the snow. This in turn meant that the firewood for that evening was wet and dripping when it went into the stove—no problem when the fire was going well but a different matter in the morning when a new fire must be built in the kitchen range.

When the pile of tree trunks and branches in the barnyard had reached the size that George believed would provide an adequate supply of wood for the forthcoming year, he contacted Vic Nichols, who brought a tractor and his big portable circular saw to the farm with which to cut the wood into stovebox length. We referred to this operation as "buzzing wood." Sometimes George hired someone to help him and Len in this operation, so that we had a three-man crew at work plus the saw operator. The operator fed into the saw the big pieces of wood that two of the others carried to him, while the third man steadied the short side of the stick and threw the severed piece on the growing pile of stove wood. On one occasion the third man was my cousin Gordon. While Gordon was taking away the cut pieces from the saw and throwing them behind him, he failed to notice that George had moved into the vicinity of the pile of cut wood and was trying to loosen a big limb from its position in the original pile. Gordon heaved a large chunk of wood over his shoulder and hit George on the back of the neck, flattening him. After giving his neck some vigorous rubbing, George pronounced himself able to continue at work. But in later years he complained a good deal about pains in his neck and on the advice of our doctor began to patronize a chiropractor. At another buzz Gordon was the victim, when the men feeding the saw swung a big limb around as they took it from the pile and hit Gordon squarely in the stomach with such force that he deposited his lunch in the snow. But he too pronounced himself ready to continue the work after a few minutes of recuperation.

Usually a long half day was sufficient for us to buzz the next year's supply of stove wood, leaving behind a tumbled woodpile that I would come to know in intimate detail during the next ten or eleven months. If the men had free time, they might take a few days to split the larger cross sections of tree trunks or large limbs and to pile the stove lengths into neat parallel ricks, but in some years they did not get around to this task, and the stove wood remained in its original higgledy-piggledy arrangement. Whatever its condition, the winter snows usually covered the pile, and I burrowed into a large white drift to find wood to stoke the various stoves during the coming evening and the following day.

SEVEN

Fowl Business and Other Supplementary Enterprise

My earliest memories of poultry on our farm place me inside the door of the henhouse on the southeast corner farm, watching a gray-black tide of hens converging on Eleta as she stood by me with a pail of chicken feed in one hand. A feather lying at my feet was striped with alternate bands of black and white. These chickens were Barred Plymouth Rock hens, a dual-purpose variety of poultry, admired by many breeders of the time because they were both good egg producers and birds that grew to the size necessary to provide a meal for a substantial family. The Barred Rocks were handsome birds although less colorful and flashy than those of some other breeds and varieties. At this time Eleta was producing a surplus of eggs for sale. I can remember her preparing them for market, wiping each egg carefully with a damp cloth to remove any spot of blood or feces from the shells and later sitting at the table in the darkened kitchen candling them—taking them one by one from a basket and placing them in the stream of light emanating from a candle placed safely behind an egg-sized round hole in a sturdy piece of suspended cardboard. If the illuminated interior of an egg showed a black or reddish spot, she discarded it, but she found few bloody eggs.

After this lapse of time, I cannot estimate the size of Eleta's flock of chickens. It was probably at its maximum in the late 1920s and early 1930s, when the number of laying hens perhaps exceeded fifty birds. Until then Eleta had hatched chicks on the farm by allowing "broody" hens to set or by using a home incubator. These methods produced comparable numbers of pullet and cockerel chicks. She marketed many of the latter as dressed poultry, and the family ate most of the rest, although she always retained a few roosters in the flock during the years when hatching took place on the farm.

By the time we moved to the northeast corner farm Eleta was obtaining chicks from a commercial hatchery in London. George brought them home in square flat cardboard boxes that had small round holes punched in the sides and interior panels dividing each container into quarters. Set down on a table in the kitchen, the boxes produced a loud chorus of cheeping. Eleta then released them in a brooder house that was some ten by twelve feet in size and heated by a small round coal-burning stove fitted with a projecting circular metal hood designed to hold heat close to the floor.

Initially Eleta spread old newspapers on the floor to facilitate cleaning. Later she put down a layer of sawdust or straw. The first few nights of residence in the brooder house were critical to the survival of the chicks. When darkness came they tended to crowd together so tightly under the protective hood of the little stove that some might smother. Eleta usually made several trips to the brooder house during the first few nights while the chicks were settling into their quarters. There she ensured that they had not packed themselves in any one location, and she stoked the stove with more coal. Even so there were some casualties in the first few nights, either from smothering or because some of the chicks were too weak to make the adjustment to life in the brooder house. Emerging from the back door of the house on a frosty spring morning and heading for the barn after breakfast, we breathed the acrid stink carried in the smoke of the brooder house stove as Eleta used its fire to dispose of the few chicks that had died during the night.

When we moved to the northeast corner farm Eleta's flock was still made up of Barred Plymouth Rock chickens. But within our first year or two on that farm she changed to White Plymouth Rocks. Egg buyers on the farmers' market in London had come to favor white eggs rather than the brown ones that Barred Rocks produced. Eleta had also discovered that the black pin feathers of the barred variety made it difficult to produce a dressed bird that was as cleanly plucked and attractively finished as those of the growers of white birds. In size and ability to produce eggs the whites were the equal of the barred variety. At about this time Eleta learned, however, that the Rocks could not match the White Leghorns as egg producers and by the mid-1930s she had shifted to that breed of chickens despite the fact that mature Leghorns were smaller than the Rocks. By now growers could specify the sex of the chicks ordered from the hatchery, and in one year at least she ordered some Rock males for sale as dressed poultry in addition to young Leghorn females. The males of the latter variety, however, made good fryers, and Eleta served them frequently on our table in our last years on the farm.

We had one brooder house while on the southeast corner farm. George had placed stout sapling skids under it and used one of the teams to haul it from the orchard on the southeast corner farm to its new location in the barnyard of the new farm. In the second year of our residence there, Eleta asked George to build a second brooder house of the same general construction and size. The front ends of these small buildings were some seven feet in height, the flat roofs sloping to back walls that measured about five feet between roof and floor. We entered through a door on the left side of the front wall. A large Plexiglass window dominated the remainder of the frontage, beginning about a foot above the floor and stretching upward for some four feet, its transparent surface nailed to the studs behind it. Above this and stretching across most of the upper front between the door and the other end was a wooden swing flap that Eleta opened for ventilation as needed. The round-hooded brooder stove sat in the middle of the floor, its smoke pipe exiting directly above through the roof.

Once the chicks were large enough to go outside, Eleta allowed them the freedom of the barnyard, but they returned to their brooder house at night, where she locked them in until morning. In the early fall we spent an evening transferring that year's generation into the henhouse, which they shared with the remainder of the flock of layers. One summer several years after our move, Eleta's White Rocks suffered a devastating epidemic of the infectious disease roup. On the veterinarian's advice she placed medicinal tablets containing potassium permanganate and other drugs in the chickens' water pails, but a good many of her birds died, antibiotics for farm livestock still being some twenty years in the future. Before confining the remaining chickens that fall, we scrubbed out the henhouse and brooder houses with a hot water, soap, and carbolic acid solution.

Eleta's birds did not suffer further sickness during our years on the farm. But the experience had been demoralizing. She cut back the scale of her chicken business thereafter, only using the newer of the brooder houses. Len and George took the old one to make a storage and entry shed at the north end of the small greenhouse that they built in the mid-1930s. The back of that structure stood a few feet from the driveway between house yard and barnyard, which provided a surface that was usually hard packed and icy in the winter. I painted white circles on the boards and used them to improve my accuracy with puck and hockey stick.

After the cement contractor completed the first-story walls and floor of the new barn, he poured the floor and foundation walls for a chicken house on the north side of the barnyard. Using siding from the old barn, George and Len built a new structure that contained three pens in line. A front door opened into the center room and the pen on the west end gave access to a fenced hen yard. Along the north side of this outside enclosure, the men built a high board fence using more of the cast-off material from the old barn. As in the exterior siding of the henhouse, they attached the boards in the fence vertically. The new building's roof of wooden shingles sloped from front to back and there was a large square window in the front wall of each room. Of these enclosures the western and central ones were approximately thirteen by thirteen feet and the eastern pen slightly narrower. The men nailed three rows of nests to the south wall of the west room, positioned between the window and the west end of the building, and they also placed a few nests on the south wall in the middle pen. They placed roosts of thin sapling trunks attached to slanted two-by-four stringers in the back of the western and central rooms. Eleta used the east end enclosure to house overflow when the flock was at its largest or for male birds, but sometimes we stored feed there or kept one or two hogs in it.

Eleta was most active in maintaining her poultry enterprise during our first few years on the northeast corner farm. At that time she was buying supplies of laying mash and oyster shell scratch for the hens. By the mid-1930s, perhaps discouraged by the losses to roup, she had cut back on her work with poultry and was using only one brooder house for the chicks; the ability of the hatchery to supply females or males in desired proportions might also have allowed her to maintain a smaller flock. And the increased emphasis that we were placing on market gardening during the mid-1930s could have given her less time to devote to poultry. Although she seemed constantly in motion, Eleta was now reaching her fifties and had been greatly dispirited after the death of my sister Eleanor. All of these factors perhaps diminished her interest in the poultry operation.

Eleta usually went to the barn and the henhouse in midmorning and again in late afternoon to feed and water the chickens and to gather the eggs. During the period when she was feeding a ration of laying mash to the hens she sometime supplemented their diet with wheat from the granary. and at later times that grain provided the major part of their ration. She started her young chickens on chick and growing mash, but they too might be fed unground wheat after they had attained some size. When building the outside enclosure at the west end of the henhouse, George and Len constructed a fence of small-paneled mesh wire that was two-tiered and rose to a height of six or seven feet. Eleta's hens revealed at once that it was not poultry proof. Some of the hens squeezed through the fence panels, some exploited gaps between the two tiers of fence, and others found gaps where the fence left the side of the building or joined the board fence at the rear of the yard. After the first year or two on this farm, Eleta gave the flock the run of the barnyard as soon as the late spring weather allowed. Typically the hens returned to the henhouse roost in the evening and continued to deposit their eggs in the nests there.

The occasional hen, however, obeyed her instincts and tried to establish a hidden nest on the upper or lower level of the barn, in the remaining heel of the straw stack, or even in the weeds behind the henhouse. Eleta instructed me to keep my eyes open for such hoards. If the hen had hidden herself well and the nest contained a full clutch or near to it, the eggs by definition were unfresh and Eleta destroyed them. I cannot remember that any of the hens succeeded in producing a hatch of chicks after Eleta switched from Barred Rocks, but I often found two or three eggs in a corner of the feeding alley in the barn or tucked into the edge of a mow beside the drive floor on the upper level. The mangers in the horse stalls were made of planks, and each contained a smaller open-topped grain box positioned at one side, into which George dumped each horse's grain ration of rolled oats. Sometimes Pomp allowed one of the entrepreneur hens to start a nest below his grain box, and several eggs might accumulate there before we noticed what was happening. A hen wandering innocently along the central feeding alley in the barn was always a tip-off that a nesting operation was under way.

Eggs in Pomp's manger provided a lasting memory. Bill Topping's fourth son Gordie, then a lad of some sixteen or seventeen years of age, came into our barn after lunch one summer day to talk with Len while he was preparing to hitch up one of the teams. As he and Gordie chatted, Len discovered a couple of fresh eggs in the manger. "Your mother sucks eggs," was a schoolyard taunt we had all heard a good many times.

"Can you eat an egg raw?" Len asked Gordie. "Of course," he replied, "but I bet you can't." Len cracked an egg against the side of the stall wall, drained the shell into his mouth and calmly swallowed yolk and white. "Your turn," he said, passing the other egg to Gordie. Not to be outdone, Gordie cracked it open and tipped the contents into his mouth. We watched in anticipation as his mouth worked and his adam's apple rose in a heroic effort to swallow. And swallow Gordie did, but then came revulsion. His neck muscles contracted, his mouth opened, and he spewed liquid egg into the muck of the stable. "Well, well," said Len, "too bad we didn't have some money down."

The eggs from Eleta's flock were a basic part of the family menu. We ate them fried, scrambled, boiled, or poached for breakfast and occasionally for supper as well. When we were ill, Eleta made eggnogs for us, flavored with vanilla extract and sporting a light dusting of nutmeg on their surface. If ordinary eggnog ceased to tempt, she sometimes separated the white from the yolk and beat each separately, so that the mixture of milk and yolk stood in the glass below a white frothy topping. Roasted chicken was a common centerpiece of Sunday dinner, and old exhausted hens often ended their careers in a stew pot topped with dumplings. In the final years on the farm, Eleta used young Leghorn cockerels as fryers for the family table.

Receipts from the sale of eggs and dressed poultry from the flock underwrote the purchase of a good portion of the groceries and other household supplies that Eleta bought. On Friday afternoon or in the early evening during the fall or winter months she selected a number of birds and carried them by their legs, protesting, to the back door of the house. There she slipped a short length of cord around their lower legs and suspended them from a low branch of the plum tree that stood at the northeast corner of the woodshed. Then she fetched her killing knife from the summer kitchen just inside the back door. This knife had a round wooden handle and a thin, slightly curved blade some three and a half inches long. Cradling the chicken's head in the palm of her left hand, she would gently force the beak open with thumb and forefinger and then slip the point of the knife blade into the throat. With a twist of the wrist she severed the jugular, and the bird was left to jerk and flutter briefly as it lost motor control and its blood drained onto the ground.

While the birds drained she brought out a steaming wash kettle of water, hot almost to the point of boiling, and she dipped the birds in it once rapidly. This, she believed, helped to release the feathers. Next Eleta took the birds into the kitchen and began to pluck their feathers as they lay on a table already prepared with a cover of newspapers. If she was taking more than two or three birds to market the following morning, George might help with the plucking. Sometimes I was pressed into this task, which the smell of hot wet chicken feathers made unpleasant and in which care must be exercised to avoid tearing the skin or leaving unsightly pin feathers embedded in it. Once the feathers were removed, Eleta lit a small can of an alcohol and wax mixture and singed off the occasional hairs found on most chickens. Then she used clean white string to bind the wings and legs close to the body and neatly wrapped and tied newspaper around the head. At this point the chicken was ready for market, and Eleta placed it with its companions in a large wicker basket to be stored in the cellar ready for transport to town early on Saturday morning. Like most farm women who sold dressed poultry in our area, she did not gut the fowls.

During the 1920s and early 1930s Eleta marketed her poultry and eggs during the fall and winter months at the Market Square in London on Saturdays in a long red-brick building with the name Covent Garden set in masonry above its end doors. Two rows of tables ran the length of the basement in this structure with back-to-back benches positioned between them. Along the exterior walls fruit merchants, butchers, and other farm suppliers maintained shops. At the tables, farm women displayed dressed poultry, eggs, butter, cottage cheese, and other dairy products as well as honey, jams, preserves, and baked goods. Here Eleta sold her poultry and eggs and sometimes butter. Her sister also sold farm products at the basement tables in Covent Garden, and over the years Eleta became acquainted with other women who set out their displays of farm goods there.

In one year of the early twentieth century, the newspaper account of prize winners at the annual exhibition sponsored by the Westminster Agricultural Society at Lambeth informed readers that David Bogue received fourteen first-prize ribbons in the poultry division of exhibits. Neither Eleta nor George, nor any of their children, shared the passion for fancy poultry that such winnings reflected. But the poultry were an important element in our farm economy, and the chickens are omnipresent actors in my recollections of the farmyard, scattered here and there and busily pecking in their search for grain from earlier feedings, or worms or insects, or mustering in an undulating white mass around Eleta as she threw grain on the ground at the foot of the barn approach or poured laying mash into narrow wooden troughs inside the henhouse. When the threshers set up the grain separator in the barnyard, threshing day provided a bonanza for the chickens. For several days afterward they thronged the threshing site to feast on spilled grain and the pile of weed seeds that the separator sieves had extracted from the grain.

There was an endless fascination in watching young chickens develop during the course of the season, growing in size, developing full sets of feathers, and evolving into roosters and hens. The antics of the young cockerels as they began to assert themselves and practice their rooster calls were quite laughable. Like many other farm boys, I tried to imitate their proclamations as well as the cluck-cluck-clucking of the hens. Of more serious concern were droopy or sick birds whose presence might indicate some kind of epidemic developing in the flock.

There were of course less attractive sides to the poultry enterprise; cleaning the henhouse, for example. This was a job Eleta sometimes delegated to me and I carried out with little enthusiasm, although the mixture of straw and droppings that I shoveled and forked from the henhouse floors was much lighter and a good deal less pungent than what came from the cow stable gutters, the horse stable, or the box stalls occupied by the bull and calves. Nor did I enjoy watching or participating in the tasks involved in preparing dressed fowl for market, although I knew that it was a necessary part of our farm life.

Eleta always watched for rats in the vicinity of the brooder houses, fearing that they would kill and eat chicks. If one appeared, George set out a couple of large spring traps in locations where he hoped that mature chickens or the barnyard cats would not wander into them. During one of our early years on the northeast corner farmer, however, it became clear that more than one or two rats had taken up residence in the barnyard. When George and the carpenters built the henhouse, they had tried to ensure a warm interior by placing board sheeting on the inside of the studs, leaving empty spaces between it and the exterior siding. Rats had gnawed passageways into these compartments and settled in, finding ample sustenance a few feet away in the mash troughs where the hens fed. Although the occasional rat blundered into our traps, it was clear as winter and spring progressed that more radical measures were needed. In those pre-warfarin days, George and Eleta feared that the use of poison might endanger the livestock. George disliked guns and tried to keep them off the premises. He often said: "If there are no guns on the place, no one will be shot on the place." The Toppings lived on the southeast corner farm at the time and the boys hunted, festooning the lilac bushes at their back door with the frozen bodies of unlucky jackrabbits in the wintertime. Young Gordie was eager to assist Len in launching a frontal assault on the rats. But even had George been willing, gunfire in the barnyard would have been dangerous.

George and Len agreed that the best strategy involved tearing out the inner sheeting on the walls of the chicken house to flush the rats into the open, where Jiggs could confront them. Should Jiggs need help, Len and Gordie set long-handled shovels conveniently at hand before they attacked the henhouse siding with pinchbar and hammer. No sign of the enemy appeared initially, although Jiggs watching with muzzle pointed and stub tail twitching, signaling that there was enemy within. But with a few more sections of siding still to be torn out, the henhouse floor and the yard immediately outside came alive with dashing gray rats. Jiggs swung into pouncing action, seizing rats by the neck, breaking their backs with a twisting upward snap of the head, and tossing them aside to find other prey. Len and Gordie seized their shovels and flailed away, sometimes hitting and sometimes missing but adding considerably to Jiggs's total. When the hunters had dealt with the first surge of rodents, Len and Gordie tore out the rest of the siding, precipitating another wave of fugitives with the same result. When the interior was clear, Jiggs and his supporters searched the weeds around the henhouse for survivors that had been foolish enough to hide there. After half an hour of great activity the hunters could find no more living rats, and the henhouse floor and adjacent barnyard were littered with several dozen dead rodents. It was Jiggs's most glorious adventure.

During a good part of her career as poultry flock manager, Eleta kept a gander and two geese in the barnyard. These birds typically produced between one and two dozen young ones, which Eleta fitted for sale on the Thanksgiving and Christmas markets. She had not kept geese for several years when we changed farms, but once reestablished, she obtained a new trio of foundation birds from my grandmother. For several years the two females nested in the vicinity of the henhouse and each successfully hatched and reared nine or ten young ones. Although one of the females had a coat that was mottled with white, all the youngsters emerged from their furry coats of gosling yellow as slate-gray replicas of their father. I never heard Eleta express affection for her chickens; they were essentially a business proposition. The geese were different.

Typically she began to feed the goslings in the barnyard at the same time that she tended the chickens. The parent birds were always reserved, keeping some distance away from her as she ladled wet mash into several dishes, supplementing it with pieces of bread and table scraps. Soon the youngsters had no inhibitions, eagerly coming to meet her and crowding around while she doled out their rations. When by themselves, the old birds seldom entered the house yard, but with the youngsters in tow, they began to anticipate their feeding time after our breakfast and again in the late afternoon, leading a ragged convoy through the barnyard gate and settling down on the lawn adjacent to our back door. When Eleta appeared the flock burst into goose talk, higher pitched, richer, and more sustained than the *quack, quack* of ducks.

If aroused by the approach of strangers or some unusual happening in the barnyard, the geese raised a chorus of warning honks that was far louder and more sustained than the barking of our dogs. Strangers emerging from their cars at either house or barn did so in the midst of a great racket.

Although the old geese led and shepherded the young ones, the latter quickly identified Eleta as their patron and were prepared to follow her in preference to their parents. Their fixation on Eleta may only have shown that the young geese knew the source of their next meal, but Eleta viewed it as a demonstration of affection that she returned in full measure. She loved to tell stories about the intelligence of her flock. Whenever she became concerned about its activities, Eleta needed only to stand in the back door and call to produce a cacophony of youthful honks that was soon followed by the appearance of the flock at the barnyard gate.

During the late spring and after summer storms, water stood in the side road ditch adjacent to the farmstead and the geese liked this little pool. There was never much auto traffic on the road, but Eleta worried that a careless motorist would run over members of the flock. She sometimes sent me to herd the big birds back into the barnyard, and I became the butt of a good deal of goose profanity as a result. Eleta never lost any birds on the road, but the goose enterprise ended in 1934 or 1935 in tragedy. Eleta's flock had suffered few losses among the goslings that year, and by October it was a handsome assembly of birds. But on a stormy night with the wind blowing from the west, and therefore away from the house, a band of outlaw dogs attacked the flock. By the time that the sounds of frightened geese penetrated to the house, almost half of the flock had been killed. On that same night the dogs killed several sheep on a farm about half a mile away. When the full details became clear, Eleta was in tears and utterly distraught. Thanksgiving market day was only a few weeks away and the loss in revenue was considerable. But in that strange kind of mental compartmentalization that many farm folk achieve, she regarded the young geese as her friends, as pets, despite the fact that she would have had to put them to the knife within weeks. The old gander died in the slaughter, and Eleta never tried to raise a crop of young geese thereafter.

In preparing the geese for sale Eleta employed many of the same procedures as in readying chickens for market, but she tried to restrict her sale of geese to the market days before Thanksgiving and Christmas. And since she prepared a dozen or so birds at the same time, George and sometimes Len helped with the plucking. A thick layer of down lay beneath the feathers of the geese, and this we carefully placed in paper sacks. Eleta used it in the winters to make a number of magnificent down comforters for members of the family. We celebrated Thanksgiving and Christmas with roast goose on the table; it was not until we left the farm that turkey appeared at festive meals in those seasons. Prior to then my acquaintance with turkeys was restricted to harvest days at the Dale farm. The water pump there stood at the back of the house in a yard patrolled by an officious turkey gobbler that saw no reason why a boy should have a drink from the pump between trips to the field.

Very briefly Eleta cultivated one other species of fowl. During one of her last years on the farm, a friend pressed a couple of guinea fowl upon her, and these handsome little birds soon made themselves at home in the barnyard, joining the chickens at feeding time. They were, however, much more opposed to confinement than chickens or geese and took wing when we tried to herd them into the chicken house. They roosted in the row of Norway spruce that ran behind the house and ended at the gate of the night pasture. They nested successfully close to the barn—I never knew exactly where, although perhaps Eleta did—and raised seven or eight chicks. In order to catch them for the table or market we went out at night with a flashlight and located them in their roosting place in the spruce trees. They were not clever enough to roost so high in the trees that we could not catch them. But capturing them was a struggle. If one missed the first grab, the sleepy bird fluttered higher in the tree. Eleta roasted a guinea fowl once to allow us to sample the quality of the meat, and the verdict was: delicious. But buyers at the farmers' market showed little interest in them, and Eleta did not retain birds for breeding purposes after the year of experiment.

When I asked George why he did not keep sheep, he replied that maintaining a flock required tight mesh fencing that was difficult to maintain. He would then reminisce about the sheep owned by his grandfather or an uncle, animals that possessed an uncanny ability to discover holes in the fence or unattended open gates. Only two of the farmers along the North Talbot Road between Lambeth and Byron kept flocks, one being the father of Eleta's friend Jessie Duncan. One afternoon when I was five or six, Eleta and I went to have tea with Jessie, who showed me the spinning wheel she kept in the front room of the house.

Farmers in the larger Lambeth community who took their milk to the cheese factory at Scottsville, south of Lambeth, used whey to provide part of the rations for hogs, and the combination of dairy cows and hogs could be a profitable one. I heard the saying that hogs were mortgage lifters repeated on more than one occasion. Obeying sanitary regulations, the officers and farm inspectors of Silverwood's Dairy maintained that hogs and milk production should not occur in close proximity, Bill Topping's dissent notwithstanding. Perhaps that rule reinforced some prejudice against the hog in George's mind. He never in my years maintained brood sows on the farm.

That prejudice was not absolute, however, and in several of our years on the northeast corner farm young hogs occupied the east compartment of the henhouse or a pen attached to that end of that building. The presence of these animals traced back to George's failure to retain the farm on the Fifth Concession. He had escaped more serious loss on that farm by reselling it on unfavorable terms and accepting a second mortgage behind the first mortgage held by the bank. The farm's new owner was a foreign-born farmer, whom George always called Tony. In those depression era years Tony found it difficult to meet his payments to the bank, let alone those owing to George. Each year George called on Tony and asked for his money. Each year Tony pleaded poverty and George suggested payment in kind, perhaps a pair of young pigs, and thus a couple of pigs would take up residence at the henhouse.

George had never worked with swine sufficiently to have any confidence in his ability to castrate the males himself, or perhaps he was too squeamish, so he had a friend perform this task if Tony's pigs were not altered prior to their arrival at our place. We fed them on skim milk, oat and barley chop, and anything else available that a hungry young porker could stomach, including potato peelings and table scraps. As we moved more deeply into market gardening in the mid-1930s, the pigs ate the sweet corn, tomatoes, lettuce, and other vegetables or fruit that we failed to sell at the farmers' market in London.

Straw bedding was typically in short supply at the barn during the weeks prior to threshing. The hog pen sometimes became messy in the extreme, a development enhanced by the pigs' tendency to throw some of their rations out of the trough and onto the floor of the pen. Eleta kept an eye on the pen, however, and championed the swine's cause. She demanded that an adequate supply of straw or chaff from the barn floor be tossed into their pen and did not allow us to cast aspersions on their inherent cleanliness. During the summers when we were most deeply involved in market gardening, we often had hired workers at the dinner table, some engaged by the month or week, others coming on a day-to-day basis from the neighborhood or from Lambeth to help with the picking. Such comments as "I'm dirty as a pig" or "It's the pig pen for you" were sure to inspire a polite rebuff from Eleta.

"You must remember," she would say, "that pigs are not dirty by nature. If you look into a pig pen where there are two levels of floor or the floor slopes, you will see that the pigs have made their bed in the cleanest part of the pen and they *keep it clean*. The poor animals only get dirty when the pen is not properly cleaned out or they are not given enough bedding." Eleta did not confine such instruction to the hired help; she set evening or Sunday visitors right on the subject of pigs and cleanliness as well. My sister Myrtle was often at the farm on weekends and during the summer, and like many public school teachers, she had strong feelings about appropriate table conversation. I never heard her admonish her mother for such lecturettes, but I sometimes caught her and Len exchanging an upward roll of the eyeballs when Eleta launched into a defense of the hog pen residents. As in most of the homes along the North Talbot Road, domestic conversation in our household was very clean. Barnyard exchanges were sometimes less so when young male neighbors or hired men dropped by. I do not know what Eleta would have done had she heard a common response there to the salutary "How are you?" which was "Oh, happy as a pig in shit."

After reaching good size, one of any pair of young pigs obtained from Tony was eaten at the family table, the other sent to the stockyards with the local trucker. In the last years of collections from Tony the hog to be slaughtered was driven down the side road toward Dingman's Creek to Fora Cornell's place, where he and his sons had developed a butcher business. As part of their trade they accepted animals from neighbors, slaughtered them, and cut the meat according to the instructions of the owner. We stored the various cuts beyond our immediate needs in a locker that we rented at a freezer storage plant near the farmers' market in London. On earlier occasions George and Len butchered a couple of the hogs themselves, and once, on a school holiday, I was able to watch.

Preparations began when Len took two large butcher knives from the kitchen knife drawer and used an emery stick to bring them to razor sharpness. George backed the car from our old garage and used a length of chain to attach a pulley to one of the cross beams above the auto stall. Through this he ran a length of hay rope with a hook on one end and a clevis on the other. Below and slightly behind the pulley arrangement in the garage, he positioned a large wooden barrel canted toward the open garage door. Meanwhile Eleta was heating a full wash boiler of water on the kitchen range. Grandmother had used a large black cast-iron kettle for maple syrup reduction, and under one Eleta built a fire near the garage to heat still more water.

Now Len released the hog and we drove him toward the gate between the barn and the house. His siesta interrupted and perhaps sensing trouble, the hog began to squeal and try to escape from us. When we reached a grassy patch Len overtook it, seized the off front leg, and flipped the animal on its side. George had been hovering with a butcher knife, which he now passed to Len, and Len plunged it into the hog's neck below the jaw. His thrust severed the jugular, blood poured out, and the squealing ceased. George placed a short piece of sapling that he had sharpened on both ends between the hind legs, piercing them at the back above the knee joints. Hitching Pomp to this, they skidded the pig, trailing blood, to the garage, where they used the pulley and rope to elevate it. It was allowed to hang for some minutes to let the blood drain completely from the body. Then they plunged it into the barrel, now full of steaming hot water. After dropping the hog into the barrel a couple of times in order to loosen its hair or bristles, they again raised it to hang from the pulley and hook. George, butcher knife in hand, now removed the offal, carefully placing the heart, liver, and bladder in a milk pail half full of cold water. That done, the men used their knives to scrape the hair off the pig's hide. Then they placed the carcass on the stoneboat and hauled it to the cool setting of the barn floor, where it was hung in preparation for butchering into quarters and derivative cuts the next day.

Since I never developed a great affection for hogs, I did not find hog slaughtering to be a disturbing experience. It would have been different had the animal been a veal calf that had sucked my fingers during the preceding months. Instead the process through which pig became pork was interesting. Jiggs was even more interested. The men shut him in the kitchen initially as a potential nuisance, but by the time that George was removing the offal from the hog Jiggs had appeared at the garage. As Len piled internal organs outside the garage, preparatory to using the stoneboat to haul them to the manure pile behind the barn, Jiggs lost all self-control. He attacked the steaming mess voraciously, gulping down large hunks of caked blood that lay on the ground or were mixed with the intestines. After a few minutes of this he retreated with a rather puzzled look on his black and white face, braced his front feet, lowered his head, and threw up. With hardly a pause he began to fill his stomach again.

As Jiggs's activity shows, we did not collect the blood of slaughtered swine. There were, however, a couple of families in the neighborhood who did and who enjoyed eating blood pudding. That treat was not part of our family's culinary tradition; years later, one of the most remembered incidents in a semester our family spent in Sweden occurred when our teenage daughter learned that she had eaten blood pudding for lunch in her school cafeteria. Pork heart and liver were a different matter, however. We usually enjoyed fresh fried liver for supper after we had slaughtered a hog. At such times we generally shared the liver with Eleta's parents, and they in turn phoned to inform us that they had saved some liver for us when they butchered hogs.

We took much of this particular hog to the freezer plant after George had divided it into roasts, chops, and other cuts. But there was some additional processing at home as well. I remember George and Eleta laying pork flanks into a salt bed and thoroughly rubbing the flesh side with the mixture of salt, saltpeter, and other ingredients that turned the meat into bacon. Eleta used the flesh and other contents of the head to make headcheese, a jellied meat loaf, the texture and smell of which I found nauseating, although George claimed that this processed meat was delicious.

George found another of Eleta's by-products less appetizing. This particular hog was quite heavy, and in dressing the meat George sliced a good deal of fat from the various cuts. Seeing this, Eleta decided to make old-fashioned home-style soap, cooking the fat and adding lye to it. When this brew had reached proper consistency she poured it into flat pans, and as it cooled in the back kitchen she cut it into squares with a knife. It was soap—that looked in consistency and color much like maple fudge. George had a sweet tooth and on his way to the barn, he popped a square into his mouth. I had heard of school teachers who forced foul-mouthed children to wash out their mouths with soap but had never experienced such discipline. If George did not exactly froth at the mouth, he did not suffer in silence either. We never dared to laugh at George, but there was some quiet snickering about this case of mistaken identity.

In the 1930s the economist John Ise published *Sod and Stubble*, the story of his family's experiences on a homestead in north-central Kansas, making his mother, Rosie, the central figure in an account of the Ises' struggles to survive in the plains country. Rosie outlived her husband by many years and, according to her son, was the driving force in the family's history. Many Rosies in the United States and Canada have failed to find a chronicler, let alone one as perceptive and sympathetic as John Ise. The last generations of American historians, however, have rightly agreed that their predecessors paid too little attention to the contributions of the farm wife, and a number of scholars have begun to right the imbalance. These efforts have greatly enriched the historical literature of North American agriculture; but in some cases they have failed to picture the complexities of interaction within the family and the farm business. So masculine a function as killing a hog affected Eleta's domestic role. As domestic worker she prepared the water for scalding the hog. As family cook she prepared the dressed meat for the table, and beyond these tasks, she assisted in converting some of the meat into bacon, cuttings from the hog's head and feet into headcheese, and its fat into soap.

Eleta also played an important role in making maple syrup and sugar, supervising the final stage in preparing those products. At some point between mid-March and mid-April George announced: "Sap's running." It was a heart-lifting announcement. By this time winter colds, sledding on the little hill in front of the house, noon hours at school spent in reading at one's desk or in some half-hearted game in the basement, and even weekend shinny on nearby ponds or "the crik" had become old stuff. It was time, George was saying, to look ahead and to do something different. Like hog butchering, the making of maple syrup was another of those farm enterprises—part subsistence, part commercial—that had come down from pioneer days and were still found on some of the farms of the North Talbot Road, although pursued on a smaller scale than formerly.

When George's father David Bogue had farmed the home place, much of the back fifty had been bush, and many of the trees there were sugar maples. He had built a sugaring shanty among the great trees to shelter a long hearth with raised sides of rocks and dirt. These supported an evaporator pan some eight to ten feet in length, and in the hearth below it David had maintained a hot fire while he was "boiling down" sap in the pan. The bottom interior surface of this receptacle was corrugated to a depth of some six inches, thus providing a much larger heating surface than a flat-bottomed pan of the same exterior dimensions would offer. I learned later that David had stoked the fire under the evaporating pan night and day when syrup making was in full swing. George recalled that his father used hot maple sap to make tea, a drink George condemned as much too sweet and also much too laxative.

When George logged the bush on the Bostwick fifty, the history of syrup and sugar making on that property ended. After George sold and then repossessed the Bostwick fifty, I often drove the milk cows from the slashing to the milking enclosure at the road. By this time there was only a low pile of rocks and sod at the site of the old sugar shanty where the evaporator pan had once boiled and steamed through crisp spring nights.

The harvesting of lumber on the Bostwick fifty had not eliminated the possibility of making maple syrup on the home farm, however. As already described, in the five or six acres of woods growing in the northeast corner of the property where we lived, a great wind storm in the 1890s had taken down the largest trees. The passing of forty years had allowed some six or seven dozen sugar maples there to reach a considerable size, while in the lowland at the west end of this little bush there were several very large trees, each capable of sustaining two sap buckets. The lie of the land had apparently protected them at the time of the big storm.

George brought much of the sugar-making equipment with us to the northeast corner farm. This included the evaporator or reduction pan, a considerable number of sap buckets, and a couple of large cast-iron kettles standing almost three feet high, which his mother had used in the last stages of boiling down sap and removing impurities. Some of the buckets were made of wooden staves and were about two-thirds the size of a milk pail.

Mixed in with them were galvanized metal containers of a later purchase, longer and slimmer in shape. During the off season, one of the sap buckets was used to store a large supply of spiles. These were small metal spouts with a hook attached below a drainage channel. When tapping trees, George used the brace and bit to bore a hole in the side of a sugar maple about two and a half feet above the ground. Into this he inserted a spile and tapped it lightly with the hammer to ensure that it was firmly in place. Then he hung a sap bucket on the hook of the spile, completing the preparation for sap collection from that particular tree. When we left each tree so fitted, we heard the drip-drip of sap falling into the bucket.

There was a rough trail into the central part of our little bush that was wide enough to accommodate a wagon or bobsled. George built a crude hearth beside this trace about midway through the woods. He dug out a fire pit and used the earth to shape low walls around it on both sides and at one end, where he left a vent for a stovepipe chimney. After the sap pails were in place George carried or skidded a supply of wood to the hearth site. When he was boiling sap, the evaporator of course sat atop the fire pit walls, but he tipped the empty pan on its side when it was not in use so that it would not fill with rain or snow. Syrup-making ventures on the northeast corner farm were never on the scale of the Bostwick fifty operation, but George made syrup in a number of the years of the 1930s and even into the 1940s, when he collected sap from the trees on foot, the horses having been sold in 1939.

I was usually in school when syrup making was under way, but I remember accompanying George to the woods on Saturdays. There he had set a large wooden barrel on a stoneboat and usually employed Pomp to pull it through the woods, dumping the contents of the sap buckets into the barrel as he came to each tree that had a bucket attached. At sugaring time snow still covered most of the ground in the woods, but the air was mild; I left my windbreaker comfortably unbuttoned and kept my mitts in my pockets. Crunching out from the stoneboat with a pail to some of the more distant trees and returning with a load of sap was simple and pleasant work. The trees stood black and stark and silent, our voices and the sounds of Pomp's harness and his occasional stamping echoing lightly back to us. Occasionally there would be the *rat-tat-tat* of a woodpecker at work, or the thinner voices of nuthatches or chickadees, lured to the vicinity of the fireplace by the possibility of finding crumbs. There were not enough trees in our stand to allow continuous reduction, so George stored sap in another large barrel and sometimes in milk cans at the fireplace, firing up only when he had enough on hand to make it worthwhile.

With the previous night's run of sap collected and the fire blazing, the supervision of the operation became one of adding to the woodpile and feeding the fire as it roared under the evaporator pan. Soon the liquid contents there were steaming and boiling and creating a frothy whitish scum on the bubbling surface. Periodically George removed this with a long-handled skimmer. He continued boiling sap in the evaporator until it had begun to thicken and change color. When he decided that the concentrated sap was ready for the final stage of finishing, he drained the evaporator through a tap in one of its lower corners and poured the liquid into a milk can for transport to the house. There Eleta put it through a final stage of concentration and purification. At this stage Grandmother Bogue had used one of the big cast-iron kettles, but Eleta employed a copper boiler long enough to extend across two stove lid openings on the kitchen range. After she had repeatedly used a round skimmer made of close-woven metal mesh to remove impurities that rose to the top of the boiling liquid, she added egg white to the syrup, which concentrated remaining bits of bark or dirt at the surface, where they could also be skimmed off. Then she and George sampled the boiling liquid until they agreed that the consistency of the maple syrup was just right. My memory tells me that they also used a thermometer to assist them in this decision, but I have no idea of the temperature they were trying to reach.

Although spring syrup making took place during many of the years while I was growing into my early teens, we never made enough maple syrup to produce much farm income. Some years Eleta took a few quarts of syrup to the farmers' market for sale, and she usually put up enough jars to provide a breakfast sweet and topping for the buckwheat pancakes she sometimes prepared. Maple syrup appeared on our table sufficiently often for me not to have considered it a particular treat. Sometimes Eleta also boiled syrup still longer to make maple sugar and put little cakes of it in my school lunches.

George recalled that when maple syrup played a more important role in our farm economy, the family celebrated the end of the process by "sugaring off." On this social occasion the family and neighbors or relatives gathered to celebrate the end of a successful season of sugar making. The hosts boiled down maple syrup to the point that it congealed into a delicious soft toffee when they poured it over pans of snow. I remember one occasion on the southeast corner farm when my siblings were allowed to invite the members of the young people's association at our church to join us in sugaring off. George dug out a supply of snow from one of the surviving snowdrifts in our orchard. Eleta brought kettles of boiling syrup to exactly the right consistency, and everyone had a great time. Our household was much more somber after Eleanor's death, and there were no more sugaring-off parties. But sometimes Eleta used maple syrup to make snow toffee as a treat for me, and I confirmed my memories of this delicious candy.

EIGHT

To Market, To Market

Our dependence on the farmers' market in London always involved more than simply the retail sales of eggs, dressed poultry, and sometimes butter. Even after we moved to the new place, George occasionally hauled a load of hay to the London market to find a buyer among the representatives of creameries, bakeries, and other firms or private individuals that still used horse-drawn vehicles. I remember a season on the southeast corner farm when our potato acreage was large enough to justify renting a mechanical potato digger. There was a young orchard of three or four acres on that farm planted mostly in Northern Spy trees. These produced fruit that exporters particularly desired for the British market.

Some of the trees in the old orchard on the northeast corner farm still bore fruit, and half a dozen Bartlett pear trees in the night pasture produced heavily in some years. During the 1930s we did not spray the fruit trees for scab or codling moth, but they produced some clean fruit and we marketed some of it. Sometimes also we had a strawberry patch sufficient in size to require hiring a few youngsters to assist in picking the berries. In 1931 or 1932 Len developed a severe infection in his antrums and sinuses that required surgery and incapacitated him for much of a year. When he recovered his health, he began to push the farm operation toward greater activity on the London market.

By the mid-1930s Len owned one of the teams and a growing number of cattle within the farm herd of Holstein-Friesians. All the revenue from milk sales, however, went to George. I believe that a different arrangement prevailed in each of the three crop years 1934, 1935, and 1936. In the first of these, Len was allowed to grow several cash crops of his own for sale on the London market; most notable was a planting of cabbage. In 1935 he rented tillable land on the northeast corner farm and paid rent, while George managed the livestock and sustaining crops as well as farming the

Bostwick fifty. In that year the men assisted carpenters to remodel the house to provide an apartment for Len, and he married Irene B. in the fall. During the following year, 1936, he and George ran the farm business in full partnership and were deeply involved in market gardening as well as maintaining the dairy herd.

Early in the shift toward greater emphasis on market gardening, the men spent much time during one winter in constructing a four-wheeled trailer, utilizing an old car chassis that Len bought. They fitted it with removable side and end gates made of wooden cross slats and stakes that fitted into metal sockets along the side of the trailer's wooden floor, the sections standing forty-eight inches in height. When fully loaded this trailer held three tiers of eleven-quart baskets. The men painted the trailer green and used it during the next several years to haul the occasional calf or other animal as well as market truck. With its sides removed, we also used the trailer to bring newly picked vegetables and fruit from the fields to the farmstead, where we prepared them for market. Len purchased a heavy brown tarpaulin of treated canvas to fit over the trailer's top when it was loaded.

Len was convinced that tomatoes provided one of the most profitable market gardening crops. He understood that it was important to bring as much of the crop as possible to market at an early stage of the season when the price was high. An eleven-quart basket of tomatoes that reached market in the first few weeks of the field-grown crop season might sell for between one and two dollars, perhaps more; later it might bring no more than thirty or thirty-five cents. To ensure that we had a good supply of strong, well-advanced young plants ready for transplanting into the field as soon as the danger of frost had passed, Len suggested that we build a small greenhouse. The men erected one on the barn side of the gate between the house and barn yards. They pulled the older of our two brooder houses into position there to serve as a storage and entry shed and sank posts in front of it around a rectangle some twelve by twenty feet in dimension. To these they nailed board siding to a height of about three feet.

Above this foundation they erected a peaked glass roof, using long glass-filled frames of a type manufactured for use in hotbeds. Within they placed two-by-four framing on either side of a central passageway and laid boards on this so that the flats of young plants stood just below the lowermost stretch of the glass panels. About one third of the way along they set a small round stove, directing the stovepipe rising from it to the far end of the structure, where it emerged below the peak of the glass roof. During the course of each fall Len stored a supply of soil in the entry shed in preparation for transplanting seedlings into wooden flats in the early spring of the following year. Initially these flats were fish boxes that Len obtained from restaurants operating in the vicinity of the market square in London.

At first we grew a well-known variety of red tomato, the Bonnie Best, still available from seed houses today. But Len noticed that pink tomatoes sustained a higher price for longer periods than did the reds, apparently because their fruit had a higher proportion of flesh and less space devoted to seeds and fluid than did the red varieties. He purchased a basket of McMullen Pinks from a market gardener whose produce he admired, and many of our tomatoes were of this pink variety during our last years on the farm. Len started the tomato seeds on wet blotting paper in the kitchen, transplanted the sprouted seeds rather thickly into flats and, when the plants were a couple of inches in height, reset them with more generous spacing either in flats or in individual cardboard containers, where they remained until we planted them in the open field. Because of the limited size of the greenhouse, Len moved some of the plants into cotton-covered cold frames adjacent to the greenhouse during the last few weeks prior to removal to their summer location.

On a gray spring day with the dirty skeletons of snowdrifts still ranged against the farmstead fences, the greenhouse was a warm little oasis. Here I sometimes sat on a Saturday morning breathing the smell of the moist warm earth in the seedling flats and using a small wooden dibble to punch holes preparatory to setting tiny plants in the flat in front of me. In one of the market gardening years Len sometimes hired young John B. from the village to work by the day, and I remember him transplanting young tomato plants on just such a day. The brother of one of my teachers at the Lambeth Continuation School, John B. was stuck at the time between high school and a decision on what he wanted to do with his future. Meanwhile he played in a local dance band, and on one greenhouse morning he explained to me at length the merits of Guy Lombardo and the Royal Canadians. John B. was a nice young fellow and less worldly than he assumed. With great seriousness, he told me on another occasion that I should not repeat in front of my mother or sister a joke I had told him.

We began to set tomato plants in the field in late May, staggering the plantings to provide a continuous harvest until the first fall frost. In 1936, the year of full partnership between Len and George, we grew several acres of this confusing plant—botanically a berry but bearing a fruit that is used as a vegetable. We planted tomato plants in the field in a couple of ways. When the planting was to be a large one, one of the men plowed a shallow furrow with the walking plow, and we took individual plants from the flats and placed them upright against the vertical side of the furrow.

Len then threw a dollop of fertilizer beside each seedling, and when we had completed a row in this fashion, the teamster used the plow to throw a wave of dirt in and around the plants. Although this method was a relatively fast one, it required a good deal of care on the part of the plowman to prevent the horses from stepping on the seedlings. I suspect that the men planted most of our tomatoes by chopping holes for the young plants with the hoe, one man wielding it, the other dropping fertilizer into the holes and setting plants in them. Thereafter we treated the tomatoes like any other row crop, using the one-horse cultivator once or twice and following with the hoe if weeds were sprouting around the young plants. These bushed out rapidly, and after this process began they outgrew any late-starting weeds.

By early July we were eagerly watching the development of the first sets on the plants, looking for the yellowish blush that indicated the beginning of ripening. Some weeks earlier a trucker had delivered a large load of new baskets, primarily eleven-quart containers. In the first year of our emphasis on tomato growing, Len had ordered baskets without the handles attached, a strategy that gave him a discount in price. But it also meant that he had to staple handles onto the baskets at a time when there was much else to do on the farm. He decided that the savings were not worth the additional trouble and thereafter ordered complete baskets. They came from the truck in bundles of four, the end sections of two baskets tucked into the matching ends of two others, all handles overlapping in the center of the bundle.

When the tomato crop was in full harvest, picking the fruit became a social process. Three or four of us started out together from a large pile of empty baskets at one end of the field, filling baskets with ripening tomatoes and carrying out full containers to the nearest end or side of the field, where Len or George picked them up with team and wagon, or car and trailer, and took them to the house yard. In removing fruit we were careful not to damage the vines where other sets of blossoms and tomatoes were at an earlier stage of growth. Sometimes one of us came to a vine where stripped leaves and blossoms and little brown pellets of excrement on the ground marked the activity of a tomato worm.

These pests might be as much as two inches in length and as big around as a fat lead pencil. Green with black spots on the sides and with little hornlike appendages at the front, they were sometimes difficult to find in the foliage of the tomato vines. If one shook the vine gently, however, the worm usually reacted by making a chattering sound in anger or fright, which led us to the worm itself. Instead of hunkering down at the approach of danger or moving into a denser cluster of leaves, it was signaling its presence. In this respect nature betrayed the tomato worm. Some of the pickers were reluctant to detach worms from the vines—"Ooh, look at the nasty thing. I'm not going to touch that." As a result I became an expert in the art of detecting these hawkmoth larvae, pulling them from the tomato stalk, and stomping on them.

Since we used eleven-quart baskets in picking tomatoes, the work was not heavy, but it involved repetitive stooping. When we had completed the task, our hands bore a thick adhesive coating of dark green that smelled strongly of tomato vines. To remove it we had to scrub energetically using a bristle brush and plenty of strong soap.

When we brought the baskets of tomatoes from the field we placed them in the garage if the weather was threatening or under the walnut tree beside the front driveway if it was a pleasant day. Then we wiped any dirt from the tomatoes with damp rags and followed that step in preparation by final packing in the baskets. If the latter were eleven-quart rather than six-quart containers, this involved arranging the tomatoes in three layers, stem end down, with the fleshy bottoms of the top tomatoes rising slightly above the upper edge of the basket. As the packer worked, he or she selected from among the different sizes of tomatoes so that the various layers were even in thickness and the space left among the tomatoes was at a minimum. We placed greener ones in the bottom layer, since these would be the last sold by storekeepers who retailed by the pound out of the basket.

Conversation ranged widely during these cleaning and packing sessions. On a few occasions Len hired our cousins Gordon and Stan to help us prepare tomatoes for market. In my eyes they were men of the world; they had worked for a time in the automobile factories of the Detroit area and told stories of their experiences there and elsewhere. If the workers in the group were all male, some of the tales would have failed the John B. test. Indeed some, I later realized, betrayed ignorance of both geography and human anatomy. Sometimes family members carried packing sessions late into Friday evening in preparation for Saturday market day.

At 5:30 A.M. on that day Len would set out in the Model A Ford, having removed its upholstery to allow as full a load of baskets as possible, and pulling the green trailer loaded with tomatoes and other vegetables. Although Saturday was our usual market day, we were raising sufficient produce in 1936 to justify trips to market on both Saturday and Wednesday. Occasionally Len made a large sale that involved returning home and putting one or two of us into the fields to pick tomatoes to fill the order. Usually such sales were to storekeepers, but I remember one in which the buyer was the institution then known as the Insane Asylum. At that time its administrators used the labor of inmates to can fruits and vegetables for their own consumption.

In a work force composed of young people, the occasional bit of what George called tomfoolery was to be expected. At times I yielded to the temptation provided by a basket of overripe tomatoes, intended for the hog pen, to test out my hard high one in the direction of another young member of the group. In turn, I also sometimes had to duck flying fruit. George once directed a selection from his meager store of poetry in my direction: "A little nonsense now and then is relished by the best of men. But with you, you rascal, it's nonsense all the time." Highly unfair, I thought, but I worked under admonition of both George and Len that I was not to bother or irritate fellow workers.

Once we had picked our first baskets of tomatoes in July we had tomatoes in bearing thereafter throughout the summer during our market gardening years. When killing frost threatened, we pulled the vines from the last planting and brought them into the barn to save the fruit, harvesting a few baskets in this way well after subfreezing nights had destroyed most outside vegetation.

After Len joined in partnership with his father-in-law in 1937, he continued to supervise preparation of a substantial crop of tomatoes in his new location and also provided George with young plants, so that we could continue to grow this vegetable for sale on the northeast corner farm. George did not have the buyer contacts among storekeepers in London that Len had built up. I suspected that some of the fruit and vegetable peddlers took advantage of George, but he was able to sell all that we produced during our last years on the farm. The tomato plant needed only sun, adequate precipitation, and a modest amount of fertilizer to thrive in most summers. In one year of the mid-1930s, however, a combination of hot days, excessive rainfall, and high humidity encouraged blight in the crop, and the late summer picking suffered as a result, but this was the only year when we had less than a bumper crop. Some time after he had joined his father-in-law, Len confided to me that he was looking forward to the day when he could afford to drop the tomato crop and market gardening from the farm enterprise. He disliked the stoop labor and the market days involved in that branch of agriculture and wanted to concentrate on dairying and to a lesser extent on hog production.

Although tomatoes were our largest market gardening crop, Len was determined to make the operation a profitable one, and he planted a sequence of crops that provided a continuous flow of marketable produce from the early summer into the late fall and even during the winter months. In the 1936 season we harvested head lettuce, yellow pencil pod snap beans, cabbages, sweet corn, potatoes, cucumbers, pepper squash, Hubbard squash, green peppers, and eggplant as well as raspberries and red kidney beans. Eggplant was a new vegetable to us, and Eleta prepared some for the family table, where it met a cool reception. She had failed to marinate the slices in salt water before cooking them. An area of muck soil stretched into the north side of the small field from the swampy part of the lower pasture, and Len decided to try celery there. The attempt was unsuccessful. The stalks of the mature plants tasted like celery, but under our care they failed to blanch properly.

Asparagus was a profitable crop and Len planned to develop a large patch. He planted a substantial quantity of seed in a foot-wide row beside the raspberry patch and kept the little seedlings weeded during the course of the 1935 growing year. The next spring we planted them in rows in a small field developed between the old orchard and the woodlot. During the rest of the growing season we allowed the little plants to grow unhindered by the knife, and they were well enough established to accept light cutting by the following year. By then Len had left, but we sold asparagus from this planting until we left the farm in 1939.

We had always grown potatoes for domestic consumption and sometimes for sale. In 1936 we planted patches at different times to produce early and later harvests. The first step in planting was to cut the seed potatoes into sections, ensuring that each section included an eye on the skin surface. From there the young sprout would issue. Next we dumped the seed potatoes in a large barrel that contained a bath of water and formaldehyde. This treatment prevented the later growth of scab on the tubers. In planting we again used one of the teams on the walking plow to make shallow furrows, into which we dropped pieces of seed potato at the correct intervals.

Thus far danger in the production of potatoes was limited to the possibility of cut thumbs or fingers while the seed was being prepared and to the hazards attendant on working with horses. But when the potato vines had begun to change into dark green clumps of stalk and leaf, small yellow and black spotted beetles made their appearance, accompanied by orange and black spotted larvae—Colorado potato beetles and their offspring. Len answered that threat by mixing arsenate of lead with slaked lime and shaking the mixture onto the vines through the bottom of a flour sack or pillowcase. Usually there was a breeze, and a white plume of airborne lime and arsenate of lead powder floated out behind him. Following Len's protracted bout with sinus and antrum infection, our doctor had advised him to get a good tan, and he usually went shirtless during much of the time that he worked in the fields. I sometimes saw his sweaty torso caked white with poisonous dust at the conclusion of a session of potato dusting. Had he continued in this type of farm economy year after year, these occasions surely would have undermined his health. On the farm even so innocuous a process as growing potatoes might have a dangerous side.

A potato patch in full white bloom was a beautiful sight, symbolizing both the esthetics of agriculture and the green of dollars in the pocket some weeks in the future. It also brought an anticipatory stir of taste buds because the first serving of new potatoes and peas that Eleta prepared in white sauce was always an early summer event. She shared our eagerness and sometimes moved the date forward by going to the potato patch and stealing a few potatoes from the side of promising hills before the plants were quite ready for digging.

The market gardening phase of our farm history was in some ways more interesting than the dairying and general farming years that preceded it. There were new crops to understand, to watch as they matured, and to harvest in the company of off-farm workers. The gardening activity, however, increased the amount of hoeing to be done, and this was not one of my favorite occupations, although it was light work. It also left me with one of my most vivid recollections of Len during those years. One afternoon I was assigned to hoe in the potato patch behind the barn. Adjacent to the potatoes was a stand of sweet corn in the small field beside the lower pasture. Quack grass always threatened row crops in the lower end of that field, and when Len returned from market he decided to attack the new sprouts of that pestiferous weed in the corn with the one-horse cultivator.

Horse power, he decided, would be provided by his thirteen-dollar standardbred mare, Winnie Mae. Much fonder of standing in the stable or under a tree in the lower pasture than working, Winnie came dancing down the headland past the potato patch pulling the green-painted cultivator on its side, Len striding alongside with one hand on the upper cultivator handle and Winnie's reins already knotted behind his waist. To this my hoe companion and I paid little attention, but soon we realized that cultivator protocol was under challenge.

Winnie was balking as Len tried to direct her between the first rows of sweet corn. "GET UP WINNIE," Len said, his voice beginning to rise. Then he slapped Winnie's flank with one side of the lines. In answer Winnie reared on her hind legs and did a little jig, coming down with her front feet on one row of corn. "DAMMIT WINNIE, YOU ARE GOING TO WORK THIS AFTERNOON."

Then he slapped her rump with both lines and Winnie plunged forward. We never knew if Winnie had ever been on a racetrack or if she had had any sulky training, but that afternoon she was determined to show that she was no plow horse—plodding calmly along ahead of the cultivator was not for her. After he had pulled out a couple of yards of corn plants with the careening cultivator, Len managed to bring Winnie down to a fast indignant walk, her head tossing, her nostrils flared. She was snorting like a 2:20 pacer coming down the stretch on a fairgrounds oval. Behind her Len followed at a half trot, the cultivator aimed midway between the rows and the small outer shovels throwing waves of dirt around the bases of the corn plants. It was the fastest bit of cultivation done on the farm that summer, and we in the potato patch thoroughly enjoyed our front-row view.

In some years Len stored a late crop of cabbages for winter sale. But the crop that he marketed most consistently during the winter months was red kidney beans. In mid- or late fall when the bean vines and pods had died down, Len pulled the beans by hand, sometimes helped by George, placing them in little piles in the field. After they had dried further for a few days, he forked them onto the wagon and hauled them to the upper barn, where he pitched them into an empty mow or piled them in a corner of the drive floor. On Friday afternoons during the winter, he swept the chaff off a section of the heavy planks of the barn floor. After throwing some forkfuls of bean vines on this area, he attacked the pile with a wooden flail. This he had constructed from two pieces of slender sapling, joining them together with a length of leather bootlace that he threaded through holes bored in the sapling ends. After he had flailed out a couple of bushels of beans he bagged them and carried them to the kitchen.

At this point there were still pieces of stem and leaf, small hardened chunks of dirt, and even little rocks mixed with the beans. That evening after the men had finished the milking and other barn chores, he dumped a pile of beans on the middle of the kitchen table, and we were all expected to sit down with a saucepan or kettle in our laps and clean beans in preparation for marketing them in London on the following morning. Home from school on Friday afternoon and with two free days ahead of me, I considered that night to be a liberty night, a night when I might go skating if there were good ice in the neighborhood, or failing that, a time when I might read the fiction I had brought home from the school or public library. Being required to forgo these delights and clean beans was refined torture.

During our first years on the northeast corner farm while the men placed major emphasis on dairying, we did not use much hired help. This was not perhaps George's wish. One spring he obtained a young Dane at the Ontario Employment Agency in London, a blond, clean-cut young fellow, fresh from Europe. I thought him very interesting because he knew only a few words of English. He would sit at the kitchen table with his dictionaries and sound out the English names of pieces of cutlery and other objects in the kitchen, telling me their Danish equivalents. George had hired him by the month, and after four weeks he asked to have his wages increased from the twenty-five dollars per month and board that George was paying him. George responded that he was not prepared to teach a man English and also pay him the going wage for experienced farm laborers. To my disappointment the young Dane packed his suitcase and George returned him to the employment agency. George replaced him with a young Yorkshireman and had a similar experience. I found the Englishman much less friendly than the Dane. I also found him to be almost equally incomprehensible, although the young man believed that we were somewhat obtuse because we had difficulty understanding him. For the first time I began to understand some of the significance of national and regional origins.

We used considerable hired help during the mid-1930s when deeply involved in market gardening. On various occasions George and Len hired men by the month at the office of the Ontario Employment Agency in London, but they never found workers who were willing to settle in for the whole summer. George and Len rose at 5:30 or 6:00 A.M. and brought in the cows and milked them before breakfast at 7:30. If a hired man was sleeping in the bedroom off the kitchen, they called him and set him to hoeing until breakfast time. Normal field work on the farm halted at around five o'clock, with supper at six, although picking might continue until a few minutes before that time. After eating we milked the cows, attended to the related barn chores, and turned the horses into the night or lower pasture. It was a long day and few hired men were prepared to work such hours. Nor was George a congenial employer. He did not hector, nor was he abusive, but he did stand on his dignity, did not like to be called by his first name, and made little effort to be friendly with hired help. In 1936 one man stuck it out for two months and then decided he had had enough. Oddly this man turned up a year or so later in the employ of one of George's good friends in the county Holstein-Friesian Breeders' Association—using a slightly different name.

Our experience with another man whom George hired at the employment agency was even less satisfactory. Hired in the summer, Tom R. soon showed signs of work aversion and began to visit young members of the family on the southeast corner who followed a relaxed work regime. Unwittingly I contributed to an incident that strained relations between employers and employee and forecast the end of Tom's days on the farm. One morning Len assigned Tom, Melvin C. from the northwest corner farm, and me to work in a patch of potatoes that needed a final hoeing before the plants were beyond danger from encroaching weeds. The planting occupied an acre or so at the east end of our middle field, running a distance of some two hundred yards from the road to the edge of the woodlot. While we were companionably hoeing our first rows, Tom announced that we would take a five-minute rest at each side of the field.

Once this arrangement had been in effect for a while, it seemed to me that we were spending a great deal of our time sitting down, engaged in pointless—and to me boring—conversation. Full of energy and competitive cussedness, I leaped up in the middle of one of Tom's ordained breaks, declared, "To heck with you guys," and hoed away at full speed. When Len arrived at the patch in midmorning to war on the potato beetles with an application of poison dust, I was a couple of rows ahead of my former companions. This led to a conference between George and Len. Should something be done about the situation? Better not precipitate an incident, they agreed. They did, however, remove me from the potato-field crew and put me on another job. But Tom's tendency to malinger or swing the lead—as George would say—was duly noted.

A few days later Len hired another worker at the employment agency; Tom immediately took the fellow under his wing, and when the two worked together they accomplished very little. Matters rapidly came to a head. After a morning when Tom's mind had obviously been elsewhere, George told him the afternoon's work would be on the Bostwick fifty, where a field of hay was ready for hauling into the barn. In the kitchen George announced that there would be sweat on Tom's shirt at suppertime. Tom was not present, but perhaps one of the other helpers passed along the word. Immediately after lunch Tom and the new hand left for the neighbors' place, where family members were playing ball in the orchard. George delivered them back to the employment agency later that afternoon.

We had much better luck with short-term workers from Lambeth or the neighborhood. Johnny B. lived in the village with his widowed mother and several school-teaching sisters and was available by the day during much of one season. We also obtained daily help in Lambeth, where a young woman and a middle-aged spinster were willing to help out when the market gardening work threatened to swamp us. A member of the county road crew lived somewhat farther down the North Talbot Road, and his younger son was sometimes available for a half or full day of work, as was one of Fora Cornell's sons. The new owner of the Pringle farm had three adult sons, and the youngest of these worked for us for a number of weeks, as did one of the sons in the Sadler family. Len heard of young people in a St. Thomas family who were willing to do gardening work and from that source obtained the services of a young man and his sister for several weeks during the summer of 1936.

The fathers of a couple of the neighbor lads who worked for us maintained milking herds, and their sons could milk, a skill that was useful when Len stayed at the market in the evening or when the business of the county Holstein-Friesian Breeders' Association took George away from home. One of these men was rough with the cattle; when old Madolyn was slow to leave the barnyard for the night pasture, he threw a stick at her and broke off one of her horns. Our herd sire of the time was growing increasingly surly, and we detected this lad hitting him on the muzzle with a fork handle when the bull shoved his nose into the feed alley through a gap in the perimeter posts of his box stall. Such incidents confirmed George's opinion that hired men were best kept away from the herd.

The Great Depression still gripped southwestern Ontario during the years 1934–36, and we invariably passed half a dozen or more young men and the occasional older one at intervals on the roadside at the outer edge of London when we returned home on Highway 2 after marketing or shopping in the city. Some had battered suitcases at their feet. Others had rolled up their possessions in a blanket and tied the bundle together with a piece of rope, and a few carried only the clothes on their backs. Some displayed their destination on a cardboard sign; others merely waved a thumb at approaching vehicles. Sometimes Len gave such hitchhikers a ride when returning from market, and he brought home a couple who had expressed an interest in finding work. Our experience with them was more satisfactory than with men obtained through the government employment agency. They worked conscientiously for us for a week or so and then took their wages and amicably went on their way.

One of them interested me a great deal. A man in his high thirties or early forties, Harry carried tattoos on both upper arms and was quiet and well-spoken. That summer a family that included a boy named Don M., a couple of years my senior, lived in the house across the North Talbot Road from our lower pasture, and Don occasionally dropped in to visit me. One evening he and I were trying to juggle green walnuts picked from the tree in our front yard. Work completed for the day, Harry walked by and picked up not three walnuts—our attainable maximum—but five, and he casually maintained all of them in the air at the same time. One Sunday afternoon, he asked for a pencil and paper and proceeded to draw a freehand portrait that faithfully reproduced the features of a woman pictured in the weekend edition of the newspaper, while giving me a few sketching tips in the process.

When my school-teacher sister returned to the house one evening from delivering a telephone message to George at the barn, Harry held open the gate between the house and barnyard for her. That mannerly gesture, she told Len, marked Harry as a most unusual addition to our work force. Unlike some of the hired men who liked to talk, Harry never volunteered any information about himself or his background, and after a fortnight he told us that he must move on. He pocketed his wages and departed, leaving us to wonder why a man with such unusual talents was on the road.

The Cornell brothers, who specialized in growing tree fruits and raspberries, sometimes used Native American laborers from the Oneida Indian reservation to pick their fruit. One day as a group of us were cleaning and packing tomatoes under the walnut tree on our front lawn, a stout, elderly Indian man walked up the drive and inquired for the owner. His name, he said, was Kenyon George, and he explained that he was trying to locate hoeing or picking work for his family. At the time, our new stand of raspberries needed hoeing. We agreed that his family could take on the job. They appeared the next day in two dilapidated cars: George, a blue-eyed son-in-law named Ireland, his wife, and several sons, daughters, and in-laws piled out of the vehicles armed with short-handled hoes and attacked the weeds in the berry patch. Twice in later years they wished to pick the berries for us when the crop was at full ripening, and on these occasions they asked to be allowed to overnight at our place. They were accompanied by a handsome young man, one of the Ireland sons, who sat in the shade or stayed with their cars while the others worked. He was blind, we discovered—the aftermath, others told us, of a binge in which he drank liquor spiked with battery acid, suffered convulsions, and lost his eyesight.

The accommodations that members of the George/Ireland family accepted for sleeping purposes would have horrified any official charged with supervision of migrant labor accommodations. One year they occupied our garage, and another time they took over the brooder house from which the chicks of that year had graduated to the henhouse some weeks earlier. They looked after their own sanitary needs. In bargaining with them, Len and George asked what they charged and, finding it reasonable, agreed to hire them without further haggling. The group hoed clean and picked clean, as the men put it, and all parties to the agreements were satisfied. None in our family expressed thoughts about the status of the Indians or hinted at the pathos and tragedy in their history. My own attitude was one of curiosity in a mind shaped by readings of Ernest Thompson Seton's *Two Little Savages*, a couple of novels by James Fenimore Cooper, and some of the verse of Pauline Johnson, the famous Indian poetess whom Eleta admired.

I have already described my roles in the care of the dairy herd and in the cultivation and harvesting of the field crops. From 1934 onward I was expected to help with the market gardening when there was work to be done. I was never paid for my time, or by the box in the case of raspberries and strawberries, as were the day workers from Lambeth and the immediate neighborhood. In two of those years, Len explained that my pay would come in the form of receipts from specialty crops that he planted for me: one year my returns were to come from a wide row of pickling onions, and in the other I was to become rich on the proceeds from several rows of popcorn. Both enterprises proved minor fiascos. The row of onions produced only one basket of little white globes, which made trip after trip to market, Len reducing the price week by week, until finally a purchaser was found who was willing to pay a dollar or two for it. None was willing to buy my ears of popcorn, and after popping some of the kernels, we agreed that the judgment of the market was probably correct.

I was not very money conscious at this stage of my life, and I cannot remember complaining about the fact that I received no specific wages. When the family went to a place of entertainment, Eleta or George usually provided me with pocket money without protest. I knew that some of the village boys received allowances, and I envied them, but I heard so much family talk about low agricultural prices and the depression that I apparently believed that such an arrangement was impossible on the farm. Eleta did help me establish a bank account at the Market Square Branch of the Bank of Montreal in London, but I had little to put in it.

Occasionally in the summer I accompanied Len to market in London, always an interesting experience and so diverting that he found me of little use as stand tender and salesperson. Covent Garden Market was a paved rectangle subdivided by sidewalks, driveways, and buildings, located on the northeast corner at the intersection of Talbot and King Streets. About two-thirds of a block to the north of this junction, Market Lane provided the northern boundary and after paralleling King Street for most of a block it looped southward to form the eastern boundary of the market square. Beyond Market Lane a rim of business buildings fronted on Talbot, Dundas, and Richmond Streets. These last two thoroughfares were London's major east-west and north-south business arteries. Facing Talbot Street was the branch of the Bank of Montreal where we had accounts and above which our lawyers, Messrs. Fraser and Thompson, had their offices. Adjacent and running through from Market Lane to Dundas Street were Cowan's Hardware and the establishment of the Ontario Trust Company.

A narrow street called Market Alley ran out to Dundas Street next to the Trust Company. In a cubbyhole on the other side of the alley was a little newsstand and tobacco shop where we bought copies of the *Saturday Evening Post* and Len's favorite periodical, the *American Magazine*. Next and running through to the market from Dundas Street was Woolworth's five-and-dime, and then came Smallman and Ingram's big department store. This enclosing rampart of buildings terminated at the intersection of Richmond and King Streets with an office building where the Ontario Department of Agriculture maintained offices on the second floor. Leaving this building and proceeding west along King Street with the market on our right, one came first to a brick and stone building that Eleta called the "comfort station." Beyond ran a covered walkway, at right angles to our path and ending at Market Lane. The roof of the walkway extended outward to cover the stands of market gardeners and fruit growers who rented their locations on a yearly basis. Partway up toward Woolworth's was the fruit stand of Stan Cornell, and at the far end George's cousin Bill sold fruit and other products that he trucked in from the Leamington and Niagara districts.

Next as we walked west on King Street's market front we came to the handsome brick market building where Eleta sold her poultry and dairy products. Paralleling the market building on the west side was a series of three sidewalks and two driveways, all the sidewalks lined by stall spaces that the city also rented out on a yearly basis. For several years we leased space on the east side of the last of these crosswalks, one stand up from King Street. Just beyond the stands that lined this walk on both sides lay the City Scales, a small building adjacent to King Street consisting of a little office and a drive-through large enough to allow the passage of loads of hay. Supporting its plank flooring was the scale used to weigh loads of livestock feed or bedding. Beyond this structure was a square area of blacktop uncrossed by concrete sidewalks; here occasional vendors set up stands on a one-day basis to sell whatever they had to offer. They displayed the usual kinds of fruits and vegetables but often quite different products as well—litters of farm pups, live poultry, fingers of cured tobacco leaves, or loads of hay.

In the summer, trucks and cars and the occasional horse-drawn vehicle were pulling into the market square by six o'clock in the morning and growers were beginning to set up their stands for the day. Len arrived at about that time, driving the Model A and, at the height of the growing season, pulling the green trailer. There was room for one vehicle in our space; when he took the trailer he found parking for the car on a nearby street. At the stand he set out a foundation of lettuce or citrus crates and laid boards over these to serve as a foundation for baskets of tomatoes, beans, cucumbers, potatoes, and pepper squash and the piles of sweet corn ears and lettuce that he spread out for examination by potential buyers.

Len emphasized that it was important to be at the market early because most of the wholesale trade with storekeepers was completed in time to allow them to return to their businesses and to add their purchases to stock on display before their local customers began to arrive. Mingling in the first crowd of potential buyers at the market square were a number of street peddlers, some with trucks and a few with pushcarts. Len called the members of a third group of potential buyers the hucksters; they maintained stands on the major routes through the market, often under the covered north-south walkway or in a similar structure running at right angles beyond the north end of the big market building. Although some hucksters grew produce of their own, they also tried to stock their stands with fruits and vegetables purchased at wholesale or bargain prices elsewhere in the market. Others survived solely on the spread between the cost of their purchases at the market and the markup at which they resold the produce.

Len tried to set our prices by taking a quick walk around in the market to learn what others were charging. Storekeeper buyers who purchased more than one basket of tomatoes, or some basic unit of other produce, expected some reduction in price, and there was often haggling about the size of such discounts, particularly by the peddlers. Two of the latter, one with a badly repaired harelip and the other with a squint eye, bargained very aggressively. Len seldom sold these men anything, but their tactics profited them. By 1939, our last year of selling tomatoes, both men had left the ranks of the pushcart peddlers and had their own stores. George sold tomatoes on several occasions to the one with the sinister squint. I suspected that he lost some dollars by doing so. Len did not cut prices in order to do business with the hucksters; although their locations on the market square were superior to ours near the City Scales, our situation was good enough and our products of sufficient quality, he believed, to sell without sharing profits with that category of buyer. Len was anxious, however, to develop his contacts with some of the grocery storekeepers who maintained large vegetable and fruit departments. One whose store was situated on the Wharncliffe Road sometimes bought as many as a dozen eleven-quart baskets of tomatoes at a time, and Len sweetened transactions of this kind by delivering the purchase to the store.

Those first few hours on a summer market day were almost indescribably exciting to me—cars and trucks turning off King and Talbot Streets into the various market square driveways, horns blaring and echoing off the backs of the buildings along Dundas and Richmond; the slam of car doors, the bang and rattle of end gates, the thud of crates and baskets being dropped on the pavement; peddlers shouting from the street to helpers or stand proprietors; and the footsteps and conversation of the buyers as they hurried along the walkways, anxious to make their purchases and return to their own businesses. All these discordant sounds combined to raise the noise to a level that was almost painful to young country ears. By nine o'clock in the morning the wholesale purchasers were gone, and on Saturdays the flow of housewives and householders along the sidewalks of the market had begun. We came to recognize regulars in these hours as well, particularly those who tried to drive hard bargains. One was a corpulent middle-aged man who always carried a string mesh shopping bag and an umbrella. I imagined him to be German in origin because he had a waxed black mustache with twisted points standing out for an inch or two on either side of his mouth.

Occasionally someone tried to barter goods in payment for our produce. Most memorable among them was the editor of the *Farmer's Advocate*, a respected agricultural journal, and we renewed our subscription in this way on a couple of occasions. I believe we paid for a subscription to the *Canadian Countryman* in the same way, a journal in which I enjoyed "The Song of the Lazy Farmer," doggerel celebrating the wrong way to do things on the farm. Sometimes Saturday market day lasted well into the evening and if I was there, Len sent me across King Street to one of a couple of Chinese restaurants for a meal. The proprietors of these establishments charged me twenty-five cents for a three-course dinner—soup, entrée, dessert, and coffee—or thirty-five cents if I decided to have steak for my main course.

Covent Garden Market square focused our off-farm interests quite remarkably. We were more frequently in Lambeth, drawn by the co-op store, drugstore, church, schools, library, blacksmith shop, Ford garage, doctor, and barbershop, but much of our income came from the market square. Although George maintained a small account at the Royal Bank in Lambeth, he did most of his banking at the Bank of Montreal branch facing Talbot Street and the market square. In addition to serving our needs, the members of the Fraser and Thompson law firm also provided at their offices above the bank legal services for the co-op store in Lambeth. We bought much of our hardware at Cowan's Hardware store, magazines at the newsstand in Market Alley, small household items at Woolworth's, and candy from that store's vast stretch of glass-fronted bins. When I was a preschoooler my oldest sister introduced me to the raptures of a banana split at Woolworth's soda fountain. We purchased clothing and shoes at Smallman and Ingram's and other stores on Dundas Street. Kingsmill's was particularly interesting because the clerks placed our money in containers that were carried on elevated tracks to a cashier sitting on a balcony at the back of the store.

In the office building on the east side of the square, beside King Street, we climbed to the second-floor suite of the ag rep, Keith Riddle, where the board of the Middlesex County Holstein-Friesian Breeders' Association met and where the Holstein-Friesian Calf Club held its organizational meeting each year. The Middlesex Creamery was located on a street adjacent to the market square, and there George sold the week's accumulation of sweet cream during the mid-and late 1930s, except when Eleta was making butter. When we had one of our animals butchered, we stored the cuts in a freezer locker at an establishment close to the square.

The London market even served as backdrop for a family romance. After some tentative relationships with other young women, Len's attention fixed upon a pert and pretty young lady whose parents farmed on the Talbot Road south of Lambeth and who marketed a variety of farm produce from a location close to ours on the market square.

The Canadian wholesale price index number for animals and their products fell by 9 percent during 1930 as compared with the preceding year. Prices dropped more sharply yet during 1931, averaging out that year at 25 percent below 1930 prices. They continued to skid downward in 1932, dropping by another 19 percent. During 1933 they held at about the same level and then began to rise slowly, to stabilize during the last years of the decade at levels some 30 percent below that of 1929. By the early 1930s the optimism that Bill Topping and George had shared when they entered into their real estate transactions of the late 1920s had faded. Farmers who derived a major part of their income from livestock were facing severe depression. In our case the situation was probably complicated by the bills stemming from Eleanor's death and by Len's illness. Much to Eleta's annoyance, George did not assume Len's doctor bills, requiring Len to pay these himself; but the illness, of course, deprived George of help on the farm.

Both George and Len would have preferred to concentrate their efforts on the dairy enterprise, although George was past fifty years old when we moved to the northeast corner farm and sometimes complained about the way in which a milking herd tied its owner down—"Twice a day without fail, rain or shine, sick or well, those cows have to be milked."

Enrolled in Stanley Warren's course in farm management at Cornell University some years later, I realized that our farm operation had not been large enough to produce an adequate income as a dairy farm, even though George supplemented the 125 acres in some years by finding rental pasture for the young cattle and dry cows during the summer months. That our cattle were purebreds may have enhanced income somewhat, but the buyers seeking replacements for the milking herds of New York and Michigan seldom offered more than a hundred dollars for a young cow. Such animals usually sold for less than this and "springer" heifers—that is, well advanced toward first freshening—fetched even less. Market gardening involved more intensive use of the farm, and Len proved that it could pay. (For more detail about the economic environment in which George and Len worked, see appendix 2.)

Whether dairying or market gardening, we were at the mercy of the weather, pests, animal and plant disease, and developments that could only be termed bad luck. As we have seen, roup decimated Eleta's poultry flock, and dogs killed almost half her geese one year. Newly freshened cows sometimes contracted garget or milk fever, as the men called it. Although our herd as a whole tested negative for brucellosis, two animals aborted their calves. One of these, Donabelle, our greatest success in the show ring, repeatedly failed to conceive and lost her calf months short of term when she finally did. A big handsome animal, so quiet and friendly that we could set a child on her back while she was standing in the field, she finally went to the stockyards as a beef animal, mourned by everyone in the family. In my third year in the calf club, one of the three heifer calves that we thought might produce a show animal died of congestion of the lungs; or at least that was the veterinarian's diagnosis.

Even successful deliveries were sometimes disappointing. Breeders preferred that all calves be heifers, and in this respect our luck was about average, the ratio close to fifty:fifty. One of Len's cows, however, dropped a fine heifer calf that was promising in every respect except that it was red and white. At that time the Holstein-Friesian breed registry refused to recognize such calves. Given the size of her midriff—barrel, we called it—another cow appeared to be carrying twins as she neared freshening, and so she was. But when she had safely delivered the calves, George reported sadly, "A freemartin, what wretched luck!" As mentioned, in such cases the female in the pair was always infertile. Two winters later George had her butchered for family beef.

The summer of 1934 was dry during a crucial period of the growing season, and our yields of both hay and small grains were far below normal expectations. When winter closed in and the cattle began their winter confinement, Len said to me, "It's going to be a hungry winter for them this year."

That winter the men tried to stretch out the supplies of feed by substituting a manger full of straw for one of the two daily feedings of hay that the cattle received in normal winters along with feedings of field corn. By the time spring recess arrived at the continuation school in mid-April, the stock of feed at the barn had dwindled to the point that there was barely enough hay left to carry the horses through their spring work. To send the cows into the pastures on the home place or at the Bostwick fifty would cut off the grass before it had a fair start. However, the ditches were beginning to green along the side road and the Bostwick Road, and there were also clumps of the previous year's growth that had dried on the stem. George banished my thoughts of a holiday devoted to reading or other recreation by decreeing that I was in charge of the cows for the next two weeks and that we would pasture them in the ditches between our two properties.

There were pickings for the hungry cows along the roads but not enough for them to settle down to contented grazing. They kept on the move and tried to explore every gateway and open fence gap between our barnyard and the gate at the Bostwick fifty. Sometimes I used my bicycle and sometimes I merely walked or trotted after and around the cattle. It was too cold to read a book, and when I settled down briefly on a sunny bank in one of the side-road ditches, a cow would walk resolutely out ahead of the herd, her eyes fixed intently on an open gate ahead. Then it was time to get up ahead of the herd and move all the cows into the ditch opposite the gate—some spring break, thought I. The younger members of the group were particularly venturesome, fast footed, and annoying. Along the mile and a half of roads between our farmyard gate and the Bostwick fifty there were only two farmsteads, well separated. As a result this stretch of road had become a favorite spot for evening drinkers, perhaps all the more so because a reputed bootlegger occupied a second house at the Dale farm. Always alert for economies in the depression years, Eleta had begun to preserve tomato juice in old liquor bottles, and while our cows were sweeping the roadsides clear of new grass in the spring of 1935, I cleared them of glass containers on my mother's behalf.

George and Len were experienced farmers, and Len attended some of the winter short courses that the ag rep organized for junior farmers. The ag rep's office was well stocked with bulletins prepared by the staff at the Ontario Agricultural College, and Len read some of those that dealt with garden crops. (Eleta brought home one dealing with bee culture, but I suspect this reflected curiosity rather than serious interest in establishing a colony of honey makers.) If dairying had its dangers, market gardening had pitfalls also, but we had no outright disasters in producing any of the crops we planted during the mid-1930s. Potato bugs and cucumber beetles appeared but were kept in check with timely applications of poison, and as described, blight struck our late tomatoes one year, reducing the yield. In general, however, we were fortunate in our production of market garden crops.

We viewed the misadventures of our last neighbors on the southeast corner, the Newcomers, with sympathy but also with some smugness. Pringle, the gentleman farmer, had been slow to submit his herd to tuberculin testing, and when he did, the veterinarian of the Ontario Department of Agriculture identified a number of reactors. Pringle's herdsman obtained permission to keep these animals for a time in Bill Topping's stable as he and his family were preparing to move into Lambeth. When the cattle went to slaughter, no one bothered to fumigate the stable. Shortly after taking over the southeast corner farm, Newcomer purchased a small herd of milking cows and young animals. He housed them in the area of the barn where Pringle's reactors had been kept. After a time he had the animals tested for TB and they tested positive. Before this herd in turn went to slaughter, one of the cows bloated, an occurrence that never happened on our farm during my years because of the care we exercised in grazing our cattle on forage crops that might produce bloat.

Newcomer planted an apple orchard, two rows of young trees stretching across the forty-rod width of his farm between the first two fields beyond his barnyard. Unfortunately, he did not encircle the lower trunks of the young trees with a protective coating of rodent-repellent paper and close-mesh chicken wire. Field mice or rabbits girdled every tree during the new orchard's first winter. After we had demonstrated that tomatoes were a profitable crop, Newcomer planted a considerable patch one year. His plants, however, had been started late, and that was the year when weather conditions encouraged the spread of blight in the late crop. Newcomer's rows of tomatoes were not spared.

In later years my cousin Gordon remarked that the agricultural depression of the 1930s was not nearly as disastrous in our area as in some parts of the United States. This I believe was true; there were not great numbers of foreclosures along the North Talbot Road. But the hard times did have impact. Pringle's hobby farm operation came to an end. Bill Topping was forced to give up farming and move into Lambeth with his family, where he and one of his sons took jobs on the county road crew. Depression-level prices for agricultural products contributed to George's decision to resell the farm on the Fifth Concession Road.

The farmer who succeeded Bill T. on the southeast corner farm did experience the ignominy of foreclosure. Jim M. came from a long-established family in the Brick Street neighborhood and had some farming experience. His son, Andy, was a pleasant young man who played long games of rummy with Len at our kitchen table on winter Sunday afternoons while we were neighbors. Jim and Andy worked hard. They were careful to ensure that Andy spread every forkful of manure from their barnyard on their fields, and Len believed that their stay on the farm had improved its fertility. But they could not satisfy their creditors. One morning in the late fall, George came into the kitchen and announced that the sheriff had stopped neighbor Jim on the side road leading to the Bostwick Road as he took his horses toward a relative's farm. The officer ordered Jim to return the horses to their stable, where they were subject to legal process, as were Jim's other farm chattels.

Some months later I stood in the back doorway of the house that we had once occupied on the southeast corner and listened to Ike Brooks, a farmer-auctioneer from the Second Concession Road, offer the farm at foreclosure sale. Ike warmed up the crowd with a string of jokes, interspersed with some squirts of tobacco juice—he was a notorious chewer—and then asked for bids. He got a few, including one from Fred M., the young farmer who had purchased the fifty acres situated south of the southeast corner farm several years earlier. But Fred's offer was insufficient to cover the reserve that the bank officers had placed, and their institution held the property until Newcomer purchased it the following spring.

NINE

Neighborhood and Family

The origins of the North Talbot Road neighborhood in which I grew up during the 1930s reached back into the first half of the nineteenth century. David and John Bogue Jr. were not patentees of the Crown; their father had purchased the title to the Bogue lands on the North Talbot Road in the early 1850s, and by that time many of the original settlers had left the area. From its earliest beginnings the neighborhood was in a constant state of replacement and renewal, down to and including the period of my recollections. George was born in 1879 and the *Illustrated Historical Atlas of the County of Middlesex* published that year lists many farm occupants along our road whose names were unknown to me except, perhaps, as characters in George's occasional reminiscing. Of the five families who occupied holdings in 1878 within the skewed rectangle bounded by the North Talbot Road, Second Concession Road, Bostwick Road, and Dale's Side Road, only the Dale family remained in the 1930s.

Elsewhere along the North Talbot Road, Cornells, Vanstones, Kilbournes, and Sadlers were still present in addition to Bogues. Interspersed among their farms were those of families who were not represented in the neighborhood when the *Atlas* of 1878 appeared. When we stopped farming at the end of the 1939 crop year, only one other member of our threshing ring could trace his family history in the neighborhood back to the 1870s. Three families in the ring became members during the 1930s. Children of the old residents had found opportunities in adjacent rural neighborhoods, on the new lands of the prairie provinces, in Lambeth or other local villages, and in the city. Household heads grew old and retired to Lambeth or died childless or, more commonly, lacking children who wished to take over the farm.

When farmers left a location and moved to another, it did not necessarily mean, as some historians have assumed, that they had failed where they were. Of course that was sometimes the case, but more often it involved a belief in and impulse toward bettering the family's economic position. George, for example, moved to a different farm on several occasions during his life, always in the belief that the new location would benefit him. Three of the farms he occupied lay within a mile of his father's place. Activity of this sort moved others out of their home neighborhoods, as the Fifth Concession purchase would have done for Len had he not become ill. In lecturing to the students in the course in farm management that I took at Cornell University, Professor Stanley Warren suggested that young men could obtain control of a farm most quickly by marrying the only child of a farmer. Although George would have liked to continue working with Len, the course Len took was a partnership with his father-in-law to increase his resources until he was able to buy a farm of his own on the Sixth Concession Road, well outside his home neighborhood. This was not quite the story that Warren had in mind, but single daughter and father-in-law did play important roles in Len and Irene's progression to full farm ownership.

While some families shared common neighborhood memories with others along the road and had a well-developed sense of place, others did not. Rather, the newer arrivals shared with the older families the sense that they were rural dwellers, deriving their sustenance from agricultural crops and animals in a common setting of soils and climate, although even in these latter respects there was a good deal of variation and exercise of special knowledge and skills. George and Len would have had no idea of how to care for the two dozen or so goats that occupied the Colemans' front pasture on the old Pringle farm while that family was producing goat's milk for the patients in the tuberculosis sanatorium at Byron. Our neighbors had no idea of the special knack involved in growing large quantities of tomatoes.

The celebrated economist and Canadian expatriate John K. Galbraith once wrote that "on coming on any form of organized activity . . . our first instinct is to inquire who is in charge." As part of Westminster Township, our neighborhood lay under the authority of the township council, headed by the reeve, and that body was in turn subordinate to the county council. During the mid-1920s George was once nominated for the position of township deputy reeve but lost out to Billy B., who lived north of the Second Concession Road on a side road leading into Byron. George showed little interest in township affairs thereafter. Until there was a reorganization of road control during the mid-1930s, however, George was a kind of road captain, supervising the conditions of Dale's Side Road running back to the Bostwick Road, and for some years he hitched a three-horse team to a road drag provided by the township and scraped that road into some semblance of smoothness as it dried out after its spring sogginess. I also remember once going with him when he threw a shovel into the car and followed a convoy of teams and wagons carrying gravel in rectangular wooden gravel boxes down the side road. The wagon drivers dumped their gravel by turning the narrow planks in the floor of the wagon box on edge, raising the rear end gate, and driving forward until all the gravel had spilled onto the road. George used his shovel to spread it evenly on the roadbed. It was the last time that hauling gravel for the side road was a horse-and-wagon operation before the town and county switched completely to the use of auto dump trucks in road maintenance. Transfer of responsibility into professional hands did not, however, ensure a weatherproof road surface. On a Saturday afternoon in the early spring of 1938 a disheveled gentleman knocked at our kitchen door and asked for help in extricating his car, which had sunk to its axles on the side road. Pomp and Prince showed their worth and I became five dollars richer.

Although the hand of local government rested lightly upon us and our neighbors, we were for a time much interested in the school board that administered the public school of School Section 17. All four of the children in our family attended this two-room brick school located at the intersection of the Third Concession Road with the North Talbot Road, half a mile south of Lambeth and three quarters of a mile distant from our corner to the north. George was a member of the school board when I was in the senior second class, my final year in the junior room of the school. The principal at this time was an inexperienced young man, and a group of boys in the senior fourth class began to test his authority. His efforts to assert control led to further challenges and the development of anarchy in the senior room. The board relieved the principal of his position, but the school year was well advanced and it was clear that no sensible public school teacher would be eager to take on the job, given the rebellion under way.

My sister Myrtle, sixteen years my senior, had been teaching public school for a number of years. Eleanor's death from streptococcic pneumonia the previous summer had shocked Myrtle deeply. She had returned to her teaching duties near Shedden at the beginning of the school year but after some weeks found it impossible to continue and returned home to recuperate. She had begun to feel better by the time board members realized that they had to fill a position few would accept. They authorized George to see whether Myrtle was able to take over the principal's position at ss 17. She agreed and during the next few weeks quelled the academic uprising. I was promoted to the junior third class at the end of that school year, the lowest level of instruction in Myrtle's senior room. On the morning of the first day of school the following September, George took me aside and told me that if ever Myrtle found it necessary to use the strap on me, I could expect another whipping from him at home. While I was a student in Myrtle's room during the next three years, I did suffer the strap on a couple of occasions and was once sent home on a rather questionable—in my opinion—interpretation of what constituted insubordination. Myrtle and Eleta, however, never informed George of these incidents.

Myrtle was an excellent teacher whose students scored well on the provincial examinations that students had to pass to enter high school, and she was also qualified to teach music. While she was at ss 17 her choruses performed well in the annual music festival held at the University of Western Ontario each spring. But as Myrtle was taking over the senior room of ss 17, the depression of the early 1930s held Canada in its grip, and some of the retired farmers in Lambeth became loud in their complaints about the burden of local taxes and the size of Myrtle's salary. It was unseemly also, they believed, that the teacher at ss 17 should be the daughter of a member of the school board. In my second or third year in my sister's room, the tax cutters packed the meeting of the school board and ousted George. In his place they elected a bachelor in his mid-thirties, without acknowledged children, who lived at the Longwoods Inn, worked on the highway, and looked after the Lambeth ice rink in wintertime. Eleta was indignant. Myrtle had risked her fragile health to take over the school in a time of crisis. Now her father had been thrown off the board and my sister could look forward to a cut in salary and perhaps even to being fired. I heard Eleta talking to George after the meeting. "Those old retired farmer skinflints in Lambeth make me sick," she said. "They don't care about the children, just their taxes, and then they come to church and sit there looking sanctimonious!"

As indicated, in Myrtle's first full year of teaching at ss 17 I moved into the junior third class in her room, and I remained a student in her room until I passed the provincial exam that qualified me to begin secondary school at the Lambeth Continuation School, where the teachers offered lower and middle high school instruction. I was fortunate in having my sister as teacher, although I would probably have had more fun under someone else. But with a lip too fast for my own good and being sufficiently bright to have spare time for recreational reading or mischief after completing class assignments, I might have been in a great deal more trouble under another teacher. One of my classmates, however, told his mother that he was glad he was not Allan Bogue because "his sister doesn't let him get away with anything."

Myrtle made me study seriously and encouraged Eleta to enroll me for elocution lessons with a Lambeth lady known for her skill in declamation. As she drilled the school chorus to compete at the musical festival in the spring of my year in the senior third class, Myrtle decided I must join the small group of boys whose voices were too undependable or flat to sing in the group. She bolstered my feelings, however, by entering me in the elocution contest and saw to it that Eleta arranged a couple of coaching sessions with one of the instructors in public speaking at the university. Professor Walker pronounced me to be "lip lazy" and explained how I could stop saying *Wen* instead of *Len* and *swing* instead of *sling*. (My "rain in Spain," however, was excellent.) My sister and I disagreed about the selection of the poem I was to recite at the festival. I wanted to deliver "I Was Born in Canada beneath the British Flag," by Pauline Johnson, with its stirring lines:

> The Dutch may have their Holland,
> The Spaniards have their Spain,
> The Yankees to the South of us,
> Must South of us remain.

But Myrtle vetoed the poem as too jingoistic. I cannot remember either the title or the content of the compromise poem we settled upon, but due to Professor Walker's tips I was rewarded with a third-prize finish and a copy of Mark Twain's *Tom Sawyer*.

My year in the junior fourth class was to be the last year at ss 17 for Myrtle and for me. Perhaps my sister would have stayed another year at Lambeth had it been necessary for me to spend a year in both the junior and senior fourth classes, but she believed I was sufficiently advanced in my work to pass out of public school by writing the provincial exams. That being the case, she asked the chairman of the school board and the district school inspector, with whom she was a favorite, to write recommendations for her and thus fortified she successfully sought employment elsewhere. During several days in June 1934, I wrote the provincial senior fourth exams at the Lambeth Continuation School in company with students from a number of other Westminster public schools. In early summer our newspaper informed us that I had passed, and a departmental certificate followed. I had exhausted the cabinet of books that constituted the senior room library at ss 17, but there I had met Kipling in the prankster persons of *Stalky & Co.* and Arthur Conan Doyle's stalwart bowmen of *The White Company* as well as Scott's *Ivanhoe*. I looked forward to exploring the library of the Lambeth Continuation School.

The school board fight brought into relief one of the fault lines in the

Lambeth community—tension between the country and the village. In this case, however, the traditional picture of a progressive, commercially oriented business center at odds with a conservative, tightfisted rural hinterland was obscured. The primary spokesmen of conservative reaction lived in the village but had earlier accumulated property as farmers. The split between village and rural hinterland was further complicated by the fact that the Farmers' Cooperative owned the major general store in Lambeth during the 1920s and early 1930s, and sometimes the farmer directors chivvied villagers who were slow in meeting the debts that they had run up on credit at the store. The conflict between Lambeth and George's cousin Bill ran somewhat truer to form. For some time Bill operated two large greenhouses just outside the village and drew his water supply from the village system. But he came to feel that he was being overcharged. A lawsuit ensued, in which he lost, and his greenhouses stood vacant thereafter.

Religious affiliation also drew some lines through the neighborhood. Ed B.—the man who cut our corn crop every year—and his family were Anglicans, worshiping at the chapel on the southwest corner at the main crossroads in Lambeth. One or two others along our stretch of the North Talbot Road were members of that church as well. Confined to bed with pleurisy for a time one winter while I was still in the junior room at ss 17, I heard George announce loudly to Eleta downstairs: "Fora C. says that the world is going to come to an end this year." As earlier mentioned, Fora and his family had begun to attend the services of a charismatic Baptist preacher in London who was prophesying that the second coming was at hand. They remained faithful to him during most of the 1930s, undeterred that the Day of Judgment had not arrived on schedule. Fora's efforts to proselytize in the neighborhood won no converts. But when George relayed his prophecy, I was in bed and feverish, still highly disturbed by my sister's death—and at the best of times I was rendered apprehensive by what I heard from the pulpit in the United Church in Lambeth. Fora's pronouncement terrified me. I was not ready for judgment. Devout church member that she was, Eleta could only assure me that she did not think Judgment Day would be arriving quite so soon. Len was more help; Fora, he said, was talking nonsense.

The United Church in Lambeth was one of the focal points in our family's social life. Eleta had been raised in a strict Methodist home and found sad comfort in her faith, particularly in the months after Eleanor died. Sunday morning breakfast on the farm was usually somewhat special—there were occasionally pancakes and almost invariably coffee instead of the tea that Eleta served at other meals. After she cleared away the dishes, Eleta usually expected that other members of the family would accompany her to church. Sometimes George took us to the service, leading us down the left center aisle behind the usher and standing aside to guide us into the pew on the right side of the aisle where we invariably sat, a little more than halfway toward the pulpit. Although he attended regularly for a year or so while he was a church steward and obligated to help count the collections, George became increasingly reluctant to go to church as the thirties advanced. Eleta, however, insisted that I accompany her. While Myrtle taught at ss 17, she sang in the choir, leaving us as we entered the church to go to the choir room and put on her robe. After the service I attended a Sunday school class that included the same village boys with whom I studied and played at school.

Intermittently the family went to special events at the church, particularly the fall chicken supper, but there was also the occasional slide show or religiously oriented speaker. Eleta attended the meetings of the Ladies Aid Society regularly. During my second year in high school that group put on a humorous play, and to the family's surprise Eleta accepted a part in it. In one year during the mid-1930s she was president of the group. Each summer the Sunday school sponsored a picnic at Springbank Park with foot races and a pickup softball game. If other family members were too busy to go, they arranged a ride for me. Both my sisters had enjoyed a summer vacation or two at Camp Onondaga, a regional girls' camp sponsored by the United Church of Canada, but the depression and the labor needs of the farm ruled out any similar experience for me. The closest I came to such a vacation was one summer when I was invited to spend a few days visiting a step-cousin named Murray Campbell on his family's farm near Watford. The following summer Murray came to visit us. He was about my age, a genuinely nice young man, and we had a great time playing catch, putting away a pint of ice cream each at the Bluebird Hall, and one night riding the roller-coaster at Springbank Park.

I cannot remember Len ever accompanying the family to the morning church service during the 1930s, although he had been active in the young people's organization and, at an earlier time, had attended meetings of the Tuxis Boys, a young men's church group. He and his friends sometimes went to the Sunday evening service, and when he began to court his future wife seriously, he sometimes took her to church on Sunday night. On those evenings his younger brother milked an extra cow.

Eleta's Methodist parents had not allowed their children to play cards with a poker deck, and Myrtle and Len presented her with a dilemma on that score. Len learned the game of rummy from friends and he began to play with Andy M. on our kitchen table on Sunday afternoons. The family of his bride-to-be were enthusiastic euchre players. The members of a family with whom Myrtle boarded close to her Shedden school taught her to play bridge, and when bridge-playing relatives from the Hamilton area visited us one winter, they organized a game. I heard Eleta expressing concern about this trend of events to George and the two agreeing to George's dictum: better here than elsewhere under worse auspices. Eleta, however, did not keep her mother abreast of these developments. Our grandmother learned of the moral decay in our branch of the family when she read the newspaper account of the Continuation School At Home held at the Longwoods Inn in the spring of my first year at the school. She was shocked to find that I had won the prize for most lone hands in the progressive euchre tournament.

The degree of religious commitment in our family obviously varied, and there was a good deal of contrast among the families of the United Church who lived along the road. The Vanstone family were the most faithful members of our church who lived nearby. They occupied the southwest corner farm but did not own an auto. It was a mile and a quarter from our corner to the church. Sometimes the Vanstones drove a horse and buggy, leaving it in the church shed beside the cars of other church members. More frequently, mother, father, and two daughters walked to the morning service and repeated that journey in time for the evening service. The father, Ed Vanstone, also walked to attend prayer meetings on Wednesday evenings. However, I never saw Ed's son Millard, a young man of about Len's age, at a church service of any kind.

Although our neighbors differed in their doctrinal views and a few families seemed to ignore the religious establishment completely, the differences in affiliation along the road did not produce squabbling. They did, however, reduce the amount of socializing between some families. Perhaps disagreement on religious grounds would have cut more deeply if there had been Roman Catholic families among us, but the area was solidly Protestant. This is not to say that religious influence was only turned to self-instruction and improvement within the local churches. Before Canadian Methodists joined with some Presbyterian elements to form the United Church of Canada, our congregation in Lambeth had been Methodist in doctrine, and after union it retained that denomination's commitment to temperance. The church pastors and lay leaders worked hard to keep Westminster Township dry whenever referendums on that subject were threatened or held.

Villagers and farm dwellers mingled in school matters, as we have seen, and worshiped together in the United and Anglican churches of the village, but members of our family at least suspected that the villagers looked down on us and exploited us when the opportunity presented itself. Some eyebrows twitched when one of the village's leading businessmen walked down the church aisle on Sunday mornings wearing a dark cutaway coat with swallow tails and gray trousers, in contrast to the somewhat shiny array of business suits scattered elsewhere in the pews. After George and his cousins cut the mature trees off the Bostwick fifty, large patches of raspberries and blackberries sprang up at the edges of the little groves of second growth that developed in the slashing. In the years before our domestic raspberries came into bearing, Eleta spent a morning or so each year picking berries there for jam. I accompanied her on one of these expeditions, and as we worked, we heard sounds suggesting that a trespasser was also present in the berry patches. We split up and executed an encircling movement. As Eleta came again into view, I sighted our quarry—one of the anti-tax retired farmers from the village and a member of our church congregation—and saw him unobtrusively hide a full six-quart basket of berries behind some bushes before he advanced to greet Eleta, an empty container in his hands. There was a strained exchange of greetings and then Eleta beckoned me to accompany her toward another part of the slashing.

"Why didn't you say something about that basket of berries that he put down?" I asked.

"Oh my, I didn't see it," she replied. "The old fox! But perhaps it is just as well. A few quarts of berries are not worth fighting over. Perhaps being caught trespassing and stealing is punishment enough."

To the best of my knowledge there were no long-simmering disagreements among neighbors along our road. But Eleta and some of her friends developed a keen sense of hostility toward one of the fruit farmers living between our corner and the Second Concession Road. His wife Alice was a cousin of George's and participated in the little luncheon gatherings of neighborhood wives that Eleta's friend Verna C. organized during some of the winters of the mid-1930s. Alice came to suspect her husband of unfaithfulness and finally took her eldest son and moved out of the household. The husband shortly installed the other woman as "housekeeper" for himself and his younger son, and Alice sued for divorce. The proceedings were unpleasant, and Eleta and Alice's other friends were indignant at the shameful way in which they believed that she had been treated. Such feelings had little impact on the erring husband, whose new housekeeper bore him another child. During those years, infidelity and divorce were viewed in our neighborhood as reprehensible in the extreme. Alice's divorce, however, did not mark the only marital separation that occurred on our stretch of road in my years there. Some years earlier, the wife of George's cousin Tink had set up separate residence with her several children. Infidelity was not at issue in this case, but Eleta's sympathy was again with the wife. Tink's parents, George admitted, "had spoiled him rotten."

George was reserved in relations with neighbors but believed in staying on good terms with them. I don't believe that he ever refused to lend a tool when asked to do so, although neither he nor his neighbors of long standing did much borrowing and the little they did was mostly among family members. Some distancing did occur over the years between the last in the series of southeast corner neighbors and our family. Initially relations had been cordial, and while Myrtle was teaching at ss 17, she and Len did some socializing with the older Newcomer children, who were in their twenties. But after her resignation from ss 17 Myrtle was only at home during parts of summers, and Len's social life was directed elsewhere. I had played somewhat at first with the youngest member of the Newcomer family, a boy several years younger than I, but became persona non grata for taking part in a family water fight, for questioning the accuracy of an "out" call that the youngest daughter made on our tennis court, and for a misdirected BB pellet. As I have described, when George sent me to the Newcomer threshing in the second year after Len's departure, Newcomer put me on a very dirty straw stack. I discovered too that when Newcomer came to our threshing as a field pitcher, he was one of those who wanted to throw several sheaves onto the load at one time, or even join with his partner in tossing up a full shock and then lead the team on to the next shock without giving the loader time to arrange the sheaves properly. In the summer when Len and George operated the farm in full partnership, they believed that members of the Newcomer family encouraged disaffection on the part of two of our hired men. Meanwhile Eleta had come to view the family with disfavor. She learned that they drank and also that they supported an effort in the mid-1930s on the part of the local "wets" to repeal the ordinance keeping Westminster Township dry. In the spring of Myrtle's last year at ss 17 she sometimes walked home for lunch and Eleta drove her back to the school. One day a man visiting Newcomer parked his car directly across from the end of our drive. Hurriedly backing the Model A out of our driveway, Eleta struck his vehicle. Newcomer and his visitor rushed out to survey the minor damage she had caused. Fearing that Myrtle would be late for school, Eleta admitted her responsibility and proposed to take Myrtle and me on to school. Newcomer's visitor demurred, wanting more information. Newcomer refused to vouch for Eleta and she flared out,

"What do you take us for, thieves?" Thereafter Newcomer had no standing whatsoever with her.

Once, George savored victory in a minor disagreement with Newcomer. The rolling contours in the first field behind our barn directed some surface drainage into the roadside ditch, and from there it passed under Dale's Side Road through a small metal culvert and into the upper corner of the field behind Newcomer's barn. The water then drained into the center of the field, where it mingled with runoff from other directions and sometimes formed a pond during the late fall and early spring. Either George or his predecessors on the southeast corner farm had run an underground line of tile diagonally across the field to discharge in the ditch along the North Talbot Road. This limited the size of any pond that developed and shortened the period during which water remained in the field. One of the younger Newcomer boys was an avid hockey player, and he asked Len where skating would be possible in the immediate neighborhood during the winter. There was often skating, Len told him, on a big pond on the old Pringle hobby farm and sometimes at a smaller one at the junction of the Second Concession and North Talbot roads as well as on Dingman's Creek. Newcomer's front field was mentioned, and Len explained that if the tile run were to be plugged, a fine skating pond might develop.

Subsequently some young men unearthed the run of tile and placed a burlap bag in the interior of one of the tiles, preventing water from flowing through. Magnificent skating ensued, but the pond persisted into the summer, rendering several acres of the field unfit for crops or pasture. Ignorant of the events that preceded the pond's stubborn persistence, Newcomer concluded that the fault lay with the Bogues. If water ceased to drain from their field onto his property, he believed, there would be no pond. Whether he propounded this theory to George who pled tradition and the power of gravity, I do not know. But Newcomer took his case to the township council and invited its members to come and view the problem—preliminary, he hoped, to requiring George Bogue to divert his water from Newcomer's land.

Quite by chance George was in our barnyard one day when a number of cars parked by the culvert on the side road, and a little knot of men gathered on the road and began to listen to a presentation by Newcomer. George guessed the subject under discussion from the location of the conclave and Newcomer's illustrative gesturing. He ambled out to join the group. A couple of the councilors, old acquaintances from George's participation in the affairs of the Farmer's Co-op and United Farmer and Progressive politics, nodded to him, and after a few minutes he eased them into a counter-seminar to explain matters something like this: It was all a bunch of silliness. The natural watercourse ran through Newcomer's field, but the field was tiled and there would have been no problem had his sons not plugged the tile run with a gunnysack. If Newcomer wanted to use more of his field, he need only remove the plug. His message delivered, George returned to our barn. After a few minutes the councilors drove off. We heard no more about rerouting the drainage from our field.

A decade later, while George was living in the farmhouse in retirement, he relished political victory in the neighborhood for the last time. Leaders in the local United Church asked him to take charge of getting out the dry vote when the local wets again tried to introduce the sale of alcoholic liquors in Westminster Township. Again liquidification and the friends of the Newcomers met defeat.

Church, school, and municipal government together provided the institutional structure within which the farmers along the North Talbot Road lived and operated their farms. We saw little manifestation of police power, although occasionally a provincial policeman or a Mountie drove along the road on the way to one of the fruit farms, where the fruit pickers from the Oneida Reservation sometimes drew their interest. Cases of theft were almost unknown in the neighborhood during the 1930s, although not completely so. For a few years in the 1930s Harvey Kilbourne lived on the side road between Fora C.'s place and Dingman Creek. In our last year of intensive market gardening I was shocked to hear that this husky and handsome young man was dead. He had fallen out of a tree while hunting raccoons with friends and broken his neck. Soon Harvey's shack had new occupants—a couple in their thirties, poorly dressed, without any means of transportation other than their feet. Following them as they walked up and down the road were two children, perhaps ten or younger in age and as poorly dressed and pinched in expression as the parents. They once called at our place looking for work or scrap metal, and Eleta, who never turned a beggar away without at least a sandwich, was frightened rather than touched. I customarily left my bicycle on our front porch. When it disappeared, our thoughts turned to our new neighbors on the side road. George reported the theft to the provincial policeman stationed in Lambeth, but we heard nothing more about the bicycle and never knew whether our suspicions were justified or unfounded. The bicycle had been a secondhand one bought to replace one that boys in the class ahead of me at Lambeth Continuation School had wrecked one afternoon while I was doing penance. But it had carried me to the Springbank Drive and back home again on school days during my fourth year of high school, and I was fearful that I might now have to walk. Eleta was firm on this issue, however; there was to be a new bicycle, or rather another secondhand one.

Farm operations along the North Talbot Road reflected the varied ways in which families worked the land to provide a living for their members. Family dynamics drove farm enterprise, and in our case family dynamics generated some friction and heat. Until the late 1920s George had been successful as farmer and community member. He had prospered as a farmer and his activities in the Farmer's Co-op, in politics, and as a Holstein-Friesian breeder gave him some claim to being a community leader. In major matters, he was an honest and well-intentioned man who thought of himself as a progressive farmer and a responsible member of the community. Within the home, however, he tended to be authoritarian and uneven in temper, capable of exploding in bursts of anger. Unquestionably he loved his family, but his vision of the children's future was restricted. He withdrew Len from school after his second year in Lambeth Continuation School without discussing the decision at any length with Eleta. However, he allowed Len to develop his own small herd of cattle and horses within the broader farm operation. He supported Myrtle through high school and Normal School. This involved some expense since she boarded in London during her upper school and Normal School years. My other sister Eleanor was on a similar path when she died following her first year at London Central Collegiate Institute.

The most athletically gifted among us, Eleanor was George's favorite among the children, according to Eleta. But Eleta felt that George was harsh and unsympathetic with the children, and Myrtle later told me that he had been stern in disciplining the older ones. I was treated more leniently, she said. Eleta believed that George nagged Len excessively. She told me of a morning on the southeast corner farm when George scolded Len for dawdling with two pails of milk that he was carrying from the west door of the barn to the milk house. When he set them down to close the door behind him, George snatched them up and started to carry them across a snowy stretch of some thirty feet to the milk house. As he strode indignantly forward, a pail in each hand, he stepped confidently on a patch of unmarked snow that concealed a layer of ice. As George's feet slipped from under him, the contents of the pails sloshed in all directions. It was an incident that apparently helped erode Eleta's respect for him.

Eleta was hardworking and fully committed to doing her full share in making the farm prosperous and the family home a comfortable one. She tended her poultry operation skillfully and canned and preserved fruit in quantity each year. Before we became deeply involved in market gardening, she planted and tended the vegetable garden. In the early days of the marriage she had shared in the milking, although she was not doing so during my childhood. Years later, however, when George was left without any help for milking except me, she sometimes came to the stable in the evening and milked one or two cows. She was busy with household chores on most evenings until well past nine o'clock, but she still found time to plant and tend flower beds in the spring and summer. During the winter she hooked rugs and made goose-down comforters. Besides faithfully attending the Ladies Aid Society meetings at the church, she served as president of the society and of the Women's Institute in Byron and greatly enjoyed the little get-togethers at lunchtime that her friend Verna C. sometimes organized among a number of the wives living along the road.

Eleta's interest focused particularly on the future of her children—perhaps to a greater extent than was the case with some of the other farm wives along the road. Her education had ended in the upper grades of public school, but as a girl she had read enthusiastically and shown some artistic talent. We still have a little winter scene that she painted in oils, charming in its proportioning and blending of colors. Eleta was determined that her children would have more education than she did and that we would do well in school. From Myrtle through the family to me, she sat down with us when our homework threatened to defeat us. Algebra was a family bugaboo, and she would take the text and read the explanations and examples and identify the places where we had gone astray. She would even take pencil and paper to show doubting offspring that her advice would guide us to the answer given in the back of the schoolbook. Thanks to the children, she sometimes boasted, she understood algebra through the Ontario middle school requirements of competency.

Long before we left the southeast corner farm, I knew that there was a continuing tension between Eleta and George. One evening they had planned to go out and I was to be in the charge of Len and Eleanor, who were still at the barn when I realized that Eleta was crying. She had been late in getting ready. As she was just about finished with her preparations, George announced that he would not go. There was a heated exchange and finally they departed, leaving me in a highly disturbed state. I was to hear this scene played out more than once as I grew up, and it never failed to leave me disconcerted and fearful. To do them justice, they usually conducted their arguments in low voices and in private. I cannot remember any loud shouting matches, but George sometimes slammed the kitchen door and I occasionally saw him kick some object out of his way as he strode off to the barn, muttering. Eleta later told me that George had been the sweetest of young men in their early marriage but had come to resent the amount of time that she devoted to the children. George never confided in me on the subject, but he believed, I am sure, that "Leta," as he called her, coddled the children.

As farmer-businessman, George entered the 1920s confident to the point of conceit. But Eleta developed reservations about his judgment. She approved heartily of our being in the Record of Performance program, but as the family commitment to Holsteins deepened, she grew increasingly critical of George's management of the dairy herd. He was inclined to accept the best offer that a potential buyer made, and this would invariably involve one of the most promising younger animals in the herd. Eleta, on the other hand, believed that the good breeder sold to cull rather than accepting the best deal of the moment. Finally, when George sold a heifer that Eleta believed should be retained for breeding purposes and milk production within the herd, she passed over a line uncrossed in their relationship up to that time. She challenged his judgment and continued to do so thereafter when she disagreed with a course he was contemplating. Apparently, however, she had failed to question the sale of the southeast corner farm and the transactions related to it—decisions that vitally affected our family life during the 1930s, probably for the worse.

Some farm wives may have become resigned to the fact that the dreams of their early married years were never realized. They may have complained that they lacked the household appliances advertised in magazines or displayed in London stores, that the futures of their children were uncertain, or that farm buildings continued to need paint. I doubt that Eleta ever became reconciled to the shortcomings of life on our farm, but I suspect that she did not fret about the state of her household appliances. Her old washing machine moved across the road with her when we changed farms. It was a topless wooden tub mounted on a metal framework, with a metal folding apron on which additional tubs might be set. Originally a small gasoline engine provided the power to run it. George modernized the washing machine by replacing its gasoline engine with an electric motor. The result was the same; in operation the machine agitated the clothes by revolving the tub, first in one direction and then in the other, the gears clanking and water splashing up and down around the clothing or bed sheets being washed. Despite its crudeness, the machine worked effectively and I never heard Eleta yearn for one of the sleek round metal machines that were available by that time. A radio and a vacuum cleaner appeared in the first few years of life on the northeast corner, and an electric toaster soon followed. But Eleta lacked a dual-burner electric plate until George gave her one as a birthday present in 1937. She was particularly grateful for this piece of household equipment because it reduced her dependence on the wood-burning kitchen range.

We did not have running water in the house until 1936 when London's Public Utility Commission allowed householders along the North Talbot Road to tap into the water system fed by new city wells being drilled adjacent to it. While renovating the old house on the northeast corner prior to our move there, George had a large new cistern dug at the back of the house and connected by hand pump to the kitchen sink, and this was our source of soft water. Collecting the runoff from rain and melting snow on the roof through connections to the eave troughs, the cistern never ran dry in our years in the house, but in summer the pump sometimes brought up mosquito wrigglers in the water.

Eleta's worries centered on other matters. She tormented herself that she had allowed Eleanor to follow too rigorous a schedule and to become run-down, thus making her vulnerable to the pneumonia from which she died. She worried that Len's sickness of the early thirties might be the prelude to tuberculosis, a disease that sentenced one of his closest school friends to the Sanatorium at Byron, She was fearful that the pleurisy I developed while in the second class at ss 17 would deteriorate into something worse.

She worried intermittently about her own health, a concern about which George was less than understanding, given, as he was, to occasional boasting that he had missed only two milkings due to sickness in his life. The doctor in Lambeth encouraged Eleta to develop her interest in gardening, to "put her hands in the earth," as he said, and she tended flower beds surrounding the house and stretching along the fence of the night pasture toward the side road, her interest centering over the years on a number of special projects: the cultivation of gladiolus, tea roses, delphiniums, and dahlias. Various large rocks came to light in the process of renovating the barn. The men used some as the foundation for the elevated runway leading to the second-story drive floor, but Eleta had them skid others to the bottom of the lawn, where she constructed a rock garden. Her creativity expressed itself in other ways as well. As we have seen, she accepted a role in a play staged by the Ladies Aid of the United Church at Lambeth. Overhearing conversation between Eleta and Myrtle in the mid-1930s, I learned that she had written several letters to the women's column in the London paper. These she kept secret from George, fearing he might scoff at such works. I did not scoff but was surprised to learn that my mother was an author named Fiddle Dee who recommended favorite recipes to other housewives.

In describing rural family life, social historians have sometimes oversim-
plified the relationships between husband and wife and also isolated them
from family relationships as a whole; have thought in terms of sun and
moon rather than constellation. Eleta and George had their visions of what
the future should hold for their children, and the children in turn cherished
their own dreams for the years ahead. In the meantime all parties interacted
in keeping with their ideas about their responsibilities as family members
and about the obligations that other members of the family owed to them.

If one ignores the influence of the oldest sister in a family one ignores a
potent force, or at least that was true in our case. Three years older than Len
and sixteen years senior to me, Myrtle taught in a succession of country
schools, all one-room institutions with the exception of her four-year stay
at ss 17, when she was principal of a two-room school. Myrtle lived at
home, suffering from "nerves" during most of the year following Eleanor's
death, and she boarded with us during the following years while she taught
at ss 17. When teaching elsewhere she came home frequently on weekends.
George or Eleta picked her up in the car on Friday afternoon and returned
her to her boarding house at the end of Sunday afternoon. During the late
1930s I usually went with Eleta as company or moral reinforcement on the
Sunday evening deliveries while George did the evening milking. At other
times during her teaching career, Myrtle often spent much of the summer
at home but also used some of the time off to improve her credentials by
taking university courses. One summer she enrolled for courses in botany
and nutrition at the Ontario Agricultural College. Myrtle played the piano
and took voice lessons from the choirmaster at Dundas Center United
Church in London, singing at times in his choir as well as at our church
in Lambeth. I knew from personal experience that she was an excellent
instructor, in complete command of her lesson materials and successfully
confident in her grasp of juvenile psychology. But despite her aplomb in
the classroom, she was sensitive and easily hurt in family matters.

Myrtle's ties with Eleta were close. As she saw more of the world, she
passed on some of her newfound knowledge to Eleta. A healthy balance of
vitamins in the diet was important, she explained, and salads and vegetables
began to appear on the family table in greater variety and number. Len was
an easy convert to changes in the menu, although George complained
at times. Lettuce was for rabbits, he said. The members of his family
had attained ripe ages on diets that emphasized meat and potatoes and
sometimes even featured pie for breakfast. But Eleta was converted. Vitamin
supplements appeared and I strangled on applications of cod-liver oil
until Eleta learned how to place the stuff in gelatin capsules. Myrtle also

influenced recreational patterns in the household. While at ss 17 she decreed that we would have a tennis court and learn to play tennis. She bought the equipment and George and Len plowed up the ground on the other side of our driveway. They ran an iron pipe through the top and bottom of a rusty old milk can and filled the can with cement to make a roller, and for several summers we played tennis on a court that sloped in several directions and was usually further subdivided by small rain channels noted for producing tricky bounces. Making good strokes and winning on that court involved knowing the lie of the land.

Quite correctly, Myrtle saw that Eleta worked too hard. Her lined face, gnarled hands, growing stoop, and limited wardrobe were all too evident to a daughter who mixed frequently with village and city women who showed their years much less obviously. One summer Myrtle took Eleta on a cruise boat that carried them through Lake Huron and Lake Superior to Port Arthur and Fort William, centers now joined as Thunder Bay. A year or so later she rented a cottage at Ipperwash on Lake Huron for two weeks, and she and Eleta entertained elements of the family there with George and Len coming up on the weekends. I was allowed a longer stay, but this vacation became less pleasant than planned when both Myrtle and I fell ill with intestinal flu.

In those years when Len and Myrtle were both at home during the summer there were some good times—fun on the tennis court, evenings when I accompanied Len to pickup softball games in which he participated, and the occasional evening or Sunday afternoon when Len said, "Let's go swimming," and we piled into the car with our swimsuits and drove along the side road to Dingman's Creek. We left the car at the road and walked through the woods along the east bank for about a third of a mile to a spot where the creek bent slightly and narrowed, so that a tree trunk could be laid across its course to raise the water level by a foot or so, making a pool slightly more than four feet deep at its lowest point. After an hour or so of splashing and cooling off we would return, much refreshed, our wet bathing suits hung on the outside mirror and the door handles of the car. Eleta cautioned us to be careful on such expeditions, reminding us that one of the farm boys who lived on the southern outskirts of Lambeth had died a few years earlier by misjudging the depth of the creek and breaking his neck when he dived in.

My brother Len has played a major role in this account, and I have acknowledged some of the influence that he had on me. I remember a good many turning points in my young life for which he was directly responsible. It was he who ordered the All-American calendars of the Holstein-Friesian

Association at which I gazed every day in the bedroom we shared on the northeast corner farm and which helped to set my understanding of the Holstein type. It was he who introduced me firsthand to the mysteries of birth, asking my help in assisting a cow with a slow delivery.

When Eleanor died, Eleta vowed that her bicycle would not be ridden by a member of the family thereafter. But Len noticed that a good many of my schoolmates were riding bicycles while I continued to trudge on foot. On a Saturday morning when Eleta and George were in London, he took the bicycle out of the woodshed, inflated the tires, and said to me, "It's time you learned to ride a bicycle." When our parents returned from London, I was riding the machine up and down the lane. Eleta was shocked, but she acquiesced in the deed already done. Since the bicycle was a girl's model and had a lowered crossbar, George traded it for a boy's bike and I joined the little squadron of bikers who traveled south on the North Talbot Road to ss 17.

While in his late teens and early twenties Len drew heavily on the little library in Lambeth. Books on the children's shelves, Tom Swift and the like, seemed poor stuff by the time that I was settled in the senior room at ss 17, and Len was a ready reference guide on more advanced tales of adventure. He set me on the track of the *Three Musketeers* series and Raphael Sabatini's *Scaramouche*, and it was his doing that the *Saturday Evening Post* and the *American Magazine* were always in the household with their exciting serials by Zane Gray and Clarence Budington Kelland. I read many of the factual articles in these magazines as well, but it was the fiction that drew me into them. I was never able to share Len's taste for the works of P. J. Wodehouse, however. Bertie and Jeeves seemed to me merely silly; at that point I had no idea of what class distinction was all about.

It was a question by Len in one of his final years on the farm that first set me thinking with some seriousness about my future. "What's Al going to be?" he asked my mother one summer day when we had come into the kitchen at midmorning for a drink of water and a brief pause to check the morning paper for the scores of the previous day's ballgames in the American and National baseball leagues. Eleta had recently remedied a long past dereliction by having me baptized and steered though the confirmation class at church, and she replied that she would be delighted if I were to become a minister. "Don't you think that would be a fine thing?" she said.

"No, I don't," said Len, "I don't think Al is cut out to be a minister."

Eleta never made the suggestion again.

By the mid-1930s Len was moving into his mid-twenties. Although Eleta believed that George should have allowed him to obtain more schooling, I never heard Len complain about it in later years. Nor did I ever hear George and Len raise their voices in argument with each other. Len did not speak yearningly of the off-farm work that our first cousins Gordon and Stan had tried. Of course, finding remunerative employment off the farm was not easy during the 1930s. Sometimes Len questioned George's judgment about farm matters, and as I have indicated, both of us were convinced that we were better judges of Holstein type and better dairy showmen than our father. Such generational rifts were usual in rural families, and occasionally George told of instances when his father had called him and his brother young smart alecks for believing that they could improve upon his methods. But there was a definite change in Len's attitude after he recovered from his illness of the early 1930s. He became the driving force in our farm enterprise, and for a time it appeared that the whole family would benefit from his leadership.

In preparation for Len's marriage in 1935, George had the front parlor and an adjacent bedroom converted into a small apartment. Here Len and his bride Irene lived until the spring of 1937. The 1936 crop year saw us involved in market gardening as never before. According to George, it was a year in which the farm "made money." It was a lively place, too, with much hired help on hand to make things interesting. That hired help added to Eleta's labors because there were extra places at the table, and Irene was expecting a baby. During the weeks of greatest pressure, we hired a girl from the village to help, but Eleta was not expert in delegating tasks. She still felt obligated to help with the packing of tomatoes, and occasionally Myrtle joined us in picking or packing as well.

In the months following this profitable season we received a great shock. Len informed George that he was going to take his cattle and horses and enter partnership with Irene's father on his farm south of Lambeth. Irene was an only daughter. Her mother missed her and was eager to help care for the baby. Her father was prepared to assist in caring for a purebred Holstein herd, although his barn was not as large or well fitted as the one that Len's stock would be leaving. I heard George and Eleta discussing this development. They were disappointed. They had remodeled the house, had seen the farm fortunes improving. Now the milk flow was to be cut in half. Len's knowledge of garden crops and marketing was to be lost as well. But, said George, "I want us to part on good terms; I want them to feel that they can come back home and visit and are truly welcome." In this it proved that George had set the right course. Irene's parents invited us thereafter to their annual gathering at New Year's, and relations between our families were cordial. Len felt it necessary to explain to me his decision to leave the northeast corner farm. George, he said, had wanted to begin investing partnership profits in upgrading the farm, and Len did not believe that it was worth it.

The next two years were lean ones on the northeast corner. Somehow we scraped by on the income from Eleta's poultry and the sale of cream, tomatoes, asparagus, raspberries, and strawberries. But we installed no new fencing, although it was badly needed along some stretches of our pasture boundaries. There were no excess animals for sale in the herd, and at my urging George purchased a couple of heifer calves to speed its growth. The harness in which Pomp and Prince performed their patient duties was studded here and there with brass rivets marking spots where George had repaired it. George was now almost sixty and Eleta only a few years younger.

To an extent that I in no way understood, the future of the farm in those years was tied to my future. Although she never said so, Eleta had come to hate the farm, the drafty house, the endless scrimping that was so much a part of the 1930s. She purchased soda crackers, for example, from the reject bins at the outlet of the McCormick Biscuit Company near the farmers' market and always bought second-day buns from the Lambeth baker. Farming had claimed one son; she had resolved that it would not take a second. Advised and supported by Myrtle, Eleta was determined that education was to be my ticket to a different lifeway. An educational specialist examining my three-year record at the Lambeth Continuation School might have responded to that proposition with a qualified "maybe."

In Lambeth two women teachers were responsible for teaching all the courses in the lower and middle high school curricula, four years of study in all. Both were new on the job in my first year of attendance. As credentials, the principal, Miss S., had only a Normal School degree, with perhaps some summer course enrichment along the way. Miss B., younger and in her first job, was the sister of Johnny B., who had sometimes worked for us. She was a member of a family of school teachers, one of whom had been Myrtle's arch rival in preparing school choruses for competition while my sister was at ss 17. Miss B. taught the courses in English, history, French, and Latin, while Miss S. taught mathematics and science for the most part. Miss B. gave the girls in the school whatever athletic coaching they received, and Miss S. did the same for the boys. With Miss B. I soon established good rapport, and she embarrassed me by informing the regional school inspector that I was a very good student.

Miss S. and I were not a good fit. I so nearly failed first-year algebra that she made me repeat it. Whereas my grades under Miss B. were mostly in the A range, they were distinctly lower with Miss S. With Miss B. I starred in history, but when the principal ventured to teach ancient history, my grade plummeted. Partly through my inattention, perhaps, I found her explanations of mathematical operations hard to follow and her exposition of other subjects uninteresting. Sometimes she hurt my feelings with tactless remarks. She seemed to favor the well-dressed, clean-smelling village boys in preference to those of us whose sweaters sometimes carried a whiff of the barnyard or the odor of the bacon that had been frying for breakfast in a farm kitchen. As principal she paid little attention to what took place on the playground or in the boys' recreation room downstairs, and there was enough bullying—even sexual abuse—to be upsetting. On one occasion I came upon the best-muscled member of our class leading the school genius by a string attached to his penis and spent the first hour of afternoon class half sick because I had opted to allow the class bell to end the torment rather than to challenge the bully.

Although they never criticized me at home for my problems with Miss S., thinking her as much to blame for them as I, Eleta and Myrtle were determined by the end of my third year to remove me from continuation school. Since in theory I could have finished middle school at Lambeth, it was necessary to seek the permission of local educational authorities to transfer to one of the secondary schools in London. Probably Myrtle attended to the paperwork, and in the early summer of 1937, Eleta came out to the barnyard where George and I were repairing the hay rack to tell us that I would be able to attend London Central Collegiate Institute in the fall. On hearing the news, George slammed down the hammer and stalked into the barn.

That gesture was the only complaint that I saw or heard George make about the decision to have me continue my secondary schooling in London. Clearly he wanted me to drop out of school and join him on the farm, looking forward to a time when I would take control of the operation. Eleta and George were engaged in a war of wills, and my future was the prize. Eventually I realized that George's decision to spend a good part of his share of the profits of the previous year of farm operations on purchasing the best young herd sire that had ever come onto the farm was a move in the same contest. He was a dedicated Holstein breeder, but he also realized, I am sure, that having such an animal on the farm made it much more attractive to me. I realized that my future was the subject of disagreement within the family. I was also concerned about my prospects but did not fully understand my options. I liked living in the country and I liked to work with animals. I believed that I could do well or at least get by in further schooling. But then what? I had no idea. Perhaps I could teach in secondary school. I suggested that I would like to go to the Ontario Agricultural College—OAC, as we all called it. Myrtle had spent a rewarding summer there, and I hoped I might soon represent our calf club in the annual dairy cattle judging competition that took place there each fall. Eleta and George agreed in vetoing the idea of enrollment at OAC. They did not have enough money to send me away to school, and the OAC student body had a reputation for rough high jinks. There was no telling what might happen to me in such an environment. But before the question of college became an immediate issue, I was to test and be tested at London Central Collegiate Institute.

On an early September morning in 1937 I bicycled north on the North Talbot Road to the Second Concession Road, where I met Ron C., the son of my mother's good friend Verna. A year ahead of me in school, Ron had taken the full four years at Lambeth Continuation School and was enrolled for his year of upper school at London Central. Together we biked north on the undulating road until we reached the crest of the "Big Hill" and coasted down to the First Concession Road, which angled into Springbank Drive. We left our bikes leaning against the woodshed of Charlie and Jeanie L., retired dairy farmers and good friends of Eleta and George. Charlie had been a member of the Farmer's Co-op board of directors. Catching the Springbank Drive bus from in front of their place, we rode into London, left the bus in front of the Hotel Belvedere on Dundas Street, and walked the additional eight or so blocks to London Central Collegiate Institute.

During the next nine months the classrooms of that venerable institution were a revelation to me. Seasoned teachers who taught only one or two subjects conducted the instruction in every one of my classes with a clarity and depth of knowledge that the over-burdened Lambeth teachers could not match. The subjects I had liked at Lambeth were now even more interesting and science and math became understandable. The teacher in my class in English composition read my short essay on making homemade bread to the class as an example to emulate. I wandered into a tryout for the boys' debating team and was selected for the team that represented the school in the Western Ontario Secondary Schools Association competition; a medal and a golden school letter materialized as a result. (The debating coach, Louise Wyatt, would still be giving me counsel when she was ninety-one.) Of course there was a downside. I was a country boy with unpolished manners and a limited wardrobe, and I was not athlete enough to impress the young city jocks; indeed the reverse applied, in the eyes of one or two particularly mouthy individuals. One of the male physical education teachers made jokes about country boys. But not all the city students were hostile and my fourth year had to be considered a success, although I did not pull quite all my grades into the A range.

Success breeds enthusiasm. I returned to London Central in the fall of 1938 hoping to do well enough in my upper school exams to win a provincial scholarship that would allow me to enter the University of Western Ontario. I took the maximum class load and worked on my schoolwork as never before. I enrolled in fifth-year algebra, geometry, and trigonometry classes and found that my old frustrations in mathematics had pretty well vanished. The mathematics teachers at London Central used the results of the first tests of the term to order the class, seating the recipient of the highest grade in the far back corner by the door. In geometry that year I ended in the second seat from the door in the back row, the prime seat occupied by another country kid, Evelyn Campbell, whose younger brother was ultimately to head the Hoover Institute at Stanford and sit on President Reagan's Security Council. In the trigonometry class, however, I attained the back-door seat. But the heavy course load and the broken trip from the country to school began to tell on me during the winter. I contracted a long, debilitating cold that left me weak and dispirited, and one night I found myself crying into my book of Latin prose. "Forget the scholarship," Eleta said, "We will find the tuition somehow." Soon after this exchange I learned that she had worked out her own solution to both her problem and mine.

Some years earlier Eleta's younger sister had decided to leave the isolated farm that the family owned on the Gore Road between Westminster and Delaware townships. She moved into London and provided living quarters for her eldest daughter and some of the latter's friends, all of whom worked for the London Life Insurance Company. This arrangement also allowed her younger son and daughter to attend London Central. Now Eleta proposed a similar arrangement. The back fifty could be sold to provide funds for the purchase of a house in London where she would keep a sufficient number of boarders to support the household. I suspect that discussion of this proposal was at times heated, but it took place when I was not present. George did not wish to continue farming if I was not to be available, and he proposed to dispose of the cattle, horses, harvested crops, and farm equipment in the fall of 1939. He believed he could keep busy as a carpenter or perhaps work for cousin Norman, who was often short of help.

George helped Eleta to move some of our belongings to our new house on Waterloo Street, two short blocks from London Central, in the early spring of 1939, and she furnished the remainder of the house with secondhand furniture. I spent the last weeks of the school year there while she put the house in order and took the first steps to obtain boarders. Aspirants for provincial scholarships were required to write provincial exams if they wished to be considered for such grants. I was not sufficiently recovered to write the exams in all of my subjects but took the tests in five subjects in which the highest grades would have given me one of the smaller awards. With the exams behind me, I returned to the farm, where George and I spent weekdays during the summer, going to the house in London on Saturday or Sunday to deliver tomatoes and potatoes and to eat at least one decent meal. That summer we harvested the hay and grain crops on both the northeast corner farm and the back fifty. We participated in the threshing ring and I went to most of the threshings, sometimes with the team and wagon. We milked the cows and separated the milk and did the usual chores in connection with the cattle. We picked and packed tomatoes, and on market mornings George left early while I did the milking.

That summer I fitted Joan Ormsby Fayne and her twin sister for the fall shows, and we tried to take special care that the bull and the other Holsteins were in good flesh in preparation for the sale that fall. George was more easygoing that summer than ever before; I believe he was relieved that the endless round of milking was soon to end. But this he never said. In midsummer Doc Bovaird, a veterinarian employed by the provincial Department of Agriculture, made his annual visit to the farm to test our cattle for TB. He returned in a few days to discover whether tell-tale knots had developed under the skin at the base of the tail of each animal where he had injected the test fluid. Having satisfied himself that all of the reactions were negative, he chatted with us, as usual, for a few minutes. "George," he said, "I hear that you are going to be selling out. You shouldn't. You have as promising a bunch of young stuff as there is around. You should stay with it."

"Oh," said George. "It's time; the boy does not want to farm."

That was hardly true. The boy did not know what he wanted at the time.

George as usual toured the county that summer with some of the directors from the Middlesex County Holstein-Friesian Breeders' Association, selecting cattle for the county herd contest at the Western Fair in London. He volunteered my services to work with the county cattle at the fair and we entered Joan in the calf class. Much under age, she did well, as noted earlier. The county Black and White Show took place in conjunction with the fall fair in Strathroy a few weeks after the Western Exhibition, and we exhibited Joan and Jane, their mother, and the herd sire as well as my club calf. George now began to make the final arrangements for his dispersal sale. Since we had not built up the numbers of cattle in our herd to the point where many buyers would be interested in coming to a sale, one of the directors of the county association added a number of his animals to ours in the dispersal. By this time classes at the university were under way and I had no wish to see Ethel, Joan and Jane, and the other animals put under the auctioneer's hammer. Their sale, however, ensured that university tuition money was available for me in the future, if I needed it.

Later that fall W. K. Riddle drove me and another member of the calf club to Guelph to compete in the annual judging competition in which calf club teams from across Ontario participated. At the conclusion of the meal ending the day's events, the master of ceremonies announced the individual and team high scores. The top individual score, he said, was 642, and there was a runner up at 641. That was my score. My partner had graded less well and we did not place as a team. So ended the Ormsby Fayne era of my life.

Epilogue

Tanned and, I believed, fit after a summer of farm work, I registered at the University of Western Ontario as a freshman in the fall of 1939, in company with many other young men who were wondering what the recent outbreak of war in Europe would mean for them. When I tried to enroll in the university contingent of the Canadian Officers Training Corps, the medical examiner informed me that I had a heart murmur and placed me in the C category of fitness for service. I was allowed, however, to join the local contingent's strength in order to fulfill my physical education requirement at the university. With this completed, the Canadian Army in its wisdom discharged me from its reserve forces at the end of my second year, only to reenlist me at the next fall's registration after its doctors decided that my condition was less serious than once thought. I was now in A category, the contingent medical officer told me. Since I was now well advanced toward a degree, I decided to stay with the army reserves until I had it in hand. In early May 1943, Eleta attended the graduation ceremonies at the University of Western Ontario to see her younger son accept his Bachelor of Arts diploma and the gold medal in the history program.

On an evening shortly afterward she watched me board a train of the Canadian Pacific Railroad to begin some two and half years of undistinguished but educational service in the Canadian Army (Active). A few months later a sergeant in the Advanced Infantry Center at Currie Barracks, Calgary, distributed the day's mail to the members of his platoon; he handed me an airmail envelope addressed in Eleta's spidery script. I opened it as we prepared to fall into formation. After a paragraph of miscellaneous information, she had written: "I must tell you that Dr. Wong operated on me recently and discovered that I have abdominal cancer. She has prescribed a course of treatment . . ."

At a break point in training some weeks later, those in our program were given leave, and I was able to spend some days at home. George had assumed nursing duties and Eleta was calm. One day she had an appointment at Victoria Hospital for treatment and suggested that I accompany her. She had no illusions about the long-run prognosis of her illness and indeed was remarkably upbeat. She believed, I suspect, that she had done all she possibly could to ensure the futures of her children and was content to let matters rest.

In February of 1944, George telegraphed that she was gone. He sold the house in London and once more moved to the small apartment in the house on the farm, having rented the rest of the house and the farm lands to others. When I returned from graduate school in 1949 to join the staff at the University of Western Ontario, he seemed to be in reasonable health for one of his age. During the war Len had purchased a good farm on the Sixth Concession Road and my sister Myrtle was happily married as well. Within a space of two years all three died.

Cancer took my sister and then my brother failed to recover from postoperative shock after a surgeon cleared his gastrointestinal tract of a food blockage. Fifteen-year-old Arthur left school to join his mother in running the farm business. Deteriorating arteries turned George into an invalid, and in late 1952 he succumbed to a heart attack. During his last months I, as his trustee, sold the farm on the northeast corner in order to provide funds with which to maintain him. The family who bought it developed a chicken business in the farmstead area but sold out after a number of years; the buyer tore down the farmstead buildings and has since rented the land to neighboring farmers. Meanwhile the new housing subdivisions of the city of London have crept steadily closer, a development probably being watched by the current owners with anticipation. Although a belt of farms still remains between our old farm and suburbia proper, the North Talbot Road is an official boundary of the City of London at our old crossroads. The walnut tree under which we packed tomatoes in front of our house some sixty years ago now rules the house yard surrounded by a grove of its seedlings.

The Dairy Herd

Herd management, biological reproduction, and milk production are key elements in the success or failure of a dairy operation. In establishing a herd of purebred Holstein-Friesian cattle, George purchased four foundation females between 1916 and the early 1920s. During the 1920s he also bought four young bulls as herd sires, the service of the last of these animals extending into the early 1930s. When my brother Len removed his animals from the herd in 1937 and joined his father-in-law in partnership, George began the task of rebuilding the milk row by purchasing two heifer calves and a new herd sire. This process ended when he held a dispersal sale in the fall of 1939. Between 1920 and 1939 he had registered seventy-eight purebred animals with the Holstein-Friesian Association of Canada, forty-six females and thirty-two males. The data in that organization's *Herd Book* series do not include entries for all of the purebred animals that were born on the farm. A few calves died at birth or before George had submitted applications for registration, and even in the prosperous 1920s, he probably did not register some bull calves from females that were not good milk-producers. When the possibility of selling young bulls for breeding stock dwindled during the mid-1930s, George submitted relatively fewer registration applications for bull calves to the breed registry. Biological odds suggest that across time our cows should have dropped approximately equal numbers of the two sexes. But several cows in the herd, notably Wooley, became highly unpopular as they delivered bull calf after bull calf, and we joked in the mid-1930s that the females were threatening to exhaust the supply of stable names provided by the first-string lineup of the New York Yankees.

From 1929 to 1936, however, George registered twenty-two heifers and sixteen bulls, losing perhaps five females before registration. A heifer died when it was several months old in 1934, and in that year one of Len's cows dropped a red and white heifer, which could not be registered under the

Table 1. Reproduction in the dairy herd (official registrations)

	Heifer calf	Bull calf		Heifer calf	Bull calf
1920	–	1	1930	4	3
1921	–	1	1931	3	3
1922	1		1932	2	2
1923	2	1	1933	5	2
1924	2	–	1934	2	3
1925	3	–	1935	3	1
1926	4	2	1936	1	1
1927	4	3	1936	–	1
1928	2	4	1938	4	1
1929	3	2	1939	1	1

Source: Compiled from the Holstein-Friesian Association of Canada, *Herd Book*, vols. 18–42.

breed rules of that time—the second such occurrence in the herd's history. One of the springing heifers aborted while on summer pasture during the early 1930s, causing George to fear that the cows might become infected with contagious abortion, or brucellosis, as we now call the disease. After repeated efforts to get Donabelle with calf, that beautiful animal finally conceived, only to throw the fetus after four or five months. We anticipated twins from another cow during these same years and she did not deceive us, but the sexes were mixed and the female was sterile, a freemartin.

Because of the gaps in the record that signify unregistered bull calves or—much less common—a calf lost at delivery or shortly afterward, we can understand the breeding and lactation management in the herd only in general terms. The females that dropped daughters after their first gestation had usually been bred at some point between their fifteenth and twenty-first month and as a result freshened during the first six months of their "two-year-old" year, that is, in the third year of their lives. The last of our cows to qualify in the Canadian Record of Performance program was not successfully bred apparently until she was twenty-six months of age. When the young animals were on summer pasture at some distance from the home place, the fact that a heifer was in season (in heat, in farm talk) might go undetected, and occasionally a breeding was unsuccessful. After the first several months of maximum milk flow, a cow's production fell off gradually until she usually "went dry" following some eleven to thirteen months of lactation. The *Herd Book* shows some instances of our cows dropping a calf eleven months after a previous calving, but usually the period from calving to calving was between a year and fifteen months in duration, occasionally longer. The herdsman who wished to maintain eight or nine cows in production at all times had to maintain a somewhat larger number of cows than that figure.

By the end of 1925, George's four foundation cows had dropped eight heifer calves, and another four arrived in the following year. By this time the members of the milking herd were almost all purebreds, and the foundation cows were still present. Of these, two dropped their last registered calves in 1926; another followed suit in the next year. Although Madolyn Fayne Segis, born in January 1917, produced her last registered calf in April 1930, she survived in the herd until the mid-1930s. Her original stable mate, Lady Veeman Segis, dropped her last registered offspring in 1926 when she was three months beyond her tenth year. Both also left long-lived daughters in the herd. Madolyn's daughter Dutchland Fayne of Walnut Lodge, born on March 10, 1926, was with us until 1936 and departed with Len in the division of the herd. During her years on the home place George registered four of her daughters and three bull calves. Her tenure in the herd, however, was considerably shorter than that of Veeman Alcartra Fayne, a second-generation animal in the Veeman line. A daughter of the original animal properly called Lady Veeman Segis but known to us as Old Veeman, Veeman Alcartra Fayne (stable-named Veeman) was born in July 1922, dropped her last heifer calf on the farm in 1939, and was still giving more milk in that lactation than some of our younger cows—a most unusual history. Her first heifer calf was Veeman Alcartra Dutchland or Young Veeman, born in 1926. I have described the accident Young Veeman suffered in our woodlot swamp that rendered her unsalable. She too was still with us in 1939.

During the 1930s the milking herd at any time included four or five middle-aged or older cows and a number of younger animals in their first, second, or third lactations. The latter females along with springing heifers that were late in their second or early in their third year of growth made up the age categories in which buyers seeking herd replacements were interested. From the late 1920s onward George probably sold a couple of such animals each year, and income derived from that source was a major addition to the income derived from the dairy herd.

When George became a purebred stockman he also committed himself to the practices of the cattle fancy. He joined the Holstein-Friesian Association of Canada, headquartered at Brantford, Ontario, and registered his animals in the association's *Herd Book* as well as joining the breed association that developed in Middlesex County. He also began to enter animals in the Record of Performance program of the Canadian Department of Agriculture. At the end of each month he sat at the kitchen table for an evening transcribing production data from the barn sheet to the reporting

Table 2. Records of performance qualifiers

Cow's name	Age (years)	Lbs. milk	Lbs. fat	% fat	Days	Year
Alcartra Pride	3	11,195	367	3.28	365	1923
Madolyn Fayne Segis	6	19,216	570	2.97	365	1923
Veeman Alcartra Fayne	2	11,357	349	3.07	365	1925
Fanny Fayne Burke	3	11,108	358	3.22	365	1925
Lady Alcartra Sarcastic	2	11,979	400	3.34	365	1926
Fanny Change Hengerveld	3	11,290	396	3.51	365	1927
Dutchland Fayne of Walnut Lodge	2	10,139	337	3.22	365	1929
Veeman Alcartra Dutchland	2	11,205	367	3.28	365	1929
Veeman Alcartra Fayne	6	14,770	452	3.06	365	1929
Larabelle Ormsby Fayne	2	10,456	389	3.72	365	1933

Source: Compiled from Canada Department of Agriculture, *The Canadian Record of Performance for Pure-Bred Dairy Cattle*, reports no. g–31.

forms provided by the federal Department of Agriculture. This was in preparation for mailing them to Ottawa in big official envelopes that went post-free thanks to the big "OHMS" lettered in the upper right-hand corner.

Only some of our cows qualified in the Record of Performance program by attaining the minimum standards for production of milk and butterfat that the department prescribed for the various age and lactation classifications. But despite that fact, it was wise to have animals "on test" because the pounds of milk and fat produced by nonqualifiers was useful information to the breeder. Table 2 provides the qualifying records of the nine cows that surpassed the departmental standards during the history of our herd along with the year in which their lactations began.

George milked all of these cows for 365 days, and his early enthusiasm is revealed by the fact that he actually milked Alcartra Pride three times a day during a period extending for 107 days and Madolyn Fayne Segis for 186 days within their 365-day lactations. Later he told of the drain on time and energy that such practice involved; milking three times a day represented an experiment in the history of the herd rather than a continuing aspect of his dairy management.

The production records listed in table 2 place an upper bound on estimates of the total production of milk or butter during any period in our herd's history. There were cows that for a time produced milk at a rate close to the level attained by cows qualifying in the ROP program but that did not sustain milk flow over time to the degree that the qualifiers did. The grain supplement George fed the cows in addition to their rations of hay and field corn was for the most part gristmill chop made of farm-grown oats and barley, and the size of the small-grain crop limited the amount of this feed available for the milk row. The cows were on reduced grain rations during the winter of 1934–35 following the poor crops of 1934. Other things being equal, cows increased their milk production, year by year, until they were fully adult animals. Veeman Alcartra Fayne appears twice in table 2, and the difference between the two records gives a good indication of the spread in production that could be expected in the history of a milk cow. The total production during the 365 days of her first lactation was 11,357 pounds of milk that contained 349 pounds of butterfat, as compared to 14,770 and 452 pounds during the lactation begun in her sixth year. Veeman had increased her production by some 30 percent in both categories and in the latter year had averaged 40 pounds or more of milk each day, twenty at each milking.

Table 2 shows variation in the butterfat content of the various cows listed. Madolyn Fayne Segis produced the most impressive milk record of the cows listed in table 2, over 19,000 pounds in the lactation begun in her sixth year, but the butterfat content of her milk was the lowest in the group, only 2.97 percent. She did, however, produce the greatest number of pounds of butterfat of all the cows in the group. At 3.51 percent, Fanny Change Hengerveld's milk carried the highest percentage of butterfat among the qualifiers of the 1920s. However Larabelle Ormsby Fayne's milk tested at 3.72 percent during the lactation that she began in 1933. Her grandmother was the low-testing Madolyn Fayne Segis.

Our first Arbogast bull, Fairmont King Korndyke Dutchland, sired daughters that produced milk flows comparable to those of the foundation matrons. In replacing the big white fellow, George returned to the Arbogast brothers for another sire, following what he believed to be the precepts of linebreeding. In general Hartog Ormsby Fayne's daughters were less productive milkers than were their dams. Larabelle's record suggests, however, that this bull may have pushed up the butterfat content of the farm milk somewhat. George's problems with Silverwood's Diary show that he was very much aware of the importance of butterfat in establishing the value of milk. But table 2 provides evidence that Eleta's charge that he lacked good judgment in his choice of animals to sell had some basis of fact. Fanny Change Hengerveld recorded the highest butterfat readings among the qualifiers of the 1920s. She also produced a string of four daughters, and George apparently sold every one of them before they had the opportunity to demonstrate their productive capabilities.

There is a distribution of two-year-old, three-year-old, and six-year-old records of performance given in table 2. This suggests that the data in it may be used as the basis for a herd average that in turn can serve in making

tentative estimates of the value of the farm's milk production. The total
butterfat product of the ten qualifiers over periods of 365 days was 3,985
pounds, a per cow average of 398.5 pounds. The records of George's actual
receipts for milk, cream, or butter have long since vanished. But we do know
the value of butter during the years of our herd history. It is also true that
the cows that qualified as milk and butterfat producers in the ROP program
were the top producers in the herd. The presence of less productive animals
pulled the herd average down. But I doubt that this pull brought the herd
performance down by more than 25 percent. That amount of depreciation
provides a lower bound of 298.9 pounds of butterfat per cow. The herd
totals calculated on the basis of a nine-cow milking herd at the two levels
would be 3,586 and 2,690 pounds of butterfat per year.

A Note on Income and Outgo

George's farm records included only his bank book, a list of the dates on which cows were serviced, and the milking record that he copied each month for submission to the Record of Performance division of the Canadian Department of Agriculture. None of these has survived. We can, however, describe some aspects of the economic environment in our region during George's last twenty years as an active farmer and provide rough and conservative estimates of returns for some major income items using 1936 as illustration.

We should first note a few exceptional income items. George realized capital gains from the resale of both his first and second farms. He also took a capital loss from the sale of the farm on the Fifth Concession Road. He inherited the Bostwick fifty acres and obtained a one-time windfall by harvesting some twenty acres of mature timber on it.

Through the 1920s George sold fluid milk and also derived some income from the sale of male animals as vealers, steers, or breeding stock after he made the transition to purebred Holsteins. Typically, I believe, he made cash sales of wheat each year and sometimes teamed a few loads of hay into the Covent Garden Market Square. The family also sold apples and potatoes and a few crates of strawberries in some years as well as small amounts of maple syrup. Income from these items was minor in nature in comparison to income from the herd or from the sale of wheat. Eleta's poultry enterprise was an important component of the farm cash income flow, providing eggs and dressed poultry for sale and making a considerable contribution to the family table besides.

Assuming that the cow row produced at a rate of 75 percent of the average of the record of performance qualifiers, a nine-cow herd would have produced 2,690 pounds of butterfat, which at twenty cents a pound (a common price in the mid-1930s) would have been worth $538. On average

George was selling two or three springing heifers or young cows each year and the same number of bull calves. The returns from these transactions would perhaps have fallen between $150 and $200 per year. The total annual value of output from the dairy herd during 1935 or 1936 was probably in the neighborhood of $700. Milk cows sold during the late 1920s at more favorable prices than during the 1930s, and this was true of dairy products as well.

Through the 1920s George usually sold some wheat shortly after thresh-ing, and he continued such sales during the 1930s, retaining a generous amount of the crop for use as chicken feed and sometimes seed. If he sold fifty bushels in 1936 at threshing time or shortly afterward, it would have produced an income item of about fifty dollars.

Poultry researchers at the Ontario Agricultural College at Guelph found considerable variation in the number of eggs that Barred Rock hens pro-duced in a year. They were most productive during their first year as layers, but prices at the market in London, Ontario, during the 1930s show that pullet eggs brought a lower price than did eggs in the Grade A large and Grade A medium categories. Maintained no doubt under optimal conditions, the Guelph hens ranged in production in their first year from something below 150 eggs to well over 200. If we assume an average production of 170 eggs per hen in a laying flock of fifty birds, we arrive at an annual product of 8,500 eggs, or 708 dozen. Egg prices on the London market showed considerable seasonal swing in the mid-1930s, but if valued at twenty-three cents per dozen, the flock's eggs would have been worth $163. Researchers discovered that the average farm family in two Ontario counties in 1935 consumed between 114.5 and 119.4 dozen eggs annually. Deduction of 120 dozen eggs from our total would reduce the number of eggs available for sale to 588 dozen and the cash value to $135. I doubt, however, that Eleta realized such returns consistently.

Depending upon season and quality, dressed chickens ranged in price on the London market during the mid-1930s from eighteen to thirty-five cents per pound. The price of cooking hens was in the lower part of the range, but such mature hens and spring roosters would have weighed between three and five pounds at sale. If Eleta marketed fifty birds as dressed poultry, she perhaps received between fifty and seventy-five dollars for them. In the years that she had geese to sell, fifteen birds would have produced approximately 225 pounds of dressed fowl, which would have been worth $56.25 if sold at twenty-five cents per pound.

Tomatoes provided our most important market gardening crop of the mid-1930s, when we planted some two to three acres of this vegetable. In discussing the cultivation of this vegetable in southwestern Ontario during the 1930s, specialists at the Ontario Agricultural College suggested that a harvest of 200 to 225 bushels per acre was a high average yield. In general our crops were good, but we were not perhaps as skilled as the growers who produced for canneries. Our green trailer could carry some thirty bushels of tomatoes packed in eleven-quart baskets, and there were days when it departed for market completely full. Occasionally it returned for still more. As with other market garden crops, the price of field tomatoes fell as greater supplies reached the market, then stabilized after a time, and might even rise a little as the season approached its end. In 1936 the price of an eleven-quart basket of field-grown tomatoes ranged from $1.05 to $1.50 on July 25. By September 12, buyers found baskets of that size available at prices ranging from twenty-five to thirty-five cents. An acre producing 180 bushels that sold for prices averaging thirty-five cents per eleven-quart basket would have produced a cash return of $207. From this sum the costs of hired labor, seeds, fertilizer, greenhouse coal, baskets, and transportation must all be subtracted to arrive at the return to family labor or land.

Intermittently over the years George had derived some income from the sale of potatoes. In the mid-1930s we increased the size of the potato patch to at least two acres. In southern Ontario during the 1920s OAC authorities reported average yields of the ubiquitous Irish Cobbler potato ranging from 123 to 185 bushels per acre. After new potatoes reached the London market in the summer of 1936, they sold there for about $1.15 per bushel for the next couple of months, an unusually high price. We sold ours in eleven-quart baskets, which perhaps allowed us to obtain an additional fifteen cents or so on the bushel price. Assuming a per-acre yield of 155 bushels and the price quoted in the *London Free Press*, the cash return on that size of planting was $178.25. This is much above the $81 per acre estimate of the Statistics Branch of the Ontario Department of Agriculture for 1936, but that agency's figure was a yearly average price for the province as a whole.

In 1936 we planted most of the front field in garden crops and utilized the small asparagus field and a couple of acres in the middle field for such crops as well. Although none of the other crops produced as much in cash return as tomatoes and potatoes, we also marketed substantial amounts of sweet corn, cucumbers, cabbages, and red kidney beans as well as lesser amounts of raspberries, peppers, pepper squash, Hubbard squash, eggplant, and even a few bunches of dill. In total these crops perhaps produced as much income as the tomato plantings.

Table 3. Farm means in the Oxford area (1931) and condensery area (1937–38)

	Oxford area (1931)					Condensery area (1937–38)		
Land utilization	Acres	Field crops	%	Livestock	No.	Operating expenses	Dollars	%
Occupied land	91.1	Wheat	3.6	Cows	7.3	Hired labor	$163	13.1
Improved land	72.7	Oats	12.0	Other cattle	6.9	Board for labor	$76	6.1
Percent improved	79.8	Other Cereals	13.1	Sheep	2.9	Family labor	$225	18.1
Field crops	52.2	Hay	17.1	Swine	6.8	Taxes	100	8.0
Improved pasture	15.9	Potatoes	0.8	Hens	143.1	Custom Work	48	3.8
Natural pasture	9.7	Roots	0.8			Fertilizer	45	3.6
Woodland	6.9	Orchards	0.7			Seed	62	5.0
		Market garden	0.3			Feed	209	16.8
						Automobile	42	3.4
						Machine repair	30	2.4
Total farm value	$8,434					Insurance (buildings)	22	1.8
Buildings per farm	3,277					Miscellaneous	223	17.9
Machinery per farm	963							

Source: Data taken from McArthur, "Farm Organization in Southern Ontario," and "Operating Expenses on Ontario Farms."

We can place George and Len's farming operation in 1936 in better perspective if we consider the picture of farming activity that agricultural economists developed during the 1930s. On the basis of the Canada Agricultural Census findings of 1931, types of farming areas in Ontario were mapped; Middlesex County was at the western edge of the "Oxford area," a subregion in which the farming was distinguished by its emphasis on dairying and poultry production. In 1937–38 the economists surveyed the dairy industry in Ontario and placed our part of Middlesex County in the "condensery area." Table 3 combines salient findings from the two investigations. Ian McArthur summarized the findings of both investigations in the issues of *Economic Annalist* noted in table 3.

In total acreage our farm exceeded the mean in our subregion, and we maintained more cattle than did the average farmer there until the last few years of George's farm operation. The more than fifteen acres that we devoted to market gardening in 1936 would not have been equaled on many dairy farms of that era. Although we fattened a few hogs taken in lieu of cash debt payments, we lacked the hog enterprise that many farmers maintained along with milking herds. Nor did we have any sheep. Although Eleta's poultry flocks may have approached the Ontario mean for a few years after our move to the northeast corner, it was much less comparable by the mid-1930s. The machinery and implements on our farm never approached the mean valuation that the agricultural economists reported for the Oxford area type of farm. However, the replacement cost of the major items of farm machinery in use on our farm would in total have equaled or surpassed the figure in table 3. George's bills for real estate taxes and the custom work involved in threshing and corn cutting were probably quite similar to those of other farmers in the condensery area.

The farm labor arrangements involved in the dairy operation and in the dairy plus market gardening enterprise were quite different. When the farm was primarily a livestock operation during the 1920s and early 1930s, George and Len and Eleta provided most of the farm labor except during a couple of weeks in the fall, when Henry did the fall plowing in preparation for planting the small grains and corn in the following spring planting season. There were in addition some incidental and short-run outlays for hired help—compensation to neighborhood or village children for picking strawberries at a few cents per quart box, the wages of an extra man or two at threshing time perhaps, and the cost of having firewood split on the woodlot of the Bostwick fifty, in which case George paid on a per-cord basis.

In this appendix I have tried particularly to highlight the kind of expense and income items with which George and Len dealt in 1936 when we combined dairying and market gardening. That year saw our greatest use of hired labor. Although they tried to maintain at least one hired man on a monthly wage from spring until early fall, George and Len obtained much of our hired help on a daily or weekly basis from Lambeth or the Lambeth-Byron neighborhood. Several young women picked and packed tomatoes or cucumbers for us, but most of the workers were male—youths or young men. Those who were involved mainly in harvesting vegetables usually worked only on the days when we were picking and preparing for the Wednesday and Saturday marketing days. Since we gave the day help a noon meal and sometimes supper as well, I believe that most of them received a dollar in addition for a full day of work. Len may have paid adult males $1.25 sometimes. Wages for the several men who were hired by the month were twenty-five dollars for that period, plus board, a figure that was above the official estimate of twenty-one dollars plus board given in the *Canada Year Book* for the mid-1930s. All told, the amount of hired work that George and Len used on the farm in 1936 would perhaps have totaled out at some seven to eight months of labor, $175 or $200 in cash, plus the additional expense of providing board for perhaps four months. At fifteen years of age my contribution in labor was fully equal to that of some of our hired male help, and my compensation was only a few dollars of pocket money and my keep, although I did have an asset in the growing animal that I owned in the dairy herd.

Table 4 presents the average prices of basic farm products and the average valuation of horses, cattle, and poultry in Ontario through the years 1920–39. In some cases these series show considerable variation from one year to another, illustrating the unpredictability of prices in the agricultural sector. Of course, the fact that farmers received higher prices for agricultural products in one year than in another did not necessarily mean that they greatly benefited. Perhaps the higher prices merely reflected a harvest year of poor crops, and the individual farmer had little surplus to send to market. The prices of goods that farmers must buy may also rise when the prices of farm produce are increasing. In general farm prices have tended to be more volatile than those of manufactured goods. Although the prices for animals and their products were apparently high during the early 1920s, Ontario farmers found that the prices they paid for goods and services were relatively higher. The relationship between the prices farmers obtained for their products and the prices they paid for goods and services was also unfavorable from 1931 through 1936, particularly in 1932 and 1933.

The late 1920s and to a lesser extent the late 1930s were years in which

Table 4. Ontario farm product prices and livestock values (in dollars)

Year	Fall wheat per bu.	Oats per bu.	Hay per ton	Potatoes per bu.	Butter per lb.	Horses each	Cows each	Other cattle each	Poultry each
1939	$.64	$.34	$7.61	$.68	$.25	$113	$49	$25	$.63
1938	.56	.28	6.92	.47	.28	98	47	28	.61
1937	1.04	.42	7.14	.36	.28	103	48	29	.62
1936	1.09	.48	8.79	.81	.25	109	43	20	.54
1935	.71	.28	7.08	.60	.25	103	41	19	.52
1934	.88	.35	12.62	.33	.24	97	37	18	.51
1933	.66	.33	8.41	.60	.23	88	38	18	.52
1932	.46	.25	7.24	.41	.23	75	43	20	.45
1931	.52	.25	8.43	.23	.27	87	53	22	.45
1930	.66	.30	10.42	.60	.34	100	73	32	.59
1929	1.24	.62	11.28	1.08	.42	110	80	36	.61
1928	1.22	.55	11.23	.56	.41	110	68	30	.63
1927	1.25	.57	11.02	.88	.40	108	61	27	.65
1926	1.25	.52	12.75	1.13	.39	108	59	27	.70
1925	1.34	.45	11.61	1.37	.39	108	59	28	.76
1924	1.34	.54	10.91	.54	.37	109	55	27	.80
1923	.96	.45	11.05	.75	.38	111	55	25	.82
1922	1.05	.43	12.03	.51	.36	109	53	24	.88
1921	1.10	.50	19.27	.88	.42	109	52	25	.97
1920	1.93	.58	24.25	.99	.58	127	86	45	1.07

Source: With one exception these data are drawn from the *Report of the Statistics Branch of the Ontario Department of Agriculture for 1939*, 44, 47. This source does not give a price for butter; the annual average price of butter per pound is taken from Urquart and Buckley, *Historical Statistics of Canada* series M238. The prices or values are given in current rather than constant dollars since these were the basis George and Len used for their decisions.

prices for farm products rose to a greater extent than did the prices farmers had to pay for farm supplies and equipment.

On the farm on the North Talbot Road there were years of hope and years of discouragement—more of the latter than of the former, unfortunately—but we survived.

Bibliography

Ankli, Robert E. "Ontario's Dairy Industry, 1880–1920." *Canadian Papers in Rural History* 8:261–75. Ganonoque ON: Langdale Press, 1992.

Armstrong, Frederick H. *The Forest City: An Illustrated History of London, Canada.* London ON: Windsor Publications, 1986.

Brown, D. M., G. A. McKay, and L. J. Chapman. *The Climate of Southern Ontario.* Climatological Studies no. 5. Ottawa: Minister of Supply and Services Canada, 1980.

Canada Department of Agriculture, Branch of the Livestock Commissioner. *The Canadian Record of Performance for Pure-Bred Dairy Cattle.* Reports no. 9–31. Ottawa: Canada Department of Agriculture, 1917–39.

Canada Soil Survey Committee. *The Canadian System of Soil Classification.* Publication 1646. Ottawa: Canada Department of Agriculture, Research Branch, 1978.

Canada Year Book. Dominion Bureau of Statistics. Ottawa: Statistics Canada, 1940.

Chapman, L. J., and D. F. Putnam. *The Physiography of Southern Ontario: Ontario Geological Survey, Special Volume.* 3rd ed. Toronto: Ontario Ministry of Natural Resources, 1984.

Crinklaw, Raymond K., Olga B. Bishop, and George P. Rickard. *Glanworth, Westminster Township: One Hundred Years of Yesterday's News, Today's History.* Lambeth ON: Crinklaw Press, 1987.

———. *The North Talbot Road, Westminster Township: One Hundred Years of Yesterday's News, Today's History.* Lambeth ON: Crinklaw Press, 1986.

———. *Westminster Township South-East of the Thames: One Hundred Years of Yesterday's News, Today's History.* Lambeth ON: Crinklaw Press, 1988.

Ermatinger, C. O. *The Talbot Regime or the First Half Century of the Talbot Settlement.* St. Thomas ON: Municipal World Limited, 1904.

Gates, Lillian F. *Land Policies of Upper Canada.* Toronto: University of Toronto Press, 1968.

Hagerty, T. P., and M. S. Kingston. *The Soils of Middlesex County.* Report no. 56 of the Ontario Centre for Soil Resource Evaluation. 2 vols. Guelph: Ontario Centre for Soil Resource Evaluation, 1992.

Hamil, Fred C. *Lake Erie Baron: The Story of Colonel Thomas Talbot.* Toronto: Macmillan Company of Canada, 1955.

———. *The Valley of the Lower Thames, 1640 to 1850.* Toronto: University of Toronto Press, 1951.

Harcourt, R., W. L. Iverson, and C. A. Cline. *Preliminary Soil Survey of Southwestern Ontario.* Bulletin 298. Guelph: Ontario Department of Agriculture, Ontario Agricultural College, 1923.

Hare, H. R. "Some Farm Management Factors Affecting Labour Earnings on Ontario Dairy Farms." *Economic Annalist* 8 (December 1938): 89–90.

Harris, R. Cole, and John Warkentin. *Canada before Confederation: A Study in Historical Geography.* New York: Oxford University Press, 1974.

History of the County of Middlesex, Canada. Toronto: W. A. and C. L. Goodspeed, 1889. Republished with introduction by Daniel Brock and index by Muriel Moon; Belleville ON: Mika Studio, 1972.

Holstein-Friesian Association of Canada. *Holstein-Friesian Herd Book: Containing a Record of All Holstein-Friesian Cattle approved and admitted for registry. . . .* Vols. 18–42. Brantford ON: Holstein-Friesian Association of Canada, 1915–39.

Hopper, W. C. "Consumption of Eggs in Farm Homes in Certain Districts of Canada." *Economic Annalist* 8 (June 1938): 46.

Hudson, S. C. "Farm Taxes on Selected Groups of Farms in Ontario, Quebec, and Nova Scotia." *Economic Annalist* 3 (June 1933): 68–69.

Illustrated Historical Atlas of the County of Middlesex Ont. Toronto: H. R. Page and Company, 1878.

Ise, John. *Sod and Stubble: The Story of a Kansas Homestead.* New York: Wilson-Erickson, 1936.

Kendall, W. W., and L. Stevenson. *Farm Barns.* Bulletin 326. Guelph: Ontario Department of Agriculture, Ontario Agricultural College, 1927.

Lewington, Peter. *Canada's Holsteins.* Markham ON: Fitzhenry and Whiteside, 1983.

Macdonald, Norman. *Canada, 1763–1841: Immigration and Settlement, the Administration of the Imperial Land Regulations.* Toronto: Longmans, Green and Company, 1939.

MacLennan, H. A., and F. W. Presant. *The Culture of Early and Late Outdoor*

Tomatoes. Bulletin 308. Guelph: Ontario Department of Agriculture, Ontario Agricultural College, 1924.

McArthur, Ian. "Farm Organization in Southern Ontario." *Economic Annalist* 8 (August 1938): 55–57.

———. "Operating Expenses on Ontario Farms." *Economic Annalist* 10 (August 1940): 51–53.

McInnis, R. M. "Perspectives on Ontario Agriculture, 1815–1930." *Canadian Papers in Rural History*, 8:17–127. Ganonoque ON: Langdale Press, 1992.

Michell, H. "The Co-Operative Store in Canada." *Queen's Quarterly*, 23 (January–March 1916): 317–38.

Miller, Orlo. *This Was London: The First Two Centuries*. Westport ON: Butternut Press, 1988.

Miller, Orlo, with Miriam Wright, Edward Phelps, and Glen C. Phillips. *London 200: An Illustrated History*. London ON: London Chamber of Commerce, 1992.

Murray, Marguerite E. *Century Farms of Westminster Township*, vol. 1. London ON: Westminster Township Historical Society, 1984.

———. *Century Farms of Westminster Township*, vol. 2. London ON: Westminster Township Historical Society, 1987.

Ontario Department of Agriculture. *Annual Report*, 1920–39. Toronto: Ontario Department of Agriculture.

———. Report of the Statistics Branch of the Ontario Department of Agriculure for 1939. Toronto: Ontario Department of Agriculture, 1940.

Orr, James E. *Historical Sketches of Westminster Township*. Lambeth ON: Westminster Township Historical Society, 1977.

Paddon, Wayne. *The Story of the Talbot Settlement, 1803–1840: A Frontier History of South Western Ontario*. N.p.: Wayne Paddon, 1976.

Poultry Department, Ontario Agricultural College. *Farm Poultry*. Bulletin 292. Guelph: Ontario Department of Agriculture, Ontario Agricultural College, 1922.

Reaman, George E. *History of the Holstein-Friesian Breed in Canada*. Toronto: Wm. Collins Sons, 1946.

———. *A History of Agriculture in Ontario*. 2 vols. Toronto: Saunders of Toronto, 1970.

Reeds, Lloyd G. "Agricultural Regions of Southern Ontario, 1880 and 1951." *Economic Geography* 35 (July 1959): 219–27.

Squirrell, W. J. *Hardy Alfalfa*. Bulletin 346. Guelph: Ontario Department of Agriculture, Ontario Agricultural College, 1929.

———. *Hay and Pasture Crops*. Bulletin 347. Guelph: Ontario Department of Agriculture, Ontario Agricultural College, 1929.

Squirrell, W. J., and A. H. MacLennan. *Potatoes*. Bulletin 339. Guelph: Ontario Department of Agriculture, Ontario Agricultural College, 1928.

Staples, Melville H. *The Challenge of Agriculture: The Story of the United Farmers of Ontario*. Toronto: George N. Morang, 1921.

St. Denis, Guy. *Byron: Pioneer Days in Westminster Township*. Edited by Frederick H. Armstrong. Lambeth ON: Crinklaw Press, 1985.

Steckley, J. C. *Dairy Cattle*. Bulletin 311. Guelph: Ontario Department of Agriculture, Ontario Agricultural College, 1925.

Theberge, John B. (ed.). *Legacy: The Natural History of Ontario*. Toronto: McClelland and Stewart, 1989.

Urquart, M. C., and K. A. H. Buckley (eds.). *Historical Statistics of Canada*. Toronto: Macmillan Company of Canada, 1965.

———. *Historical Statistics of Canada,* edited by F. H. Leacy. 2nd ed. Ottawa: Statistics Canada, 1983.

Whitaker, J. R. "Distribution of Dairy Farming in Peninsular Ontario." *Economic Geography* 16 (January 1940): 69–78.

Wood, Louis Aubrey. *A History of Farmers' Movements in Canada*. Toronto: Ryerson Press, 1924.

Zavitz, C. A. *Forty Years' Experiments with Grain Crops*. Bulletin 332. Guelph: Ontario Department of Agriculture, Ontario Agricultural College, 1927.

Index